Unconscious Christianity in Dietrich Bonhoeffer's Late Theology

Unconscious Christianity in Dietrich Bonhoeffer's Late Theology

Encounters with the Unknown Christ

Eleanor McLaughlin

LEXINGTON BOOKS/FORTRESS ACADEMIC
Lanham • Boulder • New York • London

Published by Lexington Books/Fortress Academic
Lexington Books is an imprint of The Rowman & Littlefield Publishing Group, Inc.
4501 Forbes Boulevard, Suite 200, Lanham, Maryland 20706
www.rowman.com

6 Tinworth Street, London SE11 5AL, United Kingdom

Copyright © 2020 by The Rowman & Littlefield Publishing Group, Inc.

All rights reserved. No part of this book may be reproduced in any form or by any electronic or mechanical means, including information storage and retrieval systems, without written permission from the publisher, except by a reviewer who may quote passages in a review.

British Library Cataloguing in Publication Information Available

Library of Congress Cataloging-in-Publication Data

Names: McLaughlin, Eleanor, 1982– author.
Title: Unconscious Christianity in Dietrich Bonhoeffer's late theology : encounters with the unknown Christ / Eleanor McLaughlin.
Description: Lanham : Lexington Books/Fortress Academic, 2020. | Includes bibliographical references and index. | Summary: "Eleanor McLaughlin traces the development of Bonhoeffer's work on unconscious Christianity in his writings and constructs a definition of the term, shedding light not only on Bonhoeffer's later works, but his theological development as a whole."—Provided by publisher.
Identifiers: LCCN 2019056192 (print) | LCCN 2019056193 (ebook) | ISBN 9781978708259 (cloth) | ISBN 9781978708266 (epub) | ISBN 9781978708273 (paperback)
Subjects: LCSH: Bonhoeffer, Dietrich, 1906–1945. | Christianity—Philosophy. | Christianity—Essence, genius, nature.
Classification: LCC BX4827.B57 M44 2020 (print) | LCC BX4827.B57 (ebook) | DDC 230/.044092—dc23
LC record available at https://lccn.loc.gov/2019056192
LC ebook record available at https://lccn.loc.gov/2019056193

For Luke
and
for my family, near and far

Contents

Foreword *Rowan Williams*	ix
Acknowledgments	xi
Introduction	1
Part I: Constructing a Definition of Unconscious Christianity	**25**
1 Bonhoeffer as a Member of the *Bürgertum*	27
2 Unconscious Christianity in Four Texts	55
3 Defining Unconscious Christianity	79
Part II: Situating Unconscious Christianity within Bonhoeffer's Theology	**99**
4 Unconscious Christianity in Context: Within Bonhoeffer's Late Theology and Secondary Literature	101
5 Unconscious Christianity as a Shift within Bonhoeffer's Theology	139
Conclusion: The Impact of Unconscious Christianity on Bonhoeffer Studies and Contemporary Theology	177
Appendix	195
Bibliography	201
Index	207
About the Author	211

Foreword

Rowan Williams

Dietrich Bonhoeffer continues to be an iconic figure for contemporary Christians, an exemplar of resistance to totalitarian violence and of commitment to the gospel vision of community. But this has not stopped him being a persistently contentious figure as well. How far does his involvement in direct conspiracy against Hitler help to legitimize some degree of revolutionary violence? How far do the complex speculations of his last months in prison put him alongside the most radical of doctrinal revisionists? Where exactly does he belong on the map of modern theology: with theologians of liberation, with the "death of God" radicals of the sixties, or even—as has been argued—with the more militant evangelical activists of the American religious right? Or with a Germanic tradition ultimately bound to fading categories of internal Protestant disputes, and inhabiting another intellectual world from our post-millennial landscape of uncontrolled religious plurality and widespread indifference?

That any one writer could be so diversely read and interpreted itself says something about Bonhoeffer's appeal, and about the enigmatic intricacy of his thought. It is becoming less fashionable simply to drive a wedge between an early Bonhoeffer who writes within a classical theological framework and the Bonhoeffer of the prison letters, "liberated" from any such constraints and opening the door—for good or ill—to a secularized Christian identity marked by "worldly" discipleship and doctrinal agnosticism. The continuities in his work are too strong and subtle for that to be a convincing account. But what, finally, *are* we to make of his reflections on a future Christianity that will sit light to "religious" language, and on the need to acknowledge and welcome those who are "unconsciously" Christian in their orientation? What content is left to the word "Christian" in this context?

These are the questions that Eleanor McLaughlin's searching and original book addresses. She traces the notion of "unconscious" faith back to some of Bonhoeffer's nineteenth-century predecessors and shows that he is doing something rather more theologically interesting than they could have imagined; and she also helps us disentangle his ideas from those of Karl Rahner, his Catholic near-contemporary, whose notion of the "anonymous Christian" has been very influential in theology in the last few decades. This book shows that what marks Bonhoeffer out both from his German Protestant predecessors and from Rahner is the Christological focus he brings to bear. He is from first to last a theologian concerned to understand (and to stand *with*) the God who in Jesus Christ declares solidarity with a world that is free to ignore or refuse him. And this exposed, self-forgetting solidarity is precisely the calling of believer and non-believer alike: Paradoxically, the instinctive compassion and involvement of the "unbeliever" affirms that person's alignment with the God they claim to know nothing of. As McLaughlin argues, this is very different from a purely optimistic account of some natural orientation Godward on the part of human beings: It is first and foremost a declaration about God, God's presence in Christ and activity in creation, not a thesis about human nature. To grasp its force, we need to locate Bonhoeffer's later work firmly in the context of his consistent fidelity to a deeply traditional Christology—a fidelity turned in a startlingly radical direction, indeed, but nonetheless the anchor and center of his theological world.

In spelling this out, McLaughlin offers some outstandingly clear and persuasive readings of Bonhoeffer's texts from different periods of his brief and intense career; but she also discusses the way in which Bonhoeffer in his last years and months experimented with unconventional vehicles for theology—not only poetry but fiction, in which he sought to sketch the character of the "good," Christ-aligned non-believer or half-believer. The fragments of these experiments in novel-writing are particularly interesting in fleshing out what Bonhoeffer was feeling his way toward in his mature thinking on these questions, and McLaughlin's treatment of them is especially fresh and valuable.

This is very definitely a book that shows how much Bonhoeffer has to offer for our own age. He meets us here neither as a purely "classical" theologian experimenting with a few unusual evangelistic strategies, nor as a revolutionary theological nihilist, but as a deeply thoughtful and creative Christian mind confronting the inescapable reality of a world where the Church's social and numerical dominance is a thing of the past. His ideas are provisional, not always systematic or even wholly consistent, but invariably and visibly saturated with a Christocentric and (in the widest sense) sacramental imagination. Eleanor McLaughlin succeeds in making him compelling for a new theological and ecclesial generation in this learned, original, and engaging work.

Acknowledgments

A great many individuals and organizations have contributed to the completion of this project. I first wish to thank Regent's Park College and the Oxford Centre for Christianity and Culture for providing me not only with funding but also with a community in which I could develop as a scholar. In particular the continued support of Robert Ellis, Paul Fiddes, Nicholas Wood, and the late Pamela Sue Anderson has been invaluable.

Friends and colleagues have been indispensable in this process. In particular, I would like to thank Michael Burdett, Lexi Eikelboom, Kate Kirpatrick, David Lappano, Matthew Mills, and Bethany Sollereder for their valued friendship and enlightening conversation. From the Faculty of Theology and Religion in Oxford, and the Faculty of Divinity in Cambridge, Joel Rasmussen and Rowan Williams provided helpful feedback as my work was progressing, as well as sustained and much appreciated encouragement.

The Staatsbibliothek in Berlin kindly allowed me to access to copies of some of Dietrich Bonhoeffer's manuscripts housed in their archives. I am grateful to Dorothea Barfknecht, Ralf Breslau, and their colleagues at the Staatsbibliothek in Berlin for their help and for providing me with a work space during a research trip to Berlin.

I am indebted to Johannes Zachhuber and Matthew Kirkpatrick, with whom I began exploring this topic, for sharing their expertise with me and for their skill in guiding me toward crucial questions.

I would lastly like to thank my family who have helped me throughout this project, and whose support, patience, and encouragement made this possible. Duncan and Barbara Greenland provided German language expertise and a warm welcome in London. Dick, Verna, and Neely McLaughlin contributed stimulating conversation and good food. My brothers and sisters-in-law, Sam and Lucy Greenland and Will and Fiona Greenland, gave me excellent advice and ceaseless encouragement. My parents, Janet and Jeremy Greenland, have always expressed complete confidence in me, which has enabled me to do more than I could have imagined. My mother's unwavering support over the past years has been crucial in enabling me to write this book. Most of all, thank you to Lucas McLaughlin, without whom I would not have begun, pursued, let alone completed this project.

Introduction

Churches around the world today face pressing questions relating to their place and purpose within contemporary culture. These questions pertain to the Church's relationship to society in general, to individuals within society, and to how society is led and managed. They include: How should the Church respond to the increasing secularization of society? How should the Church view those seeking a cultural or aesthetic connection to the Church rather than a spiritual one? Should the Church claim a space in public and political discourse? These questions and many other related issues are being discussed in churches and theology faculties across the globe. One of the twentieth century's greatest theologians also grappled with these questions, and left behind a valuable resource for those seeking to answer them today. That theologian was Dietrich Bonhoeffer, and the resource is his work on unconscious Christianity.

Bonhoeffer's life and thought have been extensively studied in this century and the last. His is among the best-known names to emerge from twentieth-century theology, both in academic and Church contexts. His ideas have been influential worldwide in times of political upheaval, for instance in the South African Church's struggle against apartheid.[1] However, scant attention has been paid to the idea that Bonhoeffer worked on in the final years of his life, just prior to and during his imprisonment. Bonhoeffer chose to work on the concept of *unbewußtes Christentum*, unconscious Christianity, during the most dangerous period of his life. The fact that he pursued his thinking on unconscious Christianity during a period when his own life, as well as the lives of his family, colleagues, and friends, were all under threat, indicates the great importance that he attached to this work. Indeed, after the failed assassination attempt against Hitler on 20 July 1944, he wrote to his friend

Eberhard Bethge that "the question about 'unconscious Christianity' [. . .] preoccupies me more and more."[2]

In his prison cell in Tegel, Bonhoeffer picks up the phrase "unconscious Christianity" that he had first written in the margin of his *Ethics* essay "Ultimate and Penultimate Things,"[3] and begins working on the idea through a variety of literary forms, including fiction. This intriguing fact has been largely ignored by scholarship on Bonhoeffer's later texts. This book unearths Bonhoeffer's reflections on unconscious Christianity and brings them into the forum of Bonhoeffer studies, and of theological discussion more broadly. My hope is that once this has been achieved, it will enable a discussion of unconscious Christianity and its implications within Bonhoeffer scholarship and beyond. In the conclusion of this book, I suggest ways in which the conversation around unconscious Christianity might fruitfully develop, but the aim of the present work is not to develop that subsequent conversation. Instead, my aim is to provide the tools with which to begin that conversation by constructing a definition of unconscious Christianity, one of Bonhoeffer's most important ideas. This book might seem technical, attempting to rediscover an idea from multiple disparate texts, but it is an important work that must be done. With this work, I hope to set the stage for future discussions of unconscious Christianity as a theological category.

In this book I explore Bonhoeffer's writings on unconscious Christianity, which include the fiction texts he wrote while in prison during the Second World War. I investigate the different contexts in which Bonhoeffer wrote about unconscious Christianity, and the biblical texts he links it to. Through a detective process of ascertaining Bonhoeffer's meaning every time he uses the term "unconscious Christianity," I offer a constructed definition of the phrase. This will open up new ways in which Bonhoeffer's theology can be used by the Church to make sense of its present situation.

For instance, one of the conclusions Bonhoeffer reaches in developing his thoughts on unconscious Christianity in his *Ethics* and his prison writings is that it is possible for people to be Christians without self-identifying as Christians. This idea alone speaks to contemporary debates around secularization and decreasing numbers of Church members, as well as to discussions of whom the Church actually encompasses. Unconscious Christianity could thus become an important category for thinking about the way in which the Church can respond positively to growing secularization, particularly in the context of Western Europe.

In addition, Bonhoeffer also thought that a characteristic of unconscious Christians is that they behave in a compassionate way toward disadvantaged people, and in doing so they engage with Christ.[4] This aspect of unconscious Christianity could form the background to dialogue and cooperation between the Church and organizations seeking to uphold social justice. It could also enable an engagement with society more broadly, highlighting Christianity's compassionate commitment to the disadvantaged and presenting this as a platform on which to build communal action against poverty and discrimination. I will return to the impact unconscious Christianity could have on the pressing questions facing the Church at the end of the book, when a proper understanding of Bonhoeffer's ideas on unconscious Christianity has been established.

Unconscious Christianity is not only of interest to the Church, but its importance within Bonhoeffer scholarship is also great. The definition of unconscious Christianity provided in this book will, for the first time, give scholars a common starting-point when discussing the place of unconscious Christianity within Bonhoeffer's theology. Achieving a definition of unconscious Christianity will have a fourfold impact on Bonhoeffer studies. Firstly, it enables a deeper understanding of the late theology. Secondly, it confirms that unconscious Christianity is not the same as Bonhoeffer's more well-known concept, religionless Christianity, and clarifies the difference between the two. Thirdly, it shows that there is movement within Bonhoeffer's ideas on unconscious Christianity, and points to the fluidity of Bonhoeffer's thoughts and his readiness to reassess previous convictions in the light of his changing circumstances during the last years of his life. Finally, it reveals that there is not only movement in Bonhoeffer's thoughts about unconscious Christianity, but that unconscious Christianity represents a shift within Bonhoeffer's theology.

As well as explaining what Bonhoeffer means by unconscious Christianity, this books also deals in depth with Bonhoeffer's fiction, which contains a reference to unconscious Christianity, and portrays characters described as unconscious Christians. It will become clear that Bonhoeffer's fiction must be considered theological writing.

Through this book I hope to show that while at first glance the question of unconscious Christianity appears extremely niche, its import reaches well beyond the confines of Bonhoeffer studies and into the questions faced daily by church congregations and theology faculties wishing to respond to life in the twenty-first century.

WHAT IS UNCONSCIOUS CHRISTIANITY?

Dietrich Bonhoeffer began to develop his thoughts on unconscious Christianity (*unbewußtes Christentum*) in his late theology, and it is in this context that we will be defining unconscious Christianity. Although several Bonhoeffer scholars have noted the appearance of the term in fragments dating from the prison period and shortly beforehand, no comprehensive study of unconscious Christianity has yet taken place. The fact that Bonhoeffer only mentions the term directly four times may go some way to explaining this gap in

Bonhoeffer scholarship, but it is surprising that so little attention has been given to a question that, by his own admission, preoccupied Bonhoeffer increasingly in his last months in prison. Although Bonhoeffer considered the question of unconscious Christianity over the course of several years, he never defined the concept. It is possible, however, to construct a definition of unconscious Christianity from the fragmentary texts that he left behind. In order to offer a theological definition of unconscious Christianity, this book engages in a close analysis of the texts in which Bonhoeffer mentions the term, and also of those texts in which he deals with the concept without mentioning it explicitly.

There are four texts in which Bonhoeffer mentions unconscious Christianity: the first is his *Ethics* essay "Ultimate and Penultimate Things,"[5] the second is the unfinished novel that he wrote in prison,[6] thirdly he mentions unconscious Christianity in a letter to Eberhard Bethge in July 1944,[7] and finally in some notes made in preparation for writing an outline of a new book.[8] It is likely that Bonhoeffer wrote more texts on unconscious Christianity that were lost. On the 28th of October 1944, Bethge, stationed in Italy, was carrying out his duty of reading the mail for his superior officer. On opening a telegram he read that he himself was to be taken to Berlin under guard. His immediate response was to burn the letters from Bonhoeffer that he had with him, before taking the mail to his superior. He did this in order to reduce the chances of his name being linked to that of Bonhoeffer's, who by that time had already been transferred from Tegel Military Prison to the Reich Central Security Office prison in Berlin. These last letters from Bonhoeffer to Bethge, often referred to as the "September correspondence," could well have included more thoughts on unconscious Christianity. Bonhoeffer had already written about it twice in late July/early August 1944, and in a letter dated the 24th of August Bethge had asked, "I wonder what more you have been thinking about 'unconscious Christianity'? That is so very important."[9]

Furthermore, according to a suggested reconstruction of the sequence in which Bonhoeffer had planned to order the contents of his *Ethics*, he had intended to write a chapter on "Good" which was to have followed on from "Ultimate and Penultimate Things" and "Natural Life."[10] At the end of "Ultimate and Penultimate Things," in the margin of which is one of the references to unconscious Christianity, Bonhoeffer describes unconscious Christians and the way in which confessing Christians ought to behave toward them.[11] He writes that confessing Christians should claim as Christians people who have chosen to distance themselves from Christianity, who "no longer dare to call themselves Christians."[12] Bonhoeffer ends "Ultimate and Penultimate Things" with: "The next two chapters should be understood in this *perspective*."[13] Following on from this comment, "Natural Life" can be read as an attempt on Bonhoeffer's part to convince those who choose not to self-identify as Christians that they are not so different from confessing Christians. One of the ways he does this is to highlight natural human characteristics, for example respect for parents,[14] which are shared equally by confessing Christians and others. It is possible that Bonhoeffer intended to extend this almost evangelical effort in the following chapter on the "Good."

It is a loss to this reflection on unconscious Christianity that Bonhoeffer never wrote the planned chapter on "Good." Only working notes survive. However, the fact that he meant it to be understood in the perspective of his comments at the end of "Ultimate and Penultimate Things" should be borne in mind when addressing the question of good people[15] that will arise throughout this book.

The surviving texts that refer to unconscious Christianity include sections of the fiction Bonhoeffer wrote while in prison. I suggest that the three extant pieces of fiction must be read not only as interesting autobiography about Bonhoeffer, his family, and their social background,[16] but also as theological texts in their own right. I contend that they are equal to his poetry and other prison writings in their importance in providing insight into his theological ideas while in Tegel prison.

Further to suggesting a definition of unconscious Christianity, I argue that Bonhoeffer's late theology cannot be completely grasped without an understanding of unconscious Christianity. Without taking it into consideration, Bonhoeffer's readers have no indication of how he conceives of the relationship between Christ and good people, a subject that Bonhoeffer himself says that theology has not sufficiently addressed.[17] Without an awareness of unconscious Christianity readers cannot see the full complexity of the prison texts. With an understanding of unconscious Christianity, readers will be able to more fully see how Bonhoeffer attempts to offer a theological explanation of how Christ is in relationship with good people.

A question that is often asked in connection with Bonhoeffer's work on unconscious Christianity is whether it is connected to Karl Rahner's concept of anonymous Christianity. While there are some similarities between the two concepts, they are by no means identical. In order to make the distinction between the two terms clear, it is worth spending some time looking at Rahner's description of the anonymous Christian. To do this, we will also briefly discuss Rahner's understanding of humanity in relationship to God, as his thoughts on the anonymous Christian depend on his theological anthropology. It will then become clear as we proceed that a different question preoccupies Bonhoeffer when he writes about unconscious Christianity.

BOOK STRUCTURE

The introduction to the book provides the background to Bonhoeffer's term "unconscious Christianity," outlining how it had previously been used in German Protestant theology by Richard Rothe and Martin Rade. Here I also introduce Karl Rahner's work on the anonymous Christian, to allow for a comparison between it and Bonhoeffer's unconscious Christianity to develop throughout the text. The introduction ends with notes on terminology.

The first part of the book, comprising the first three chapters, builds toward a constructed definition of unconscious Christianity as it appears in Bonhoeffer's late theology. I build this definition in three stages. The first chapter is biographical, focusing in particular on a description of the *Bürgertum*,[18] the social class of which the Bonhoeffer family were a part and in which Bonhoeffer grew up. The analysis of *bürgerlich* society and its values that features in this chapter will provide the necessary background for understanding more about not only Bonhoeffer's social and religious background, but also the setting in which his fiction takes place.

The second chapter discusses Bonhoeffer's fiction, which has been largely overlooked in Bonhoeffer scholarship, and sets out why it must be considered theological. I also examine Bonhoeffer's experimentation with various literary forms. In an attempt to make Christianity accessible to people with no theological knowledge, Bonhoeffer begins by writing a play, which he abandons to write a novel, before leaving that unfinished to complete a short story. Finally he turns to poetry. In the first two literary forms, he writes about his familiar *bürgerlich* society. His characters discuss ideas about God and religion explicitly. Remarkably, in his short story any words relating to God, the Church, theology, or Christianity are completely absent, and there is no direct reference to *bürgerlich* society. He continues to use poetry to explore complex theological ideas until shortly before his death.[19] I then turn to a description of the four texts in which Bonhoeffer mentions unconscious Christianity. I give an overview of each text, outlining the context in which it was written and the way in which Bonhoeffer addresses unconscious Christianity within it. With an awareness of the fiction as theological writing, as well as of the other instances in which Bonhoeffer mentions unconscious Christianity, it is possible to begin defining unconscious Christianity as Bonhoeffer presents it in each separate text.

In the first section of chapter 3, I propose a definition of unconscious Christianity for each text in which it is mentioned. This series of definitions traces the way in which Bonhoeffer develops the concept of unconscious Christianity over the course of time. I then assemble the definitions of unconscious Christianity arrived at after analysis of each text, and consider whether they can be taken together as forming a definition of one unified concept. I suggest that rather than describing a rigidly structured concept, these definitions point instead toward an evolving idea of unconscious Christianity. However, despite the fluid nature of Bonhoeffer's thoughts on unconscious Christianity, I contend that it is possible to put forward a definition of it that encompasses the various elements that he considered to be part of the concept, while acknowledging the direction in which Bonhoeffer was moving as he articulated his ideas on the subject.

The second part of the book, consisting of the last two chapters, and the conclusion build on the definition of unconscious Christianity arrived at in chapter 3. The last two chapters and the conclusion can be pictured as three widening concentric circles. They each expand on the information presented in chapter 3, broadening their focus to include a comparison with the other theological ideas Bonhoeffer developed in prison, tackling the question of continuity and change within Bonhoeffer's work, and identifying issues raised by the definition of unconscious Christianity.

In chapter 4 I show how unconscious Christianity fits in with the other, more well-known, ideas that Bonhoeffer developed during his imprisonment. This chapter contains analyses of the relationship between unconscious Christianity and two other central ideas from the Tegel theology: the world come of age and religionless Christianity. While this chapter does not aim to show whether unconscious Christianity is compatible with an exhaustive list of Bonhoeffer's theological concepts from the prison texts, it demonstrates how an understanding of unconscious Christianity adds depth to the reader's perception of other theological ideas from this period. It becomes clear that considering unconscious Christianity as an important theological idea broadens the reader's view of the theology that Bonhoeffer developed in prison. I then turn to a discussion of how unconscious Christianity has been addressed in Bonhoeffer scholarship, and suggest that the definition of it proposed in this book fits alongside, and adds significantly to, the existing conversation in this field.

The fifth chapter addresses the question of whether unconscious Christianity can be traced back to Bonhoeffer's earlier theological work, or whether it represents a new departure in his thinking. Engaging with some of Bonhoeffer's earlier writing and authors from both sides of the debate, I argue that unconscious Christianity represents a shift in his theology that should not be overlooked.[20]

The conclusion addresses the implications of my definition of unconscious Christianity for Bonhoeffer scholarship and theological thinking more broadly. To demonstrate how my research could inform Bonhoeffer scholarship, I ask what unconscious Christianity reveals about the way in which Bonhoeffer viewed the future of Christianity in a postwar world. I present a comparison between unconscious Christianity and promising godlessness,[21] suggesting that the latter might be related to, or even be a form of, unconscious Christianity. I draw attention to the many theological ideas that Bonhoeffer addresses in his fiction, and show how a close study of the fiction in conjunction with the other prison texts enriches our understanding of the Tegel theology, and the theological letters to Bethge in particular.

Finally, I discuss how my findings can impact how the Church relates to society. I point to ways in which the concept of unconscious Christianity as defined in this book is a useful addition to contemporary theological discussion. I suggest that consideration of unconscious Christianity would benefit specific categories of theological reflection which deal with the relationship between theology and society, and conclude that Bonhoeffer's concept is still not only relevant but useful in theology's assessment of the state of Christianity in Europe today.[22]

KARL RAHNER AND THE ANONYMOUS CHRISTIAN

Rahner begins his essay "Anonymous Christians" by outlining two opposing principles. The first is that Christian faith is necessary for salvation, and the second is "the universal salvific will of God's love and omnipotence."[23] He sees only one way in which to reconcile the two, and that is by affirming the capacity of all human beings to be members of the Church. This is not an abstract capacity, but a "real and historically concrete one."[24] This reasoning brings him to affirm the following:

> But this means in its turn that there must be degrees of membership of the Church, not only in ascending order from being baptised, through the acceptance of the fullness of the Christian faith and the recognition of the visible head of the Church, to the living community of the Eucharist, indeed to the realisation of holiness, but also in descending order from the explicitness of baptism into a non-official and anonymous Christianity which can and should yet be called Christianity in a meaningful sense, even though it itself cannot and would not describe itself as such.[25]

Rahner makes it clear in this passage that he thinks there are different types of Christianity, but considers them to be on different levels of a hierarchical scale. There are higher and lower "degrees of membership" of the Church. Anonymous Christianity figures on the lower end of the scale. The view that there are different forms of Christian expression is akin to Bonhoeffer's understanding of Christianity, as we will see further on in this investigation. However, we will also find that Rahner's opinion that these different forms of Christian expression are part of a hierarchical structure is vastly different to Bonhoeffer's view.

Nadia Delicata underlines Rahner's idea that some forms of Christianity are higher up on the hierarchical scale than others while making the point that Rahner counters his own claim for God's universal salvific will by arguing that receiving baptism for no other reason than to pay lip service to Christianity "is not enough to truly receive God's Gift of salvation."[26]

> While it is a greater good to recognize the Christ explicitly and not only implicitly, to become a member of the body of Christ through baptism and not only anonymously, water baptism without metanoia and an authentic desire to become like Christ is insufficient for our transformation to become children of God.[27]

Rahner's dismissal of performing Christian rituals without desiring to become like Christ echoes Bonhoeffer's critique of pious people in *Life Together*,[28] his comments on hopeless godlessness "dressed up in religious-Christian finery,"[29] and his writing about religious people refusing to suffer alongside Christ, to which we will turn in chapter 4.[30] Crucially, both theologians condemn empty religious actions, and neither the anonymous Christian nor the unconscious Christian performs any such actions. However, despite this similarity, and the fact that both men agree that Christianity can be expressed in different forms by different people, Rahner's view of anonymous Christianity as being at the bottom of a many-tiered hierarchy divides it from Bonhoeffer's unconscious Christianity, as we will see in chapter 4.

Underpinning Rahner's view of anonymous Christianity is his idea that God constantly pours out God's grace to humanity, and his subsequent theological anthropology. For Rahner, when God gives God's grace to humanity, God is in fact communicating Godself. This self-communication of God to humanity presupposes, argues Rahner, that humans are capable of hearing and of bearing witness to this self-communication. More than that, humans expect to hear this self-communication, even though they can't of course demand God to reveal Godself to them.[31] Another way that Rahner talks about this human expectation is by saying that humanity has a constant "tendency towards God, which is on occasion quite implicit and incoherent and yet always completely permeates man's being and existence."[32]

For Rahner, the incarnation is the peak of God's self-communication to us. This has repercussions for humanity itself. He writes:

> Man is accordingly in the most basic definition that which God becomes if he sets out to show himself in the region of the extra-divine. And conversely, formulating it from the point of view of man: man is he who realises himself when he gives himself away into the incomprehensible mystery of God. Seen in this way, the incarnation of God is the uniquely supreme case of the actualisation of man's nature in general.[33]

Because of this connection that he posits between what human nature is and how it relates to Christ, Rahner can affirm that anyone who "really accepts *himself completely*"[34] accepts God's revelation. Further, he is able to make a connection between those who accept God's self-communication, which is God's grace, and a form of Christianity: "And anyone who has let himself be taken hold of by this grace can be called with every right an 'anonymous Christian.'"

This might later lead the individual to affirm faith in God in a formal ecclesiastical context, and for Rahner it is to be hoped that this will be the case, but Rahner describes this anonymous relationship to God as more than simply an internal disposition:

> Prior to the explicitness of official ecclesiastical faith this acceptance can be present in an implicit form whereby a person undertakes and lives the duty of each day in the quiet sincerity of patience, in devotion to his material duties and the demands made upon him by the persons under his care. What he is then taking upon himself is therefore not merely his basic relationship with the silent mystery of the Creator-God.[35]

According to Rahner, anonymous Christianity must necessarily go hand in hand with "a *certain* making visible and tangible of the anonymous relationship,"[36] which might look like the "duty of each day" described above. This is based on Rahner's understanding of the Church as being more than an inner reality: if someone is a member of the Church, this membership must be expressed differently than in a "merely intangible inner way."[37] He gives another example of an anonymous Christian expressing his relationship with God through a "loving humaneness,"[38] but does not go into detail about what this might entail. We will return to some of the actions that Rahner describes as belonging to the anonymous Christian, and will see that they bear some resemblance to the actions Bonhoeffer ascribes to unconscious Christians. However, it will become increasingly apparent that Rahner's idea of the anonymous Christian emerges from a theology that stands in sharp contrast to Bonhoeffer's, and that the two types of theological anthropology that the thinkers present are very different to each other. Indeed, the theological structures and assumptions surrounding anonymous Christianity and unconscious Christianity are so at odds with each other that the superficial similarities between the two ideas can't hide the wide gulf that separates them.

Rahner on the Future of Society

Bonhoeffer's and Rahner's views on the future of society highlight the way in which their opinions on how humanity and God relate to each other diverge. I will be referring to Bonhoeffer's views on this subject at various points throughout this book, and these points will provide the opportunity to compare Bonhoeffer's opinion to Rahner's. For the time being, it's sufficient to note that both theologians agree that society in the West is heading toward a time in which people will no longer share Christianity as a common reference point. Raoul Dederen remarks that Rahner views the Christianity and the Church of his day as existing in a cultural context in which the general public, aware of the empirical sciences and their methods, will be "in a quite definite sense a-theistic."[39] According to Dederen, Rahner argues that awareness of the empirical sciences does not necessarily exclude faith and any reference to God, but that the a-theistic nature of society will only increase in the years to come. This sounds very similar to the way in which Bonhoeffer views society, as we will see in due course. Both theologians acknowledge the recent advances of the empirical sciences and their impact on Christian faith. Both see a resulting decrease of Christian faith as the default position in society, which Bonhoeffer refers to as moving away from the "working hypothesis: God."[40] However, their views on how humanity responds to increasing knowledge of the world and mastery over technology differ greatly. As will be explained in more detail in chapter 4, Bonhoeffer thinks that in the world come of age humanity ceases to need God. However, George Lindbeck calls our attention to the fact that for Rahner, humanity's moving away from religion is only a passing phenomenon. According to Lindbeck, Rahner posits that despite his view of society just outlined, the world will still be "a world overshadowed by that wordless mystery that we call God."[41] Humanity will continue to subjugate the world, only to realize that human anxiety and craving for the infinite remain. According to Rahner, as humanity's technological control over the world increases, the question of religion will in all likelihood arise again.[42] Lindbeck sums up Rahner's view as follows: As humanity increases its understanding of, and mastery over, the world, there is an intensification of the separation between the world and God. As a result, humanity will renew its call to God as a God who is outside the world. In Bonhoefferean terms, this situation forces humanity to adopt the view of the *homo religiosus*. As we will see in the discussion of religionless Christianity in chapter 4, Bonhoeffer describes the religious person as someone who thinks of God as being outside the world, instead of perceiving God as suffering within the world. When faced with suffering, the religious person seeks help from a God who is akin to a *deus ex machina*, instead of trying to perceive God as active within the world. This view of God in relation to the world is precisely the view that Bonhoeffer deplores.[43]

I've noted that Rahner thinks humanity has a "tendency" toward God. This permeating tendency toward God, which will trigger a return to a religious seeking of God in the technological age, is what allows the individual to perceive God's saving word, even though this might be done unconsciously. Delicata underlines Rahner's idea that the very essence of being human is to be seeking the divine at all times. She describes this seeking as having "the right 'antennae' to receive God's communication."[44] Human beings desire the Holy Spirit, and for their restless hearts to be at rest in God. Delicata writes: "Our 'restlessness' is a clear sign of our 'searching,' of our seeking the one who fulfils our desire for transcendence."[45]

There is no restlessness in Bonhoeffer's conception of humanity in the world come of age. As will become clear, Bonhoeffer thinks that humanity in this new context has no need for a relationship with the transcendent, being able to solve its own problems without recourse to Christianity.[46] The difference between the two men's understanding of humanity's relationship with God helps to highlight another difference between unconscious Christianity and anonymous Christianity. Delicata explains Rahner's view that God desires to communicate with all human beings, and that "in our humanity we are all blessed with the desire to seek transcendence and to become 'like God.'"[47] The encounter with the divine can happen without a formal recognition of Jesus as Savior, and without baptism. She continues:

> Rahner calls these numerous men and women who are desirous of "God," and receive and embrace the gift of God's self-communication—even if only in the hiddenness of their hearts—"anonymous Christians." They can be religious others, committed to various religious paths; they can be secular others, claiming no overt allegiance to any religion; but they must be desirous of authentic transcendence, walking on a spiritual path, seeking the divine Spirit of holiness.[48]

The importance of desiring "authentic transcendence," and of seeking "the divine Spirit of holiness" is unique to anonymous Christianity. We will see later on in the book that the unconscious Christian neither desires transcendence, nor wishes to seek a divine Spirit, and that if she does seek anything in a conscious manner, it is to value the worldly, the concrete, giving help to people who are suffering in the world. Furthermore, the unconscious Christian does not wish to seek a divine Spirit. We will see that in some cases, the unconscious Christian has consciously rejected any attempt at engaging with God, even though an unconscious encounter with Christ occurs.[49]

This is of necessity a cursory appraisal of some differences and similarities between unconscious Christianity and anonymous Christianity. However, it has sufficed to show that although some similarities might at first suggest that both terms refer to the same idea, examining them in more depth immediately reveals that this is not the case. There is some kinship between the anonymous Christian and the unconscious Christian, but Rahner and Bonhoeffer were working within very different theological frameworks, which led them to very different views about how people relate, unwittingly, to Christ. The definition of unconscious Christianity that I propose in this book enables a methodical comparison between Rahner's anonymous Christian and Bonhoeffer's unconscious Christianity that hitherto was not possible because of the lack of any clear definition of unconscious Christianity in Bonhoeffer's theology. However, it can be said at the outset that Rahner's articulation of anonymous Christianity is not simply a repetition of what had come before in Bonhoeffer's work on unconscious Christianity.

APPROACHING FRAGMENTARY TEXTS

The question of how to treat the fragments that survive from the Tegel years is a contentious one in Bonhoeffer scholarship. For instance, Eric Mascall writes that the prison theology should not be taken "*au pied de la lettre*," as it was written "under conditions of grave physical and emotional distress."[50] However, Ferdinand Schlingensiepen notes that "Many commentators after the Second World War, including even Karl Barth, wanted to ascribe Bonhoeffer's new theological ideas to the shock of his arrest and imprisonment; but he had already left that far behind when he began expressing his new insights."[51] Schlingensiepen refers here to the difference between the early part of Bonhoeffer's imprisonment, in which he considered suicide and suffered, albeit only for a short time, from what Bethge terms *tristita*,[52] and the period beginning in spring 1944, which Schlingensiepen describes as follows: "In April 1944 he came to a watershed; the style and content of his letters changed so fundamentally that not even the 20th of July, with the news that once again the coup d'état had failed, could alter them any longer."[53] James W. Woelfel cites Thomas F. Torrance as describing the fragments as "stray sentences of an exaggerated kind penned under the stress of Nazi oppression in Buchenwald."[54] Woelfel states that Torrance rejects the theological ideas from the prison period "by means of what I would call psychological innuendo, a familiar conservative way of lightly dismissing the prison writings."[55] He continues: "To dismiss the 'Christianity without religion' project by psychological innuendo is not only somewhat irresponsibly facile; it is also an unfair and inaccurate portrayal of Bonhoeffer himself."[56] Woelfel argues that although Bonhoeffer and other prisoners of the regime were treated harshly and subjected to severe privations, "there is absolutely no evidence in the prison writings or in the accounts of Eberhard Bethge and of fellow prisoners to show that the 'non-religious' reflections are in any way the ecstatic product of excessive psychological strain."[57]

Woelfel does not claim that the prison texts define Bonhoeffer's theology. However, he argues for a reading of the texts that does not diminish their value due to the conditions in which they were written. For Woelfel, the fragmentary nature of the Tegel writings prevents them from being considered as defining Bonhoeffer's theology. Here I go further than Woelfel is prepared to go, and propose that in spite of its fragmentary form, the Tegel material must be allowed to define Bonhoeffer's late theology. From it, it is possible to build a definition of unconscious Christianity that is essential to a complete understanding of Bonhoeffer's theology.

There are of course difficulties involved in constructing a coherent definition of unconscious Christianity from the fragments surviving from the Tegel years. In the matter of how to approach fragmentary texts, I take my cue from Bonhoeffer's own thoughts on the fragmentary nature of life, and Heinrich Ott's suggestions on how to read the late fragments. In a letter to his parents reflecting on the difference between their generation and his own, Bonhoeffer writes:

> Moreover—our generation may no longer expect a life that unfolds fully, both professionally and personally so that it becomes a balanced and fulfilled whole, as was still possible for your generation. [. . .] Probably that is why we feel especially strongly how unfinished and fragmentary our lives are. But precisely that which is fragmentary may point to a higher fulfillment, which can no longer be achieved by human effort. That is the only way I can think, especially when confronted with the deaths of so many of my best former students. Even when the violence of outward events breaks our lives in pieces, as the bombs do our houses, everything possible must be done to keep in view the way all this was planned and intended to be. At the very least, it will still be possible to recognize from what kind of material here we build or must build.[58]

Bonhoeffer's own words annihilate the opinion, popular among some Bonhoeffer scholars, that his prison writings should be discarded due to their incomplete nature. Ott refers to this letter in his comments on how to read Bonhoeffer's fragments, noting that:

> What Bonhoeffer here says expressly about his life must also be true of his work, which was so closely bound up with that life. For interpretation of his work the basis must be to recognize "how the whole was planned and thought out," or at least "what material was used here for building."[59]

Taking Bonhoeffer's idea that that which is fragmentary can point to a higher fulfilment, this book is based on the presupposition that by examining the fragments of Bonhoeffer's late theology, it is possible to perceive an outline of Bonhoeffer's late theology as a whole. The fragments reveal Bonhoeffer's theological intentions. At the very least, they allow us to see the theological material that Bonhoeffer uses to build his late theology.

While this work relies on the idea that fragments can point to a whole, it is also important to recognize the unfinished nature of these fragments. Ott reflects on the qualities of letter-writing, noting that the writer must allow for his text to be questioned by its reader, and must be prepared to receive a counterargument in reply. The letter-writer must, therefore, perceive letter-writing as an ongoing dialogue, rather than an opportunity to set down his thoughts as though in a treatise. Ott writes of the prison letters that: "The latest and possibly most essential thoughts of Bonhoeffer, the goal of his mind's pilgrimage, meet us in this peculiar mediating form between the finality of a work and a living discussion of the present day."[60] He therefore proposes reading the prison fragments in a dialogical manner, remaining aware that the thoughts expressed in these texts are not intended as set in stone by their author, but that Bonhoeffer was prepared to refine his ideas in the light of the responses he received from his correspondent. Heinz Eduard Tödt agrees with this assessment, writing that the Tegel letters are "experimental, unguarded, bold, trusting that the reader, the intimate friend, will understand, complete, and add more to thoughts that had remained unfinished in the shortness of time."[61]

This book treats the fragments as able to point toward the prison theology as a whole, while recognizing the fluid and unfinished nature of this part of Bonhoeffer's work. It tries to heed the warning issued by Wayne Whitson Floyd Jr. that the prison texts should not be "domesticated," but that:

> They must be allowed to remain "radical" in the truest sense, for they go directly to the root of issues, saying things that perhaps *should* have been obvious to Christians even in the 1940s, but certainly still haven't been entertained by much of the church even a half-century later.[62]

Floyd is correct not only in his assessment of the radical nature of some of the ideas in Bonhoeffer's prison texts, but also in his indictment of the lack of serious attention given by the Church to these ideas.

ORIGINS OF THE TERM "UNCONSCIOUS CHRISTIANITY"

When he wrote "*Unbewußtes Christentum*" in the margin of his *Ethics*, Bonhoeffer was not coining a phrase new to German theology. On the contrary, it had already been used by both Richard Rothe and Martin Rade, editor of *Die Christliche Welt*. There is no direct evidence to show that Bonhoeffer had read either man's account of unconscious Christianity. However, it is more than mere speculation to suggest that Bonhoeffer would have been aware that the term was already part of German Protestant theological discourse. It is therefore useful to understand how the term was used by Bonhoeffer's predecessors, in order to see how his view of unconscious Christianity relates to their own.

Richard Rothe

Richard Rothe is credited as being the first person to use the term *unconscious Christianity*. Described by Martin Rade as "A really undogmatic, non-ecclesiastical, modern Christian, but not at all an unconscious one!"[63] Rothe was a theology professor at Heidelberg from 1837 until his death in 1867.[64]

He refers to unconscious Christianity in his 1862 essay "Zur Orientierung über die gegenwärtige Aufgabe der deutsch-evangelischen Kirche."[65] In the paper, Rothe assesses the development of the Lutheran Church since the eighteenth-century European Revival. He argues that an increasingly pietistic understanding and practice of Christianity over the last century has alienated a large part of the population, of which a majority are intellectuals. The forsaking of the Church by the intellectual classes has produced two unfortunate consequences. The first affects the clergy: they are no longer challenged by the intellectuals among their parishioners to take modern culture seriously and to develop their own views on how the Church should relate to modern culture. The second affects those who have chosen to distance themselves from the Church: their choice is calmly accepted by those remaining within the Church, and nothing is being done to draw them back within the community. Rothe writes: "It weighs on my conscience to accept to leave numerous classes of our population to their fate, which the Church is on the point of doing."[66] Rothe argues that until the Kingdom of the Spirit is established on earth and renders all churches superfluous, something needs to be done in order to turn the Church away from its pietistic tendencies and its emphasis on orthodox dogma, and toward forming a real bond with human culture and society.[67] This would enable people to truly belong to the Church whilst also truly being part of contemporary culture.

To this end, Rothe suggests a down-to-earth approach that should be adopted by all Church members:

> We spiritual people—as the Church appoints us to be—should be leaders to Christ among our communities. We should (as long as this is humanly possible) help them to come to belong to Christ, in the truest sense of the word, and be true and right Christians through real, living, personal faith.[68]

Rothe highlights the need for Church members to be active members of society. If they are not integrated into their lay communities, how can they become leaders showing the way to Christ within these communities? Rothe calls for an end to the hostility between believers and unbelievers, both of whom in fact belong to the Church. Rade, who offers an overview of Rothe's position in his article "Unbewusstes Christentum,"[69] whose title reflects the importance of the concept of unconscious Christianity within Rothe's essay, explains that according to Rothe, the Church will not lose anything by widening its boundaries to include these new members:

> Fortunately, the church will not lose anything by this. Because the brothers, who currently stand outside and should be won by this new way, are in reality not the "unbelievers" and the "unchristians" which the churchly people hold them to be.[70]

In Rothe's view, the people outside the Church are in fact neither unbelievers nor non-Christians. Their belief and Christianity are not obvious to those observing them from within the Church. Rothe adds that Christianity is sometimes absent from traditions established by the Church, only to reveal itself unexpectedly in situations that lack any external links to institutional Christianity.[71] According to Rothe, therefore, Christianity is confined neither to the institutional Church, nor to those who make up its congregations. This should be recognized by the Church, and a conscious effort should be made to celebrate the latent Christianity in society, as well as condemn the attitude within the Church that labels all those outside it as unbelieving non-Christians. Rothe concludes that what the Church needs is a new version of the apostle Paul:

> Oh, how much our generation needs a new Paul, a new holy Apostle, to convict our unconscious Christians of their Christianity, and thereby at the same time our Judeo-Christians of the un-Christianness of their legal, i.e. conventional Christianity, with the power of the Spirit![72]

Reinhold Bernhardt assesses Rothe's stance in terms of a tension between the Church and Christendom. In this context, he writes, Christendom should be understood neither as the historical religion of Christianity, nor as the individual's religion, but as the spiritual power of God that shapes the world, emanating from Christ and operating through history.[73] Bernhardt explains that according to Rothe, secularization is not to be lamented over, but greeted as a providential phenomenon. Although the Church's function is reduced within secularized society,[74] such a reduction is not applicable to Christ: "Christ shines not only out of the Gospel, but also '*with ever increasing clarity* out of all of his works of world history over the past eighteen centuries.'"[75]

Bernhardt defines Rothe's idea of unconscious Christianity as being a spiritual reality within ecclesiastical Christianity understood as a historical, social entity. Unconscious Christians are baptized, and are therefore nominally members of the Church, but they have now distanced themselves internally from it.[76] They are part of Christendom, in that they participate in God's history-shaping power through their engagement with the historical, social world in which God is at work. In this view of unconscious Christianity therefore, unconscious Christians stand in tension between the Church to which they nominally belong, and the world toward which they have turned. According to Rothe, God is at work equally in both spheres.

Indeed, despite the unconscious Christians' internal turning away from the Church, Rothe thinks that the Holy Spirit expresses the Spirit's self in unconscious Christianity just as much as in conscious Christianity. Bernhardt highlights the idea that the Holy Spirit, when expressing the Spirit's self in unconscious Christianity, is doing so "in his moral essence and his striving for the Kingdom of God."[77] Thus morality and the striving for God's Kingdom are central to Rothe's understanding of the activity of the Holy Spirit within unconscious Christianity.

However, as Bernhardt points out, Rothe thinks that unconscious Christians often are not aware that morality is at the heart of the Christian faith. This is due to the false conception, held by those outside the Church, of what faith is. People outside the Church perceive faith as accepting theological statements. According to Rothe's thesis that the Holy Spirit is at work in unconscious Christians expressing the Spirit's moral essence and striving for the Kingdom of God, unconscious Christians display Christian morality, and act in such a way as to further God's Kingdom. However, because they do not understand Christian faith correctly, they are unable to make the connection between their own actions and Christian faith. Rothe argues that the Church must help to make this connection clear. The Church must reveal Christianity's moral essence to those who misunderstand Christian faith, and, furthermore, must allow it to take the place previously occupied within their consciousness by theological ideology. Bernhardt cites a sermon in which Rothe uses the term "unconscious Christianity" for the first time and in which he says that:

> You will now become aware of real faith in Jesus, that is already in existence in you, but that you have not recognised until now, because a false idea of it blinded your eyes—it will turn what has been until now your *unconscious* Christianity into *conscious* Christianity.[78]

When Rothe refers to unconscious Christianity, he means a Christianity that is prevalent in people who have turned away from the Church, and who are considered by many still within it as unbelievers and non-Christians. However, this is a false perception: Christianity is indeed possible outside the institutional Church, because of God's power at work in history. The Holy Spirit is expressing the Spirit's self through unconscious Christians, showing that God is at work equally in those who do and those who don't adhere to the Church. It is the Church's responsibility to teach unconscious Christians what real faith in Christ is, and to lead unconscious Christians to a true belief in Christ. This entails a recognition of the moral center of Christian faith, instead of a dogged attachment to theological theses.

Martin Rade

Martin Rade is another important figure in the development of the term "unconscious Christianity." Distancing himself from Rothe's positive view of the progression of history and the idea that every advance made by humanity can be traced back to Christ, Rade also refutes the idea that there is a latent Christianity within society simply by virtue of God's involvement in human history. He argues that it is not enough for an individual to be an active member of society for her to be a Christian, unconscious or otherwise.

Rade begins his 1905 article "Unbewusstes Christentum" with a definition of unconscious Christianity: "Unconscious Christianity is a Christianity that one does not know one has. Others know about it, and call it Christianity, they claim it as Christianity."[79] This definition highlights two important points in Rade's understanding of unconscious Christianity. Firstly, people are able to recognize unconscious Christianity in others, and secondly, they claim it as a type of Christianity. This is a different viewpoint than Rothe's, who emphasizes the problem of people within the Church not recognizing unconscious Christianity as a type of Christianity, and not being interested in claiming it as such.

Rade also differs from Rothe's opinion about the central place of morality within Christianity. Bernhardt points out that for Rade, the primary effect of the incarnation is not the Christianization of culture, but rather the creation of the possibility for humanity of a relationship with God.[80] Thus, while Rade argues with Rothe that unconscious Christians should be made aware of their Christianity, he does so because unconscious Christians would then be aware of their relationship with God, not because unconscious Christians are already displaying Christian morality through their actions. Rade also rejects the idea that theological concepts should be removed from people's understanding of the Christian faith, writing:

> What is necessary for the unconscious Christian to become a conscious Christian? First of all, certainly not a reduction of the contents of the sermon or the confession, as if the world were to be had by the lowest bidder. On the contrary: more content, more tradition, more confession![81]

He adds that it is necessary that the unconscious Christian should be given complete freedom to decide whether to take up the offer of learning more about Christianity, stressing the importance of the genuine personal relationship to the truth, and, ultimately, to God. Being a Christian is something special, different from simply being a member of society, and therefore a freely made decision to step out of the ordinary is crucial is if the distinction between Christianity and the world is to be maintained.

Both Rothe and Rade agree that unconscious Christians are people who are Christian without realizing this to be the case. They also both agree that steps must be taken by the Church to convince unconscious Christians of their Christianity, and to draw them into the Church. However, their recommendations for how to do so differ greatly, due to their contrasting views on society and the progression of history. Furthermore, their opinion concerning who recognizes unconscious Christians as such are at odds with each other.

Therefore, despite some agreement, Rothe and Rade disagree on how unconscious Christians are viewed by others, and how they relate to conscious Christians, the Church, and society. This shows that there was no unified concept of unconscious Christianity within German Protestant theology at this time. In constructing a definition of unconscious Christianity as used by Bonhoeffer, I will refer back to Rothe and Rade's views of unconscious Christianity, in order to assess to what extent Bonhoeffer is in agreement with his predecessors.

A FEW NOTES ON STYLE AND TERMINOLOGY

When referring to Bonhoeffer's late theology, I mean specifically his *Ethics* and his prison texts. In this I follow Bethge's analysis, discussed in chapter 4, of three distinct periods in Bonhoeffer's life. The writing I refer to as the late theology is that which emerges from the period Bethge refers to as "Liberation."[82]

I engage with both Renate Bethge and Eberhard Bethge in this book. Due to Eberhard's more substantial work on Bonhoeffer's life and theology, and to the frequency with which I refer to it, I will hereafter refer to him only as "Bethge." I will give Renate Bethge's name in full when I refer to her and her contribution to Bonhoeffer studies.

I use the term "good people" throughout this text. By good people, I mean people whom Bonhoeffer describes as doing good things, or as being part of the "human and the good" that should be "claimed for Christ."[83] Bonhoeffer uses the term "good people" in his late theology,[84] and where I cite his use of the term, I put the words in quotation marks.

Bonhoeffer's term "*unbewußt*" is translated throughout this book as "unconscious." The meaning of being "unconscious" of something in this context is to be unaware of something. The term "unwitting" conveys a similar meaning. "Unconscious" in this context does not refer to the conditions of being asleep, in a faint, or knocked out. I have deliberately chosen the term "unconscious" instead of "subconscious," based on the fact that Bonhoeffer uses the term "*unbewußt*" and not "*unterbewußt*."[85] "Unconscious" is also the term in standard use in Bonhoeffer scholarship.

When I identify unconscious Christianity as representing a shift within Bonhoeffer's theology, I take the term "shift" to be defined as it is in the Concise Oxford English Dictionary: "a slight change in position, direction, or tendency."[86] I therefore do not mean that unconscious Christianity brings about a change so radical in Bonhoeffer's theology that one would have to entirely separate the theology before the appearance of unconscious Christianity from that which comes after it. The term "shift" allows for development within one same overarching pattern, for a change that does not bring about a cutting off from that which precedes it. Indeed, I argue that Bonhoeffer develops his ideas on unconscious Christianity over the period in which he writes about it, instead of seeing unconscious Christianity as a unit that he injects, ready-made, into his theology. There is no clean break between his theology before and after the addition of unconscious Christianity. However, it marks a change in Bonhoeffer's position on the importance of self-identification within Christianity, and a change in direction regarding the forms in which he imagines Christianity can be expressed.

NOTES

1. For a succinct summary of Bonhoeffer's influence on the struggle against apartheid in South Africa, as well as examples of his influence in other political contexts, see Christiane Tietz, *Theologian of Resistance: The Life and Thought of Dietrich Bonhoeffer*, trans. Victoria J. Barnett (Minneapolis: Fortress Press, 2016), 116–17. For a more in-depth account of the relevance of Bonhoeffer's theology for the South African context, see John de Gruchy, *Bonhoeffer and South Africa: Theology in Dialogue* (Grand Rapids, Michigan: William B. Eerdmans Publishing Company), 1984.
2. Dietrich Bonhoeffer, *Letters and Papers from Prison*, DBWE vol. 8, ed. John W. de Gruchy, trans. Isabel Best, Lisa E. Dahill, Reinhard Krauss, and Nancy Lukens (Minneapolis: Fortress Press, 2010), 489.
3. See Dietrich Bonhoeffer, *Ethics*, DBWE vol. 6, ed. Clifford J. Green, trans. Reinhard Krauss, Charles C. West, and Douglas W. Stott (Minneapolis: Fortress Press, 2009), 146–70. The term "unconscious Christianity" is scribbled in the margin at the end of the manuscript. The last page of the "Ultimate and Penultimate Things" manuscript is reproduced in the appendix, document 1.
4. This will be discussed in chapter 3.
5. Bonhoeffer, *Ethics*, 170.
6. Dietrich Bonhoeffer, *Fiction from Tegel Prison*, DBWE vol. 7, ed. Clifford J. Green, trans. Nancy Lukens (Minneapolis: Fortress Press 2010), 71–182.
7. Bonhoeffer, *Letters and Papers from Prison*, 489–90.
8. Bonhoeffer, *Letters and Papers from Prison*, 491. These will henceforth be referred to as "Notes II," as that is the title under which they appear in *Letters and Papers from Prison*.
9. Bonhoeffer, *Letters and Papers from Prison*, 522.
10. See Ilse Tödt, Heinz Eduard Tödt, Ernst Feil, and Clifford Green, Editors' Afterword to the German Edition of Bonhoeffer, *Ethics*, 447–48.
11. For a full discussion of unconscious Christianity in "Ultimate and Penultimate Things," see chapter 3.
12. Bonhoeffer, *Ethics*, 170.
13. Bonhoeffer, *Ethics*, 170.
14. Bonhoeffer, *Ethics*, 177.
15. For an explanation of my use of the term "good people," see my comments on terminology at the end of the introduction.
16. This is how the fiction has mostly been read among Bonhoeffer scholars to date. See Clifford J. Green's introduction to the English edition of Bonhoeffer, *Fiction from Tegel Prison*, 9.
17. Bonhoeffer, *Ethics*, 348 and following. Bonhoeffer formulates the question thus: "The question is what it means that the good find Christ. In other words, what is the relation of Jesus Christ to those who are good and that which is good?"
18. Usually translated in Bonhoeffer scholarship as "upper middle class" or "educated middle class."

19. The last extant poem by Bonhoeffer, "By Powers of Good" was sent to Maria von Wedemeyer on the 19th of December 1944. A note on it reads "New Year, 1945." See Bonhoeffer, *Letters and Papers from Prison*, 548–50.
20. For my definition of the term "shift," see my comments on terminology at the end of the introduction.
21. See Bonhoeffer, *Ethics*, 124.
22. As I specify in my concluding discussion, I confine my comments to the state of Christianity in Western Europe. For my reasons for doing this, see the conclusion.
23. Karl Rahner, *Theological Investigations, vol. 6, Concerning Vatican Council II*, trans. Karl-H. Kruger and Boniface Kruger (London: Darton, Longman and Todd; New York: Seabury Press, 1969), 391.
24. Rahner, *Theological Investigations*, 391.
25. Rahner, *Theological Investigations*, 391.
26. Nadia Delicata, "Revisiting Karl Rahner's 'Anonymous Christian': Towards a Christian Theology of the Religions Grounded in the Kenotic Ethic of Imitatio Christi" (paper presented at *Engaging Particularities IV: New Directions in Comparative Theology, Interreligious Dialogue, Theology of Religions and Missiology Conference*, Boston College, Massachusetts, 17–19 March 2006), (Chestnut Hill, MA: Theology Dept., Boston College, 2006), 4. http://dlib.bc.edu/islandora/object/bc-ir:102756.
27. Delicata, "Revisiting Karl Rahner's 'Anonymous Christian,'" 4.
28. See Dietrich Bonhoeffer, *Life Together and Prayerbook of the Bible*, DBWE vol. 5, ed. Geffrey B. Kelly, trans. Daniel W. Bloesch and James H. Burtness (Minneapolis: Fortress Press, 2005), 38f.
29. Bonhoeffer, *Ethics*, 124.
30. See Bonhoeffer, *Letters and Papers from Prison*, 480, and also chapter 4.
31. See Rahner, *Theological Investigations*, 392.
32. Rahner, *Theological Investigations*, 392–93.
33. Rahner, *Theological Investigations*, 393.
34. Rahner, *Theological Investigations*, 394.
35. Rahner, *Theological Investigations*, 394.
36. Rahner, *Theological Investigations*, 392.
37. Rahner, *Theological Investigations*, 392.
38. Rahner, *Theological Investigations*, 395.
39. Raoul Dederen, "Karl Rahner's *The Shape of the Church to Come*: A Review Article" in *Andrews University Seminary Studies* Vol. XIV (1976), 219.
40. See Bonhoeffer, *Letters and Papers from Prison*, 425–26.
41. George A. Lindbeck, "Thought of Karl Rahner, S J," *Christianity and Crisis* 25, no. 17 (October 18, 1965): 214.
42. Lindbeck, "Thought of Karl Rahner, S J," 214. Here Lindbeck references Rahner, *Mission and Grace: Essays in Pastoral Theology* (London: Sheed and Ward, 1963), vol. 1, 1–55, vol. 2, 105–15, and Rahner, *Free Speech in the Church* (London & New York: Sheed and Ward, c. 1959).
43. For a more detailed discussion of these ideas, see chapter 4.
44. Delicata, "Revisiting Karl Rahner's 'Anonymous Christian,'" 2.
45. Delicata, "Revisiting Karl Rahner's 'Anonymous Christian,'" 2. Delicata cites Karl Rahner, *Foundations of Christian Faith: An Introduction to the Idea of Christianity*, trans. William V. Dych, (New York: Crossroad, 1999), 318.
46. See Bonhoeffer, *Letters and Papers from Prison*, 406.
47. Delicata, "Revisiting Karl Rahner's 'Anonymous Christian,'" 3.
48. Delicata, "Revisiting Karl Rahner's 'Anonymous Christian,'" 3.
49. This will be discussed in relation to Bonhoeffer's description of people in his essay "Ultimate and Penultimate Things" in his *Ethics*. See in particular *Ethics*, 170.
50. E. H. Mascall, *The Secularization of Christianity: An Analysis and a Critique* (New York: Holt, Rinehart & Winston, 1965), 41.
51. Ferdinand Schlingensiepen, *Dietrich Bonhoeffer, 1906–1945: Martyr, Thinker, Man of Resistance* (New York: T&T Clark, 2010), 350.

52. See Eberhard Bethge, *Dietrich Bonhoeffer: Theologian, Christian, Contemporary*, ed. Edwin Robertson, trans. Eric Mosbacher (London: Collins, 1970), 735–36.
53. Schlingensiepen, *Dietrich Bonhoeffer, 1906–1945*, 249.
54. James W. Woelfel, *Bonhoeffer's Theology: Classical and Revolutionary* (Nashville: Abingdon Press, 1970), 293. The article Woelfel cites appeared in *The Scotsman* on the 28th of May 1966. Woelfel points out that in fact the Tegel material was written in Tegel prison in Berlin, not in Buchenwald. Bonhoeffer was only moved to Buchenwald in early 1945, and by then he was not allowed any contact with the outside world.
55. Woelfel, *Bonhoeffer's Theology*, 293.
56. Woelfel, *Bonhoeffer's Theology*, 294.
57. Woelfel, *Bonhoeffer's Theology*, 293.
58. Bonhoeffer, *Letters and Papers from Prison*, 301.
59. Heinrich Ott, *Reality and Faith: The Theological Legacy of Dietrich Bonhoeffer* (London: Lutterworth Press, 1971), 65.
60. Ott, *Reality and Faith*, 94.
61. Heinz Eduard Tödt, *Authentic Faith: Bonhoeffer's Theological Ethics in Context*, ed. Glen Harold Stassen, trans. David Stassen and Ilse Tödt (Grand Rapids, MI & Cambridge, UK: William B. Eerdmans Publishing Company, 2007), 42.
62. Wayne Whitson Floyd Jr., "Bonhoeffer's Literary Legacy," in *The Cambridge Companion to Dietrich Bonhoeffer*, ed. John W. de Gruchy (Cambridge: Cambridge University Press, 1999), 86.
63. Martin Rade, "Unbewusstes Christentum," in *Seite zur Christlichen Welt*, 53 (1905): 5. The original reads: "Ein ausgesprochen undogmatischer, unkirchlicher, moderner Christ, aber gar kein unbewusster!" All translations relating to Rade's article are by the author.
64. In fact Rothe took a five-year break from his Heidelberg professorship between 1849 and 1854. He was invited to Bonn to take up the position of university preacher and theology professor.
65. Richard Rothe, "Zur Orientierung über die gegenwärtige Aufgabe der deutsch-evangelischen Kirche" in *Allgemeine Kirchliche Zeitschrift: Ein Organ für die evangelische Geistlichkeit und Gemeinde*, (1862). In English the title reads: "On the orientation of the present-day task of the German Evangelical Church." All translations relating to Rothe's article are by the author.
66. Rothe is quoted in Rade, 6. The original reads: "Es drängt mich im Gewissen, mich der zahlreichen Klasse unsrer Bevölkerung anzunehmen, welche die Kirche im Begriff steht, ihrem Schiksal zu überlassen."
67. The term translated here as the Kingdom of the Spirit is "Reich des Geistes" (see Rade, 7). As Johannes Zachhuber notes, the German term "Geist" can be translated in English as both "mind" and "spirit." See Johannes Zachhuber, *Theology as Science in Nineteenth-Century Germany: From F. C. Baur to Ernst Troeltsch* (Oxford: Oxford University Press, 2013), 65. The eschatological meaning of "Reich des Geistes" here shows that it should be translated in this instance as "Kingdom of the Spirit."
68. Rothe, "Zur Orientierung über die gegenwärtige Aufgabe der deutsch-evangelischen Kirche," 39. The original reads: "Wir Geistliche—dazu beruft uns die Kirche—sollen unsern Gemeinden Führer zu Christo sein, sollen ihnen (so weit dies in menschlicher Macht steht,) dazu helfen, daß sie wahre, rechte Christen, durch wirklichen, lebendigen, persönlichen Glauben Christo, im eigentlichten Sinne des Worts, angehörig werden."
69. See Rade, "Unbewusstes Christentum," 5–10.
70. Rade, "Unbewusstes Christentum," 7. The original reads: "Zum Glück wird die Kirche dabei nichts verlieren. Denn die Brüder, die jetzt draussen stehen und auf diesem neuen Wege gewonnen werden sollen, sind in Wirklichkeit nicht die 'Ungläubigen' und 'Unchristen,' wofür die Kirchlichen sie halten."
71. See Rothe, "Zur Orientierung über die gegenwärtige Aufgabe der deutsch-evangelischen Kirche," 59.
72. Rothe, "Zur Orientierung über die gegenwärtige Aufgabe der deutsch-evangelischen Kirche," 67. The original reads: "O wie hoch thäte doch unserm Geschlecht ein neuer Paulus noth, ein neuer Heidenapostel, der unsere unbewußten Christen von ihrem Christenthum und

damit zugleich unsere Judenchristen von der Unchristlichkeit ihres gesetzlichen, d. h. conventionellen Christenthums mit Geistesmacht überführte!"

73. See Reinhold Bernhardt, "Christentum ohne Christusglaube: Die Rede von 'unbewusstem Christentum' und 'latenter Kirche' im 19. und 20. Jahrhundert.," in *"Zur Kirche Gehören," Festheft für Christine Lienemann-Perrin zu ihrer Emeritierung am 18. Mai 2010*, Theologische Zeitschrift 2/66 (Basel University: 2010), 4 of the document sent to the author by Bernhardt. All translations relating to this article are by the author.

74. Bernhardt writes that it is reduced "an den göttlichen Grund des Verchristlichungsprozesses und an dessen Zielbestimmung der Gottesgemeinschaft zu erinnern." (In English, this reads: reduced to "remembering the divine foundation of the process of Christianization and its goal for God's community.")

75. Bernhardt, "Christentum ohne Christusglaube," 5. The original reads: "Christus leuchtet nicht nur aus dem Evangelium entgegen, sondern auch 'aus seinem ganzen weltgeschichtlichen Werke während dieser achtzehn Jahrhunderte *mit immer steigender Deutlichkeit*.'" Emphasis Bernhardt's. Here, Bernhardt is quoting from Rothe's 1857 sermon "Der Kampf zwischen Glauben und Unglauben an Jesum in den Herzen der Kinder unserer Zeit."

76. See Bernhardt, "Christentum ohne Christusglaube," 6.

77. Bernhardt, "Christentum ohne Christusglaube," 5. The original reads: "in seiner sittlichen Substanz und seiner Streberichtung auf das Reich Gottes."

78. Bernhardt, "Christentum ohne Christusglaube," 6. Bernhardt cites Richard Rothe, "Der Kampf zwischen Glauben und Unglauben an Jesum in den Herzen der Kinder underer Zeit" in Richard Rothe, *Nachgelassene Predigten*, ed. D. Schenkel, Elberfeld, 1869, 324. The original reads: "Ihr werdet nun dem wirklichen, bereits in Euch vorhandenen Glauben an Jesum, den ihr bisher nicht erkanntet, weil eine falsche Vorstellung von ihm euer Auge blendete, inne werden—es wird euch euer bisher unbewußtes Christentum bewußt werden."

79. Rade, "Unbewusstes Christentum," 4. The original reads: "Unbewusstes Christentum ist ein Christentum, von dem man nicht weiss, dass man es hat. Andre wissen darum und nennen es Christentum, nehmen es in Anspruch als Christentum."

80. See Bernhardt, "Christentum ohne Christusglaube," 10.

81. Rade, "Unbewusstes Christentum," 19–20. The original reads: "Was also tut den unbewussten Christen not, damit sie bewusste werden? Erstens ganz gewiss nicht Verkürzung des Inhalts der Predigt oder des Bekenntnisses, wie wenn die Welt für den Mindestbietenden zu haben wäre. Im Gegenteil: mehr Inhalt, mehr Tradition, mehr Bekenntnis!"

82. See chapter 5.

83. Bonhoeffer, *Ethics*, 169.

84. See for example Bonhoeffer, *Ethics*, 348.

85. See Michael Craig Miller, "Unconscious or Subconscious?" in *Harvard Health Publications* (01.08.2010), www.health.harvard.edu/blog/unconscious-or-subconscious-20100801255 (accessed on the 14th of April 2014). Miller writes: "As for the term 'subconscious,' Freud used it interchangeably with 'unconscious' at the outset. The words are similarly close but not identical in German (subconscious is das Unterbewusste; unconscious is das Unbewusste). But he eventually stuck with the latter term to avoid confusion. He couldn't have predicted that the confusion would still exist after more than 100 years of discussion."

86. Concise Oxford English Dictionary, tenth edition, revised, ed. Judy Pearsall (Oxford: Oxford University Press, 2002), 1321–22.

Part I

Constructing a Definition of Unconscious Christianity

Chapter One

Bonhoeffer as a Member of the *Bürgertum*

INTRODUCTION

The connection between Bonhoeffer's life and his theological thought has often been highlighted in Bonhoeffer scholarship. The different contexts in which Bonhoeffer found himself throughout his life left clear traces in his theology. This is particularly the case, I contend, for his development of the idea of unconscious Christianity. This chapter focuses on a particular aspect of Bonhoeffer's life that is especially crucial to understand in order to construct a coherent definition of unconscious Christianity: the cultural context in which Bonhoeffer grew up. As Jonathan Sorum notes:

> The cultural inheritance Bonhoeffer received through his family is of central importance for understanding his thought. Moreover, far from receding, this inheritance grew in importance to him as he developed as a theologian.[1]

The fact that Bonhoeffer thought increasingly about his background during the last years of his life is clear from his prison writing, which contains not only letters in which he expresses his yearning for his familiar surroundings and friends,[2] but also fiction whose social setting is the same as the one in which Bonhoeffer spent his childhood and part of his adult life. I agree with Sorum that in order to understand Bonhoeffer's theology it is vital to have a clear picture of Bonhoeffer's social and family context. I therefore pay particular attention to the *bürgerlich* class to which the Bonhoeffers belonged, and the specific family atmosphere in which Bonhoeffer spent his childhood. It is evident that an important element of Bonhoeffer's family background is the concept of *Bürgertum,* which has so far been translated as "middle class" or "educated middle class." The complexity of this term has already been noted by Bonhoeffer scholars.³ An analysis of what is meant by the term *Bürgertum* therefore features prominently in this chapter, as a correct comprehension of it is essential to understanding not only Bonhoeffer's family's social and religious background, but also the setting in which his fiction, which will be central to my later discussion, takes place. It will also enable the discussion of the link between Christianity and the *Bürgertum*, which features in chapter 3.

This chapter is divided into four parts. The first is a short outline of Bonhoeffer's life and work, providing the necessary factual basis for the following investigation of his late theology. In the second part I explain the concept of the *Bürgertum*. The third part focuses on the Bonhoeffer family home, the family's particular habits and way of life. Part four is a case study of the character Hans Brake from Bonhoeffer's fiction. Through this case study, I give concrete examples of the behavior that was expected from members of the *Bürgertum*, and show how Bonhoeffer's upbringing influenced his later life.

A BRIEF SKETCH OF BONHOEFFER'S LIFE

What follows is an overview of the salient events in Bonhoeffer's life, highlighting elements that are germane to the discussion of *Bürgertum* below. This overview provides the context to points discussed later in this book.⁴

Bonhoeffer decided to become a theologian during his early teens,⁵ and began his theological studies in Tübingen in 1923. The next year he returned to Berlin, and in 1927 he completed his thesis *Sanctorum Communio*, thereby gaining his doctorate. After a year spent in Barcelona as a pastoral assistant to the German congregation there, Bonhoeffer returned to Berlin, where he completed his postdoctoral degree with his thesis *Act and Being*. He spent the following year at Union Theological Seminary in New York, and after travelling to Cuba and Mexico he returned to Berlin to work as an adjunct lecturer in systematic theology. The year 1931 also saw Bonhoeffer ordained as a pastor in the Lutheran Church. His interest in ecumenical matters took root during this period, and he started building a network of friends in the European ecumenical church through his attendance at several ecumenical conferences throughout Europe.⁶ In the summer of 1933, Bonhoeffer, Martin Niemöller, and other concerned Christian leaders in Germany formed the Pastor's Emergency League. This step, along with his participation in the formulation of the Bethel Confession, was the starting point of Bonhoeffer's involvement in the Church struggle. The issues relating to the legitimacy or otherwise of the Reich Church followed Bonhoeffer into his two-year ministry as pastor of two German expatriate churches in London, where he often found himself involved in arguments with the Reich Church hierarchy.

Taking leave of his London parishes in August 1935, Bonhoeffer moved to Finkenwalde to become the leader of the Confessing Church seminary there.[7] Bonhoeffer remained at Finkenwalde until the seminary's closure by the Gestapo in August 1937. In February of the same year, Bonhoeffer's right to teach at Berlin University was withdrawn. During his time in Finkenwalde, Bonhoeffer had kept up his ecumenical and international contacts, even taking his students on a trip to Sweden and Denmark in spring 1936. Up until March 1940 Bonhoeffer continued teaching seminarians by means of the collective pastorates, of which there were two, situated in Köslin and Schlawe.[8]

In September 1938 Bonhoeffer and Bethge helped Bonhoeffer's twin sister Sabine Leibholz-Bonhoeffer and her family immigrate to England.[9] The following year, Bonhoeffer left Germany for the United States, intending to give lectures and work in a parish church,[10] but he returned to Germany less than two months after his departure. In a letter to Reinhold Niebuhr, who had arranged for Bonhoeffer to give a series of lectures at Union Theological Seminary, Bonhoeffer explained his decision to return to Germany in July 1939 despite the dangers he knew he would encounter there:

> I would have no right to take part in the restoration of Christian life in Germany after the war if I did not share with my nation the trials of this present time. Christians in Germany will find themselves faced with a terrible alternative of whether to desire the defeat of their nation in order that Christian civilization may survive or to desire the victory of their nation and thereby the destruction of our civilization. I know which of these alternatives I must choose, but I cannot make this choice in security.[11]

The sense of duty to share in the suffering that the outbreak of war would inflict on his fellow citizens is clear in this letter. The responsibility that Bonhoeffer felt toward his country and fellow-citizens, in particular his Jewish fellow-citizens, is highlighted by Bethge in an interview with Keith Clements.[12] Clements asks Bethge about people who "would have been aghast at the thought that the head of state had been killed and that there had been Christian pastors involved in it." Bethge turns Clements's question on its head, replying that it is not a question of "How could [. . .] Bonhoeffer do such a thing?" but rather "How could he *not* have done it?"[13]

KC: "In view of what was happening to the Jews?"

EB: "Of course, in view of what was happening to the Jews. Not to do anything, not to lift your hand for the Jews, this was a much bigger guilt,

> quite another guilt to the guilt of stopping the leader and his perpetrators!"
>
> KC: "So that really to have done nothing would have preserved his own innocence but would have made him guilty of the—"
>
> EB: "—I mean this is the real motive all the time: how could he as a member of this kind of educated, responsible, political family of Germany—how could he sit down and let these things go on being done all the time?"[14]

Clements also asks Bethge about Bonhoeffer's choice to join the *Abwehr*[15] instead of becoming a conscientious objector:

> KC: "Wouldn't simple pacifism have been a much more straightforward way of Christian witness?"
>
> EB: "That way [by becoming a conscientious objector], he would have solved the problem of a Christian who would like to show there's no blessing in taking up arms, there's only blessing in peace. But besides that very serious, very honourable position, the whole problem of the killing of thousands and thousands of Jews would not have been affected. Being German, and belonging to the kind of class who had furthered and nourished that anti-semitic atmosphere in which Hitler made it possible to come even to the Auschwitz solution, he had a responsibility. So giving that answer [of becoming a conscientious objector], or considering the whole question under the view of a straightforward pacifist principle, would have isolated this witness from the reality, that he was still accountable for the killing of the Jews."[16]

Here Bethge highlights the link between Bonhoeffer's social and family background and the way in which he acted during the Second World War. The sense of responsibility imparted by being "a member of this kind of educated, responsible, political family of Germany," which was at the same time "the kind of class who had furthered and nourished that anti-semitic atmosphere in which Hitler made it possible to come even to the Auschwitz solution" dictated Bonhoeffer's participation in the Resistance movement instead of embracing pacifism. Sorum agrees that Bonhoeffer's cultural background informed his decision to become a member of the Resistance:

> It cannot be emphasized enough that Bonhoeffer entered into the conspiracy to overthrow Hitler, not as a Christian *per se*, but as a German, and especially as an inheritor of a particular German cultural tradition, that of the *Bildungsbürgertum*. The prime representatives of this tradition were his fellow

conspirators. These people, who were ready to sacrifice everything in order to preserve the values of their tradition in the face of the Hitler regime, were the inspiration both for Bonhoeffer's theological reflections on "the world come of age" and also for his prison fiction.[17]

I will return to the link that Sorum points to here between Bonhoeffer's *bürgerlich* coconspirators and his later theological writing in chapter 5. Bonhoeffer's brother-in-law, Hans von Dohnanyi, was one such conspirator. Through him Bonhoeffer came into contact with, and eventually became part of, the Resistance movement in Germany. Bonhoeffer's parents' home became a meeting place at which members of the Resistance could gather political information. In fact, several other members of Bonhoeffer's family became in some way involved in the Resistance movement, most notably his brother Klaus, their sister Christine von Dohnanyi, and their brother-in-law Rüdiger Schleicher. Bonhoeffer became a member of the *Abwehr* in October 1940 and worked under Admiral Canaris, who was opposed to Hitler's regime. Posted to the *Abwehr*'s Munich office, Bonhoeffer was also still officially employed by the Old Prussian Council of Brethren, who allowed him leave in order to work on his *Ethics*. Thus began the period in which Bonhoeffer "had to lead two lives."[18] As a pastor he continued to correspond with his former seminarians, to lead small group discussions where possible, and to conduct funerals. As a member of the Resistance, he traveled within Europe to inform the Allies, through his international ecumenical contacts, of the reality of the situation in Germany and to negotiate help from the Allies in the event of the Resistance securing Hitler's overthrow. He was able to do this under the cover of his official role in the *Abwehr*.

During one of Bonhoeffer's visits to his friend Ruth von Kleist-Retzow at her Klein-Krössin estate,[19] Maria von Wedemeyer was also present. Bonhoeffer and von Wedemeyer became engaged in January 1943, only three months before the former's arrest on the 5th of April. During the first months he spent in Tegel Military Interrogation prison, Bonhoeffer was hopeful for an early release.[20] When hopes of an early trial receded, Bonhoeffer held out instead for a successful coup against Hitler. With the failure of the assassination attempt of the 20th of July 1944, Bonhoeffer then thought that he might be kept alive in prison until the Allies' invasion of Germany. However the discovery of the military intelligence resistance group's secret files in Zossen on the 22nd of September 1944 made this expectation impossible. Because of the information discovered in these files, Hitler ordered the execution of the Canaris group on the 5th of April 1945. Bonhoeffer was moved from Tegel to the Gestapo prison in Prinz Albrecht Strasse on the 8th of October 1944. From there he was taken in February 1945 to Buchenwald concentration camp, and thence to Flossenbürg concentration camp. At Flossenbürg he was executed along with coconspirators Wilhelm Canaris and Hans Oster.

News of Bonhoeffer's death reached his family and friends slowly, due to the confusion following the Allied invasion of Germany.[21] His parents had learned of their son's death in July, and it was confirmed as they listened to a BBC radio broadcast of Bishop George Bell conducting a memorial service for Dietrich at Holy Trinity Church in Kingsway in London on the 27th of July 1945. At a time when, following the discovery of the Nazi concentration camps and their horrors, Germans were reviled and abused in England, people of both nationalities came together to mourn the passing of Dietrich Bonhoeffer, his brother Klaus, and their brothers-in-law Hans von Dohnanyi and Rüdiger Schleicher.[22] In leading the memorial service alongside Franz Hildebrandt and Julius Rieger,[23] Bell embodied Bonhoeffer's conviction that there is a "Universal Christian brotherhood which rises above all national interests."[24] During his sermon, Bell said of Bonhoeffer:

> His death is a death for Germany—indeed for Europe too . . . his death, like his life, marks a fact of the deepest value in the witness of the Confessing Church. As one of a noble company of martyrs of differing traditions, he represents both the resistance of the believing soul, in the name of God, to the assault of evil, and also the moral and political revolt of the human conscience against injustice and cruelty. [. . .]
>
> For him and Klaus . . . there is the resurrection from the dead; for Germany redemption and resurrection, if God pleases to lead the nation through men animated by his spirit, holy and humble and brave like him; for the Church, not only in that Germany which he loved, but the Church Universal which was greater to him than nations, the hope of a new life.[25]

THE *BÜRGERTUM*

In order to understand what pushed Bonhoeffer to his stance of responsible action just outlined, it is necessary to understand the social class to which the Bonhoeffers belonged. They were members of the *Bürgertum*, which has so far been translated in most Bonhoeffer scholarship as middle-class, or educated upper-middle class.[26] Clifford J. Green, the editor of *Fiction from Tegel Prison*, which contains Bonhoeffer's own descriptions of members of this social group, writes that the *Bürgertum*:

> [. . .] might well include people of aristocratic heritage who espouse middle-class values, as well as people who are less economically privileged, but who are committed to building community and providing responsible leadership.[27]

Here Green underlines two aspects that are of vital importance to members of the *Bürgertum*: the willingness to both build community and provide responsible leadership within that community. Historian David Blackbourn draws attention to the claim made by members of the *Bürgertum* that they act for the public good and represent the general interest of the community in which they live and work.[28] Bonhoeffer himself also mentions the attributes of striving for the good of the community and taking on responsibility in public life in a letter to Bethge in which he talks about some of the characters in his fiction, themselves members of the *Bürgertum*, growing up and taking on the responsibilities of public office, and striving for the good of the community:

> The children of the two families connected by friendship grow up gradually into the responsible tasks and offices of a small town and attempt together the creation of common life, mayor, teacher, pastor, physician, engineer.[29]

In this excerpt Bonhoeffer lists some of the main public offices held by members of the *Bürgertum*, and, more specifically, the *Bildungsbürgertum* to which Bonhoeffer's family belonged. The differentiation between the *Besitzbürgertum* and the *Bildungsbürgertum* can be put in terms of "'makers' and 'thinkers.'"[30] The people who made up the *Besitzbürgertum* were business owners, department store founders, and heads of manufacturing companies. They were economically powerful, and their emergence is linked to the industrialization of Germany. The other part of the *Bürgertum*, the *Bildungsbürgertum*, were academics, clergymen, teachers, and members of similar professional groups. These professions were, of course, predominantly occupied by men, which makes the fact that Bonhoeffer's mother was a trained teacher all the more noteworthy. Indeed, Blackbourn describes the traditional *bürgerlich* household as including: "material resources and security, the domestic servants, and the presence of a non-working mother."[31] The material and financial security that Blackbourn refers to here produced in those who enjoyed it a personal sense of security in their own status and identity. This is evidenced by an anecdote related by Thomas Mann, who makes a humorous case for Goethe as the ultimate representative of the *bürgerlich* age.[32] The character traits that Mann attributes to Goethe, confirming the position ascribed to him, include patience, industry, endurance, moderation, carefulness, and caution. Mann recounts an exchange between Goethe and an Englishman, in which Goethe states that had he been born in England, he would never have made the error (*sottise*) of being born in the lower classes. Mann says of Goethe's comment: "That is the bourgeois sense of security, the psychology of the aristocratic consciousness, that one can never, under any circumstances, be other than privileged and favoured."[33]

Bonhoeffer also portrays his *bürgerlich* characters as having this sense of security, which gives them a quiet self-assuredness that is sometimes perceived by members of other social classes as arrogance. This is especially clear in his fiction in a dialogue between Christoph, the son of a *bürgerlich* family, and another young man who grew up in his aunt's tavern near the docks, among sailors and prostitutes. When confronted by the other's anger and contempt, Christoph does not back away, but says:

> I come from what people call a good family, that is, from an old, distinguished, educated middle-class family [Bürgerfamilie], and I'm not one of those who are ashamed to admit it. On the contrary, I know what quiet strength you find in a good middle-class home.[34]

The family, to which Bonhoeffer draws attention in the above excerpt, was a valued part of *bürgerlich* life. It provided a sphere in which the *bürgerlich* "public" male[35] could retreat from the world and enjoy the comforts of a well-ordered home that his wife provided for him. There was a clear hierarchical structure within the family, in which the wife and children were subordinate to the husband. This pattern is reflected in Bonhoeffer's own home, as will be discussed below. The family was also the locus through which the *bürgerlich* class could externalize its values and introduce them into society more generally. This echoes the desire of the *Bürgertum* to exert responsible leadership within society and display their superior values to the lower classes, in order that these should be "civilized."[36] It should be noted in passing that although Bonhoeffer adhered to the view that the *Bürgertum* ought to lead the lower strata of society by example,[37] in a sermon given during his time in London, he spoke of the socially "stronger" members of society needing to "look up to" the disadvantaged, and "devote" themselves to them.[38] This attitude reveals a distinction between Bonhoeffer's outlook and that of the *Bürgertum* in general, which is evident in his treatment of Frau Karstensen in *Novel*.[39] His concern for lower social classes is also clear in his call to the Church to reach out to and "win" the proletariat in *Sanctorum Communio*.[40]

Mann also refers to the *bürgerlich* practice of trying to improve the community in general, describing Goethe's inner desire to strive for the good of the community in the following terms: "His heart's real desire is to do good to men, to benefit the world."[41] This strongly resembles Bonhoeffer's portrayal of his characters as trying to work together for the good of the community. Mann relates another anecdote in which Goethe, then age seventy-nine, makes his guests, who are gathered at his house for a party, wait for him while he stays in his office surveying all the work on his desk still to be done. When the party finally sends someone to ask him to join them, he says that posterity would not be served if old men always came when they were called, and never finished their work. Mann concludes:

> A touching little episode, and one can pay no higher tribute to middle class morality than by ascribing to it this trait of faithful industry. One may do so, I suppose; for the love of labour and effort, the ascetic faith in it, belong to a

society that supplies a religious, a Protestant basis for the bourgeois attitude to life; it has been defined as the spiritual pendant to the bourgeois state.[42]

This linking of *bürgerlich* morality and Protestant faith is key to understanding Bonhoeffer's thoughts on the necessity of Christian faith as the basis for a *bürgerlich* attitude of responsibility in the sphere of the state. It should be noted however that Bonhoeffer's attitude in this respect is not representative of his class in general. As Blackbourn points out, another unifying element of the Protestant majority of the *bürgerlich* classes was a commitment to secularization and secular culture.[43] In his fiction Bonhoeffer investigates the idea that without Christian faith there can be no responsible leadership in the state, and responsible leadership is one of the vital elements of the *bürgerlich* life.[44] It should be made clear, however, that for Bonhoeffer responsible leadership is not an exclusively *bürgerlich* trait. In their conversation about a new elite that is needed to lead Germany in a responsible manner, the two characters Christoph and Ulrich do not restrict themselves to considering only members of the *Bürgertum*, and they also highlight ways in which the *Bürgertum* has failed in its responsibility to provide good leadership.[45] Indeed, it is important to remember Green's definition of *Bürgertum*, which includes people from both the upper and lower classes, provided they are committed to the moral values associated with the *Bürgertum*.

While Bonhoeffer addresses himself to the future with great energy, especially in his prison writings, he does not abandon the *bürgerlich* values that his childhood instilled in him. Instead, Bonhoeffer sees how the values and practices gained from his *bürgerlich* upbringing equip him to face the future in a responsible way. He illustrates this in a sermon for the baptism service of his godson, the son of Eberhard and Renate Bethge. Here Bonhoeffer comments on how the baby's inheritance of the *bürgerlich* way of life will impact his life:

> The cosmopolitan culture of the old middle-class [*bürgerlich*] tradition represented by your mother's home has created, in those who inherit it, a proud awareness of being called to high responsibility in public service, intellectual achievement and leadership, and a deep-rooted obligation to be guardians of a great historical heritage and intellectual tradition. This will endow you, even before you are aware of it, with a way of thinking and acting that you can never lose without being untrue to yourself.[46]

The baby's mother, Renate Bethge, is the daughter of Bonhoeffer's sister Ursula and Rüdiger Schleicher. Based on the description of Ursula given by Leibholz-Bonhoeffer,[47] and Schlingensiepen's claim that in writing about Klara Brake in *Novel* Bonhoeffer is in fact describing Ursula,[48] it is possible to assume that Renate's home that Bonhoeffer refers to here would have been extremely similar to Bonhoeffer's own, and certainly the tradition it represents is his own. It is therefore possible to read these comments as ones that Bonhoeffer could equally apply to himself.

In this section I noted some ways in which Bonhoeffer and his family depart from the norms of the *bürgerlich* class. A final comment on the *Bürgertum* in general, made by Blackbourn, that adds to the distinctive character of the Bonhoeffer family is that the *Bürgertum* is generally perceived to embody a tendency to retreat from the political realm and "cultivate its own garden."[49] Members of this class step back into the privacy of their family homes, their businesses, professional lives, and academic studies, to the detriment of engaging with political questions. This has led some to accuse the *Bürgertum* of adopting a weak attitude toward the rise of Hitler, a question that Bonhoeffer himself addresses in his fiction.[50] The Bonhoeffer family could not be accused of ignoring Hitler's rise to power, nor of failing to act concretely to remove him from power, as the arrest of Christine von Dohnanyi, and the deaths of Klaus and Dietrich Bonhoeffer, and their brothers-in-law Rüdiger Schleicher and Hans von Dohnanyi attest. This is an important difference between the Bonhoeffers and the majority of their social class, but it is not the only one, and it is therefore important to outline their particular way of life and family practices in order to have a complete picture of the context in which Bonhoeffer grew up. In the following section I turn to a description of Bonhoeffer's immediate family and the ways in which their specific version of the *bürgerlich* way of life informed the way he later thought and acted.

THE BONHOEFFER FAMILY

There are two sources that allow us to gain an insight into the family and social context in which Bonhoeffer grew up. The first is made up of the numerous biographies that have been written about him, the most useful of which in this instance must be the material by his twin sister, Sabine Leibholz-Bonhoeffer, and other family recollections, as they comprise the most intimate portraits of the theologian as a child, and can most faithfully reflect the atmosphere of the Bonhoeffer family home. The second is the fiction that Bonhoeffer wrote in prison. While I consider the fiction texts primarily as theological writing, as I show in the following chapter, the fiction also offers rich insights into Bonhoeffer's own childhood. Though not intended primarily as autobiography, the novel that Bonhoeffer left unfinished contains several passages that scholars consider to be descriptive of his family and home.[51] Commenting on the fiction, Renate and Eberhard Bethge note that in every character in *Drama* and *Novel* "quite often very different people are combined."[52] They also point out, "one should be cautious about making too simple and too direct identifications with people from his family and associates."[53] Despite this caveat, the Bethges agree that some characters are directly identifiable with members of Bonhoeffer's own family,[54] and all the surviving pieces of fiction feature characters who come from Bonhoeffer's own social background. Indeed, Bonhoeffer writes to Bethge: "You would recognize many characteristics familiar to you in the story, and you yourself also appear in it."[55] Sorum goes so far as to describe Bonhoeffer's fiction as "his attempt, in the last year of his life, to body forth this cultural inheritance as lovingly as he could."[56] While the fiction must not be interpreted as simple autobiography, and while its theological import must not be undervalued, it can at the same time be used as a resource from which it is possible to gain insight into Bonhoeffer's life and social context. In order to present a detailed picture of Bonhoeffer's family, home, and social background, I draw on both the biographical sources and Bonhoeffer's fiction.

The family into which Dietrich Bonhoeffer was born on the 4th of February 1906 was wealthy, educated, and large. The family was close, not only in terms of their relationships with each other, but also geographically speaking. When Dietrich moved to Barcelona in early 1928, in order to become the chaplain to the German congregation there, he was the first of the siblings to live outside Germany. Despite this, the Bonhoeffers were very outward looking, interested in other people and cultures,[57] and often traveling abroad. Bonhoeffer's years of work and study in Spain, New York, and London gave him new perspectives on the world, and particularly on Germany, but it was not only his experiences in Europe and the United States that taught him to question prevailing political views. The Bonhoeffer family home was also a place in which dissenting political ideas were aired and discussed. As Schlingensiepen notes:

> During his formative years at school and university, Germany was a republic which was increasingly bitterly resented by a majority of the population, though not in Bonhoeffer's parents' home or by the people who visited there. Thus to have a different political opinion from that of the majority was nothing unusual to him.[58]

The Bonhoeffers moved to Berlin from Breslau in 1912 when Karl Bonhoeffer was appointed as head of psychiatry and neurology at the University of Berlin. The house in which Bonhoeffer spent most of his life was in the Grunewald area of Berlin, a residential district of large country houses that had been planned by Otto von Bismarck.[59] Listing its residents as including merchants, artists, and scholars, Schlingensiepen writes: "The Bonhoeffers could hardly have found more stimulating surroundings in Berlin."[60] The house in Grunewald was home to Bonhoeffer's parents, his seven siblings,[61] and, from 1925 onward, his grandmother. It also housed Bonhoeffer's father's surgery, which meant that the children had to learn to keep quiet when patients were in the house.[62]

Bonhoeffer's mother, Paula Bonhoeffer née von Hase, ensured the smooth running of the household, and was helped in this task by several servants. The standard of living to which the Bonhoeffer children became accustomed, and the importance that their mother attributed to this standard, becomes obvious when reading Sabine Leibholz-Bonhoeffer's autobiography, in particular her descriptions of the places in which she, her husband, and children lived while refugees in the United Kingdom: "I was glad my mother could not see the cramped quarters in which we had to live as refugees for so many years. How she would have cast about right and left to try to bring us some help!"[63] Leibholz-Bonhoeffer's reflections on becoming used to the hardships of refugee life ("financial restrictions; cold, cramped quarters; the loss of our house, our car, and our servants"[64]) tie in with the emphasis on quality that Bonhoeffer makes when describing the Brake home in *Novel*:

> This foyer with its long coat rack would hardly give a visitor the impression of an elegant residence. One did, however, immediately see that the wood and metal used in this bright space were top-quality, solid material and painstakingly polished and cared for. A thick, plaited mat covered the parquet floor. There was no need for the children to run across Persian rugs before they knew how to keep their shoes clean—that was the mother's opinion.[65]

In the Bonhoeffer household, we can infer from this passage, quality items and materials were valued and looked after, but ostentation was frowned upon.

As well as organizing the household, Paula Bonhoeffer had other duties. Being a qualified teacher, she undertook the first few years of her older children's education herself, and "gave each of her eight children three years of serious religious instruction."[66] Schlingensiepen points out that this insistence on religious education was not common practice among people of the Bonhoeffers' class. Their mother was not the only person who helped form their ideas about religion. Their governess, Maria Horn, was a devout Christian and member of the Moravian community.[67] Her sister Käthe was also a member of the household staff. She was in charge of the three youngest Bonhoeffer siblings and taught them for their first year of schooling at home.[68] Sabine Leibholz-Bonhoeffer recounts a dramatic episode in which Maria Horn rescued the Bonhoeffers' kindergarten teacher from drowning in a mountain lake, which illustrates the governess's own religious faith and practice. After managing to bring the woman safely back to the shore, Horn "said a long prayer of thanksgiving."[69] The Bonhoeffer family observed Christian practices, such as saying grace before meals, singing hymns, and attending confirmation classes.[70] In Sabine Leibholz-Bonhoeffer's recollections, their mother features strongly as encouraging all these activities, and Leibholz-Bonhoeffer refers to her as having "a strong and believing soul."[71]

In *Novel*, the young man Christoph sums up his parents' religious outlook by saying: "You can't say they're Christians, at least not in the customary sense of the word. They don't go to Church. They only say grace before meals because of Little Brother."[72] While this assessment could perhaps be said to be Bonhoeffer's own view of his family, it is clear that in fact Christian practices played a much more important part in daily life than simply instilling certain rituals into the life of the youngest sibling. This is further suggested in *Novel* itself, in a conversation between the young Klara Brake and a new acquaintance, Frau von Bremer. In the conversation between the two women, it becomes evident that a lot of the responsibilities involved in the running of the household have been taken on by Klara, and that she perceives her vocation in life as living at home and perhaps, later on, marrying and having a family.[73] In describing Klara's daily routine Bonhoeffer emphasizes the place of the Bible in the family home, particularly among the women of the house. Although she does not mention it to Frau von Bremer, the reader knows that Klara "read a chapter of the Bible every morning before she began her housework."[74] Klara's grandmother, whom she looks after in the mornings, also reads her Bible daily. It is clear from the way in which Bonhoeffer presents both these characters that it is their reading of the Bible that informs their actions. Frau von Bremer discerns in Klara a steadfastness that she attributes to a happy family life,[75] but that Bonhoeffer also links to her rootedness in the Word of God. Klara's grandmother Karoline, for whom the Word of God and its true proclamation are of extreme importance, is presented here as the wiser, older woman who slowly educates Klara and opens her granddaughter's eyes to other ways of life that are alien to her:

> While Klara was by her simple and straightforward nature inclined to reject— or even quick to condemn—everything different or strange, she would become thoughtful whenever her grandmother would tell stories of the differences in human circumstances, customs, and ways of life that she had seen during her long life.[76]

Even though both women are assiduous readers of the Bible (and, as far as we know, the only members of the Brake family to be so inclined), and meet together every morning for half an hour, they do not discuss the Bible, but talk about "everyday things and events, about the little changes that every day brings even to the most orderly household."[77] When, however, the conversation strays to the Church, and Christianity, Klara is surprised by her grandmother's "blunt and unrelenting judgment,"[78] evidence that Bonhoeffer's *bürgerlich* characters differentiate between the Word of God found in

Scripture, and the corrupted version of it preached by the Reich Church.[79] It is evident that Klara is very much influenced by her grandmother's views, and gives a lot of thought to what she says. Furthermore, in addition to thinking over her grandmother's ideas, Klara learns on a more practical level to "love her everyday tasks,"[80] thanks to the time they spend together.[81]

From the evidence of the fiction, and of Bonhoeffer's biographers, it is clear that the young Bonhoeffers were aware of what Christianity was and what Christians believed. Later in their lives, it was not only Dietrich who articulated a firm Christian faith. His older sister Christine wrote these lines to her children from prison, after her arrest on the same day as her husband Hans von Dohnanyi and Bonhoeffer himself. Christine's words echo the reserve about speaking of religious matters that Bonhoeffer articulates in *Novel*:

> We have, you know, never spoken much with each other about religious things. Not everyone can speak about these things. But I want to say to you that I am so convinced that all things work together for good to those who love God—and our entire life has proved it again and again—that, in all the loneliness and worry about all of you, I was never really in despair even for a moment. You will probably be surprised to hear this from me, a person whom you no doubt have thought stood quite removed from all these matters of faith. Well, that's just how I am—I must actually be in prison to express such things.[82]

Outlining her opinion about the type of Christianity practiced by the Brake family in *Novel*, Renate Bethge refers to Klara's silence on the subject of reading the Bible, mentioned above, and writes: "In the Brake family Christianity is not exactly unconscious. Rather there is a reserve about speaking of it."[83] This reserve, which was general among the Bonhoeffer family,[84] could be attributed to the personality of Karl Bonhoeffer, whose description by Leibholz-Bonhoeffer is worth quoting extensively because it sheds much light on the family atmosphere in which the young Bonhoeffers formed their own opinions and sensitivities.

> He taught us by example, by the manner and form in which he conducted his daily life. He spoke little, conveying his judgments by a raised eyebrow, a joke, or occasionally a gently ironic smile. He had an extraordinarily clear eye for the genuine, the spontaneous, the creative. He let us feel how much he respected warm-hearted, selfless, and self-controlled behavior, and he trusted us to stand by the weaker party. Above all, he hoped that we would learn to distinguish the essential from the inessential, and would come to recognize our own limitations. His great tolerance left no room for narrowmindedness, and broadened the horizons of our home. He took it for granted that we would try to do what was right and he expected much from us, but we could always count on his kindness and fairness in judgment. [...] He had too firm a grip on

his own emotions to allow himself ever to speak a word to us that was not wholly suitable. His dislike of clichés did at times make some of us inarticulate and uncertain of ourselves. But it had the effect that as adults we no longer had any taste for catchwords, gossip, or loquacity.[85]

In both *Drama* and *Novel*, Bonhoeffer portrays the father of the Brake family as very similar to his own father. Eberhard and Renate Bethge write that the parents in Bonhoeffer's fiction "clearly correspond to Bonhoeffer's own parents."[86] Hans, like Bonhoeffer's own father, Karl, is an eminent doctor, and in *Novel* is portrayed as often coming home tired after a day's work, and being extremely generous with his time and money. There is a strong resemblance between the fictitious Hans Brake and the real Karl Bonhoeffer. Reserve and care for others, particularly for the weak, both feature prominently in Bonhoeffer's description of Herr Brake in his fiction.[87] Bonhoeffer also gives his readers a snapshot of Hans Brake as a child, and through this he reveals that Herr Brake's values and actions toward others have remained the same since his youth.[88] A close study of the character Hans Brake reveals what he expects from his children, and, by extension, delivers an interesting insight into the sort of behavior that was expected of the young Bonhoeffers.

CASE STUDY: HANS BRAKE AND THE *BÜRGERLICH* WAY OF LIFE

Bonhoeffer makes abundant reference to Herr Hans Brake and the values he instils in his children in the early sections of *Novel*. Hans's influence is present throughout the novel, as his personality and opinions dominate his children's upbringing and help form their own views on a variety of subjects, ranging from music and art, to what names may be considered suitable for children of their own social status. It is clear to the reader that Hans's values are not a collection of unconnected ideas, forced onto the younger generation simply to keep them in line with tradition, but rather, they emerge from a consistent worldview, based on respect of, and care for, the other and taking into account the social position of the family. An example of the extent to which their father's influence is accepted by the numerous Brake children concerns the youngest Brake brother. His name is Ekkehard, but he is known by everyone as "Little Brother."

> He was, incidentally, the only member of the Brake family who was not called by the name given him at baptism. Ordinarily it was something like a family principle that all diminutives, pet names, and nicknames were avoided. "That's a privilege of the aristocracy and film stars, to call their children Mautz and Koko and Pippy," the father had once said in passing at the table. And as sometimes happens, it had been a foregone conclusion with the children after this casually dropped joke that such silly extravagances were unnecessary.

> And, as we know, young people are often quick to turn questions of taste into moral judgments. And so they couldn't get enough of spending their time making fun of the greengrocer's children, whose names were Thekla and Armin. In fact, they almost thought it was to their own credit that their own names were neither silly not literary nor theatrical, but sensible middle-class names, though not all that run-of-the-mill. They all agreed that "Ekkehard" transcended the limits of the permissible, which were as doggedly observed as they were hard to define.[89]

In this anecdote, Hans's own understanding of what "sensible middle-class names" should be is passed on to his children by his casual joking reference to other social strata and their habits. His opinion is picked up willingly by his own children, who endorse it with such energy that it makes them change their behavior toward members of these other classes. This example shows that Hans does not force his children to conform to a certain tradition, but that their embracing of his values happens naturally in the environment he has created for them, and that, in this instance at any rate, they freely choose to carry the values of the previous generation into their own.

Through another character, the young Klara Brake, Bonhoeffer presents a second instance of Hans's taste influencing that of his offspring. In her conversation with Frau Sophie von Bremer, Klara explains that her last task every day is to play from *The Well-Tempered Clavier* to her father when he returns home from work late in the evening. Klara continues:

> "We're all especially fond of Bach," she added. "There isn't a Good Friday when we don't all listen to the *St. Matthew Passion* together, and hardly a year passes without our hearing the Mass in B Minor. For the past few months we've been studying together the *The Art of the Fugue* under Ulrich's direction. I just can't understand why people find this music so hard to understand; for me it's the clearest and most transparent music there is. But Mother doesn't think quite the same way. She prefers Brahms and Richard Strauss and sings their songs very beautifully."[90]

This passage reveals more than just the fact that Hans's musical tastes have influenced the whole family in their enjoyment of music. It also shows that their interest in music is taken a step further than simple enjoyment, and that the children work hard to be able to play pieces together. This is, again, an appropriation on the part of the children of a specific aesthetic taste introduced initially by their father. They have accepted his opinion, here, his liking for Bach above other musicians, and have validated it by learning the music in question. It is also interesting to note that their mother, while her tastes are acknowledged, does not exert the same type of influence over them than does her husband. Renate does not embroider on the theme of Brahms and her mother's other favorite musicians. This could be down to Bonhoeffer's view that the husband is ultimately responsible for the whole family,[91] or simply that this musical anecdote comes straight from his own experience of making music with his family, and that it reflects the different roles played by various members of his own family. Indeed, Renate Bethge and Ilse Tödt point out the similarities between this scene and others that often occurred in the Bonhoeffer household.[92]

Both of the above examples show how Hans's views influence his children's actions, even though in these instances Hans is not actively trying to shape their behavior. However, Bonhoeffer also gives examples of Hans's parental reprimands toward his children when they behave inappropriately. For instance, he recounts an incident in which Christoph had visited a house in which hung portraits of various family patriarchs in full official regalia. Having been brought up in a household in which self-aggrandizement is considered in bad taste, Christoph had "boldly spoken of 'nouveau riche' taste."[93] Hans scolds his son in the following terms:

> Dear boy, remember this. It is inappropriate for you to judge people like that at your age. If they are kind enough to invite you into their home, it is not fitting to criticize the way they live and furnish their home. That is an abuse of the law of hospitality. Listen to me and don't forget it. You still have to learn how good it is that people are different, and you must not take offense at external things. It is foolish to compare all the time and to judge everyone by the same measuring stick.[94]

Hans says this even though he "secretly agreed with him and was glad to see how certain his instincts were."[95] He is not therefore seeking to correct the intuition that led Christoph to condemn the vulgarity of the family portraits, but is trying to teach his son how to act toward others, to be gracious and respect certain social mores, such as, in this instance, the law of hospitality.

Christoph calmly accepts his father's judgment, which points to the extent to which the children are shaped by their father's ideas. Bonhoeffer writes: "Since his father's word was the standard by which Christoph measured everything, a reply to this statement was out of the question."[96] This unquestioning acceptance of their father's authority is not shared by Christoph's eldest brother, Franz. In what is perhaps the strongest example Bonhoeffer gives of how Hans Brake tries to exercise his influence over his children, Franz does not display the same accommodating attitude as Christoph. During a musical evening in the Brake household, Franz roundly criticizes his father for spending money on music lessons for his children, saying that "the artificial cultivation of musical achievements in people who lacked talent was an injustice and the money should be made available instead to train especially talented working-class people."[97] Hans reprimands him sharply, and reminds him that due to his medical practice in the city, he knows more about poverty than Franz does. However, in this case it is unclear whether Franz accepts his father's admonishment. He does not directly challenge

Hans's authority, but leaves the room instead of meekly acquiescing to his father's statements.

The editors of the original German version of the fiction point to an excerpt from a letter written by Bonhoeffer from prison in April 1944 in which he considers the effect of his father's personality on his own development: "I don't think I have ever changed much, except perhaps at the time of my first impressions abroad, and under the first conscious influence of Papa's personality."[98] Bonhoeffer is keenly aware of the ways in which his father's personality has influenced his own, and in another letter even acknowledges the process to which he is indebted for his ability to articulate his thoughts clearly:

> I've found that one of the most powerful factors in our upbringing at home was the way we were given so many hurdles to overcome (having to do with sticking to the point, being clear, natural, tactful; keeping things simple, etc.) before we were ready to formulate our own ideas.[99]

Looking at the above examples taken from the fiction alongside aspects of Bonhoeffer's real home life enables a clear view of some of the lessons learned by the young Bonhoeffers from their father and their *bürgerlich* upbringing. It also reveals a little of how Bonhoeffer viewed the *Bürgertum* and other social classes.

The example of the nicknames given above indicates that Bonhoeffer perceives *bürgerlich* people as feeling secure in their own identity, as has already been noted. They have no need to aspire to join the ranks of the aristocracy or share in the glamour of film stars, and therefore reject the frivolous nicknames of those social groups. On the other hand, they also differentiate themselves from the working classes, who in this example try to elevate themselves by naming their children after characters in literary and religious works.[100] This self-assurance is a defining feature of the *Bürgertum* according to Bonhoeffer.

The family's dedication to learning and playing music together is something that springs out of every Bonhoeffer biography, and it is not surprising to find it mentioned in the fiction.[101] Being trained to have good taste is something that Leibholz-Bonhoeffer refers to in connection with her daughters and the circumstances in which they grew up as refugees. She writes:

> My thoughts hardly ever turned back to my house and furniture. I must admit, however, that some years later, when our daughters were growing up, I did feel rather differently about this. Then we had to put up with so much ugliness in the furnished lodgings in which we had to live that I often feared that our daughters would never again have any opportunity to acquire an eye for beauty in household things.[102]

Leibholz-Bonhoeffer grieves over her daughters' lack of opportunity to learn to recognize beauty in everyday things. In contrast with her daughters, Leibholz-Bonhoeffer benefited from growing up in aesthetically pleasing surroundings that allowed her to develop an appreciation for the beautiful. This appreciation was cultivated in concrete, household things, in visual art, and in music. The young Bonhoeffers are taught an appreciation of beauty, based on quality. As noted previously, they also learn to recognize vulgarity and ostentation. This ability to tell the difference between real quality and faked quality is echoed in Bonhoeffer's work when he discusses being able to recognize reality for what it is, without being taken in by faked realities.[103] The insistence on the appreciation of music in both Bonhoeffer's own writing and his many biographies shows how much music was valued in the Bonhoeffer household. From the way in which the young Bonhoeffers worked on improving their musical skills, it is plain that they were also expected to strive for beauty and quality in their own lives.

The ability to recognize quality and denounce ostentation, however, was combined with care for others who did not share the same standards. Hans's reproof of Christoph's criticism of the "nouveau riche" taste he had witnessed in someone else's home illustrates the importance of the respect for alterity that was central to the Bonhoeffers' way of life, and, according to Bonhoeffer, that of the *Bürgertum* more generally. Not only must the *bürgerlich* person respect the other, and accept the limitations that other imposes on him, but he must also realize that alterity is a good thing in and of itself. Hans reminds Christoph: "You still have to learn how good it is that people are different."[104] Hans's speech highlights an aspect of the fiction to which Nancy Lukens draws attention. Lukens highlights the importance of the "Other" in Bonhoeffer's thinking.[105] This is already clear in his early writing, particularly in *Creation and Fall*, when he discusses the limit embodied in the other, which is in fact a blessing to any human subject.[106] In the example under discussion here, not only does Hans (the other, in relation to Christoph) place a firm limit on Christoph's behavior, but he also points out how respect for alterity must in itself limit Christoph's behavior. Alterity is in itself a good thing, and thus, to be limited by the other is also good.

Indeed, in all his fiction, Bonhoeffer presents characters who are challenged by others. His characters do not necessarily change their attitudes and behavioral patterns because of this challenge, but the challenge by the other is a constant feature of his fiction writing.[107] Lukens writes, of both Bonhoeffer and Adam von Trott, also a conspirator against Hitler and member of the Kreisau circle, who was executed in August 1944:

> They placed a high value on the challenges of alterity, i.e. facing in the Other the limits of one's own thinking and claims. Thus the importance of dialogue in the context of relationships across political, cultural, religious, gender, class,

racial and national boundaries cannot be underestimated as an antidote to monolithic thinking and behavior in the context of Nazi culture.[108]

The value that Bonhoeffer places on alterity and the challenges that taking alterity seriously brings can be seen throughout his work, particularly in his fiction and his portrayal of Hans Brake.[109]

SOME PRELIMINARY CONCLUSIONS

This examination of Hans Brake and the ways in which he influences his children and their behavior has revealed several features of Bonhoeffer's own upbringing and the life of the *Bürgertum* more widely. Obedience to the head of the household, self-assuredness and a sense of security in belonging to a particular social circle, an appreciation of beauty, based on quality, and care for others that acknowledges alterity as good in itself, are all components of the *bürgerlich* life.

Bonhoeffer's own sense of security gained from belonging to the *Bürgertum* is clear from the following excerpt of a letter to Bethge. In it, Bonhoeffer describes the pangs of homesickness he experiences in prison. He compares his own way of dealing with the feelings of longing for his loved ones with his observations of how other prisoners, belonging to lower social classes, cope with separation:

> Some people have been so shaken from early on in their lives that they can no longer, so to speak, manage any great longing. They have given up extending their inner "bowstring" of tension[110] over long periods of time and create for themselves surrogate pleasures that can be more easily satisfied. That is the sad fate of the proletarian classes and the ruin of all spiritual fruitfulness. It truly may not be said that it is good for people to be beaten up by life early and often. In most cases it simply breaks a person. To be sure, such people are better hardened for times like ours but also infinitely coarser. If *we* are forcibly separated for a long time from the people we love, then we *cannot* procure for ourselves a cheap substitute from other people like most others do—I don't mean out of moral scruples but simply because of our very being. The substitute repulses us. We simply have to wait and wait; we suffer indescribably from the separation; we have to experience longing practically to the point of becoming ill—and only in this way do we sustain communion with the people we love, even if in a very painful way.[111]

Bonhoeffer shows compassion for those who are not able to bear the pain of separation in the same way that he and his *bürgerlich* equals can, and attributes their lack of endurance to the difficult lives they have led. However, he does not conceal the fact that the *Bürgertum* are able to withstand the pressure of being separated from their loved ones, while the masses are not. This is because of the *bürgerlich* discipline of being able to maintain extended the "inner 'bowstring' of tension," something the masses cannot do. Thus, unlike, the masses, the *Bürgertum* retain an authentic relationship with those from whom they are separated.

In his fiction, Bonhoeffer doesn't hesitate to present members of the *Bürgertum* as superior to others. In the opening section of *Novel*, he contrasts Frau Karoline Brake, an "agile and stately figure, who presented a rare picture of moderation and dignity in her gray dress, gray silk parasol, gray hair, and the dry gray skin of her intelligent face" with Frau Warmblut, a short, plump, bustling woman who struggles to catch up with her elegant neighbor on the way home from church, finally appearing before her "breathless with a shiny, red face."[112] Equally, in his depiction of high school students later in *Novel*, the young Hans Brake's comportment is superior to all his other classmates', except for the young Harald von Bremer, who is part of an aristocratic family.[113] John A. Moses offers an excellent analysis of Bonhoeffer's portrayal of the *Gymnasium*:

> What is remarkable for the Anglo-Saxon educated reader is the basic assumption, on the part of all boys, that there are permanent inequalities between and among the boys based on family background, and this is accepted as quite normal. Instead of a situation in which the point of departure was that all boys are socially equal, and all have a degree of ability to contribute to team effort accordingly, in the German *Gymnasium* it was expected that one from better family background would become spokesman for the class. He would clearly have to be superior and brighter and also stronger physically. And so, there was a competition between obvious candidates; each one having a constituency among the masses, so to speak.
>
> [...]
>
> What I think Bonhoeffer is saying is that it was expected of a son of the *Bildungsbürgertum* at that time and particularly in that country town situation, to demonstrate his ability to lead and set the example. This was a social obligation, a case of *noblesse oblige*, in German: *Adel verpflichtet*.[114]

The outcome of the struggle for the position of class leader between Harald von Bremer and Hans Brake is that the two boys become friends. Moses notes that by becoming friends the two boys are "not only demonstrating the solidarity of their class, but also the supremacy of noble values."[115] The other result of the resolved clash between Brake and von Bremer is that the cliques that had existed beforehand are brought together under their joint leadership. Due to this consolidation of the various factions within the classroom, the boys who had thrived on creating intrigue among their fellow-students become marginalized. Bonhoeffer thereby depicts justice as having been done.

Moses's commentary confirms the view that Bonhoeffer, at this point in his life, had a strong sense of the superiority of the *Bürgertum*, and that, in his view, this sense of superiority was shared by all *bürgerlich* people. According to Moses, Bonhoeffer later realized that this view was unique to the Germans among the European social elite.[116] Ruth Zerner underlines the clash between Bonhoeffer's views of societal structures and his desire to follow the gospel. Citing Thomas I. Day, she writes:

> At least one student of Bonhoeffer's writings during the year 1943 has observed "the contradiction between the Gospel to which he was trying to be true and the authoritarian structures in which he was trying to live."[117]

Discussing the conversation between Ulrich and Christoph on a new elite,[118] Zerner argues that in writing this passage,

> [Bonhoeffer] touches on the unresolved conflict that obviously troubled him: between the Christian teaching of equality before God epitomized in St. Paul's assertion that in Christ there is neither Jew nor Gentile, slave nor free, man nor woman, since all are one in Christ, and the common-sense conviction that there must be distinctions between the upper and lower levels of society, "that everything depends on the right people being on top." Here Bonhoeffer recognizes that his proposal for a Christian elite to solve social and political problems rests on a shaky theological foundation. He fails to resolve the dilemma.[119]

Bonhoeffer's failure to align his theological and sociological views does not stem from a lack of awareness of the problem. His background and upbringing influence his theology and, although in the case of his views on social hierarchy this can make for uncomfortable reading in the twenty-first century, I will argue that it prompted him to develop the concept of unconscious Christianity, which is of theological relevance today. As Jonathan Sorum puts it:

> Bonhoeffer's culture was by no means identical with our own. His instincts were aristocratic rather than democratic; and he and his co-conspirators hoped for a third way in a future Germany that would reject both the totalitarianism of Soviet communism and the extreme individualism of western democracy. Even if we do not find his cultural ideal amenable, our encounter with a counter-cultural Christian ideal may still be fruitful.[120]

In this chapter I have provided a picture of who Dietrich Bonhoeffer was, and from what sort of background, both familial and societal, he emerged. This image of Bonhoeffer, with his inheritance of *bürgerlich* values and behavior, will remain as the backdrop for the rest of this book, and will impact the definition of unconscious Christianity that I will work toward in the following two chapters. To begin constructing this definition, I turn in the next chapter to the texts in which Bonhoeffer mentions unconscious Christianity.

NOTES

1. Jonathan Sorum, "Another Look at Bonhoeffer," in the *Lutheran Quarterly*, Volume XVIII (2004): 473.
2. See for example Bonhoeffer, *Letters and Papers from Prison*, 118–19, 176, 227.
3. See Clifford J. Green, Editor's Introduction to the English edition of Bonhoeffer, *Fiction from Tegel Prison*, 19.
4. For more biographies providing much more detail than is possible here, see the bibliography.
5. See Schlingensiepen, *Dietrich Bonhoeffer, 1906–1945*, 16.
6. For further details about the ecumenical conferences that Bonhoeffer attended and spoke at during the years 1931–1937, see Schlingensiepen, *Dietrich Bonhoeffer, 1906–1945*, 423–26.
7. Bonhoeffer had in fact already been working with the seminarians from April of the same year, when the seminary was housed at Zingsthof, but he officially left his London parishes in August.
8. Schlingensiepen, *Dietrich Bonhoeffer, 1906–1945*, 243. Köslin and Schlawe were both part of Pomerania during this period. They are now Polish cities.
9. Sabine Leibholz-Bonhoeffer's husband, Gerhard Leibholz, was of Jewish descent. He began encountering difficulties in his professional life in 1933, and the family was eventually forced to flee Germany. For a full account of the Leibholz-Bonhoeffer family's prewar and wartime experiences, see Leibholz-Bonhoeffer, *The Bonhoeffers: Portrait of a Family* (Chicago: Covenant Publications, 1994).
10. See Leibholz-Bonhoeffer, *The Bonhoeffers*, 44.
11. Letter cited in Leibholz-Bonhoeffer, *The Bonhoeffers*, 44.
12. Keith Clements, *What Freedom? The Persistent Challenge of Dietrich Bonhoeffer* (Bristol: Bristol Baptist College, 1990).
13. Clements, *What Freedom?* 36.
14. Clements, *What Freedom?* 36.
15. Military Intelligence.
16. Clements, *What Freedom?* 29.
17. Sorum, "Another Look at Bonhoeffer," 473.
18. Schlingensiepen, *Dietrich Bonhoeffer, 1906–1945*, 246.
19. The two had met while Bonhoeffer was leading the Finkenwalde seminary. Ruth von Kleist-Retzow had an apartment in Stettin and became part of the Confessing Church congregation that Bonhoeffer started there. Her granddaughter Maria von Wedemeyer had occasionally attended the church services at Finkenwalde with her, and so had already met Bonhoeffer.
20. See Bonhoeffer, *Letters and Papers from Prison*, 224.
21. See Schlingensiepen, *Dietrich Bonhoeffer, 1906–1945*, 380, and Bonhoeffer, *Letters and Papers from Prison*, 562–63.
22. Hans von Dohnanyi was executed in Sachsenhausen on the 9th of April 1945. Klaus Bonhoeffer and Rüdiger Schleicher were shot in the back of the neck outside Lehrterstrasse prison on the 22nd of April 1945.
23. German pastors of expatriate congregations in England. The former had had to flee Germany in 1937 due to his Jewish ancestry and involvement with the Confessing Church.
24. Peter Raina, *George Bell: The Greatest Churchman—A Portrait in Letters* (London: Churches Together in Britain and Ireland, 2006), 284. This is part of the message that Bonhoeffer asked Captain Payne Best, the British Intelligence Service agent, who met Bonhoeffer and was with Bonhoeffer the day before his execution, to give to George Bell. The whole message is recorded as: "Tell him that for me this is the end but also the beginning—with him I believe in the principle of our Universal Christian brotherhood which rises above all national interests, and that our victory is certain—tell him too that I have never forgotten his words at our last meeting." The meeting he refers to was in Stockholm on the 1st of June 1942.
25. Schlingensiepen, *Dietrich Bonhoeffer, 1906–1945*, 380–81.
26. See for example Bonhoeffer, *Letters and Papers from Prison*, 181. Due to the inadequacies of these translations, and the negative connotations attached to the English terms "bour-

geoisie" and "bourgeois," I will use the German terms *Bürgertum* and *bürgerlich* throughout this book.

27. Bonhoeffer, *Fiction from Tegel Prison*, 19.
28. See David Blackbourn, "The German Bourgeoisie: An Introduction," in *The German Bourgeoisie*, ed. David Blackbourn and Richard J. Evans (London & New York: Routledge, 1993), 6.
29. Bonhoeffer, *Letters and Papers from Prison*, 182.
30. See Blackbourn, "The German Bourgeoisie: An Introduction," 3.
31. Blackbourn, "The German Bourgeoisie: An Introduction," 11.
32. See Thomas Mann: "Goethe as Representative of the Bourgeois Age," in Thomas Mann, *Essays of Three Decades*, trans. H. T. Lowe-Porter (London: Specker & Warburg, 1947). The lecture, given to mark the hundredth anniversary of Goethe's death, was subsequently published as a pamphlet, entitled *Goethe als Repräsentant des bürgerlichen Zeitalters* (Belin: S. Fischer Verlag., 1932).
33. Mann, "Goethe as Representative of the Bourgeois Age," 84.
34. Bonhoeffer, *Fiction from Tegel Prison*, 64.
35. See Blackbourn, "The German Bourgeoisie: An Introduction," 10.
36. See Blackbourn, "The German Bourgeoisie: An Introduction," 11. Blackbourn lists some of the values embraced by the Bürgertum as "a widely shared belief in hard work, competition, achievement (Leistung), and the rewards and recognition that should flow from these; in rationality and the rule of law, in the taming of nature, and in the importance of living life by rules. Correct table manners, sartorial codes, the emphasis placed on cleanliness and hygiene, and the importance attached to timetables (whether in the school or on the railway) [. . .] To this roster of beliefs (they were, of course, perceived as virtues) one should certainly add a powerful shared idea of 'independence,' which rested on economic security, the possession of sufficient time and money to plan ahead, and certain minimum standards of education and literacy" (9). For an example of the importance of hygiene in the Bonhoeffer household, see Leibholz-Bonhoeffer, *The Bonhoeffers*, 6, where she describes the routine followed if one of the Bonhoeffer children fell ill: "If we could not have baths, we were made to lie on several towels and were soaped all over from head to foot. If we spent a bad night, or broke out in a sweat, someone in charge would bring fresh linen and rub us with French spirits."
37. This is evident throughout his play and his novel, and in the way he refers to the fiction when writing to Bethge. See for example Bonhoeffer, *Fiction from Tegel Prison*, 31, 77–80, 104–5, and Bonhoeffer, *Letters and Papers from Prison*, 182.
38. See Dietrich Bonhoeffer, *London, 1933–1935*, DBWE vol. 13, ed. Keith Clements, trans. Isabel Best (Minneapolis: Fortress Press, 2007), 403: "The Christian relation between the strong and the weak is that the strong has to look up to the weak and never look down." Bonhoeffer uses the dichotomy of strength and weakness to refer to physical, mental, moral, and social inequalities.
39. This character will be discussed in chapter 3.
40. See Dietrich Bonhoeffer, *Sanctorum Communio*, DBWE vol. 1, ed. Clifford J. Green, trans. Reinhard Krauss and Nancy Lukens (Minneapolis: Fortress Press, 1998), 272. The section "Church and Proletariat" (Bonhoeffer, *Sanctorum Communio*, 271–74) was included in Bonhoeffer's dissertation but not in the first published version of *Sanctorum Communio*. It appears now in the footnotes of the DBWE edition.
41. Mann, "Goethe as Representative of the Bourgeois Age," 70.
42. Mann, "Goethe as Representative of the Bourgeois Age," 75.
43. See Blackbourn, "The German Bourgeoisie: An Introduction," 9.
44. See Christoph and Ulrich's conversation in Bonhoeffer, *Fiction from Tegel Prison*, 104–6.
45. See Bonhoeffer, *Fiction from Tegel Prison*, 102f.
46. Bonhoeffer, *Letters and Papers from Prison*, 384.
47. See Leibholz-Bonhoeffer, *The Bonhoeffers*, 24–26.
48. See Ferdinand Schlingensiepen, "Die Darstellung von gelebtem Glauben und unbewusstem Christentum in Dietrich Bonhoeffers 'Fragmente aus Tegel.'" in *Dietrich Bonhoeffers*

Christentum, eds. Florian Schmitz and Christiane Tietz (Gütersloh: Gütersloher Verlag., 2011), 276.

49. Blackbourn, "The German Bourgeoisie: An Introduction," 25.

50. See for example Bonhoeffer, *Fiction from Tegel Prison*, 103.

51. See for example Bonhoeffer, *Fiction from Tegel Prison*, 81, footnote 37, in which Renate Bethge and Ilse Tödt state that the coat hooks that Bonhoeffer describes as being in the hall of the Brake family home did "in fact exist for the eight brothers and sisters in the big house at Wangenheimstrasse 14 in Berlin-Grunewald." Such is the consensus that the fiction sheds light on Bonhoeffer's own childhood and family experiences, that some authors use it as if it were a factual account of Bonhoeffer's early life. See for example Charles Marsh, *Strange Glory: A Life of Dietrich Bonhoeffer* (London: SPCK, 2014) in which the author recounts episodes from *Novel* as if they had happened to the Bonhoeffer family. Marsh correctly cites Bonhoeffer, *Fiction from Tegel Prison*, as his reference for the events he relates, but presents them in his book as factual occurrences in Bonhoeffer's life. See for example Marsh, 13: "Eating the simple meal, luxuriating in the 'the [sic] energy of the forest, sun, water, each other's company . . . and freedom itself,' the boy could sense 'in the depths of his being' the infinite everywhere alive." Marsh cites Bonhoeffer, *Fiction from Tegel Prison*, 97–98, in which Bonhoeffer writes of the young Brakes' day out in a forest. The closest part of the text to that which Marsh cites reads: "They [the Brake children] ate in silence, and along with the nourishing food, each of these young people took in the energy of forest, sun, water, each other's company, their family, their native land, and freedom itself. They received all this more or less consciously as one great gift in the depths of their being." Bonhoeffer, *Fiction from Tegel Prison*, 98. See also Marsh, 15, for a similar use of the fiction, this time pertaining to Bonhoeffer's eldest brother, Karl-Friedrich.

52. Renate and Eberhard Bethge, Introduction to Bonhoeffer, *Fiction from Tegel Prison: Gathering Up the Past*, eds. Renate and Eberhard Bethge with Clifford Green, trans. Ursula Hoffmann (Philadelphia: Fortress Press, 1981), 5.

53. Renate and Eberhard Bethge, Introduction to Bonhoeffer, *Fiction from Prison: Gathering Up the Past*, 5.

54. Renate and Eberhard Bethge, Introduction to Bonhoeffer, *Fiction from Prison: Gathering Up the Past*, 5.

55. Bonhoeffer, *Letters and Papers from Prison*, 182. Bonhoeffer refers here to his novel.

56. Sorum, "Another Look at Bonhoeffer," 473.

57. See for example Sabine Leibholz-Bonhoeffer, *The Bonhoeffers*, 21, where she describes her brother Klaus mixing with Russian émigrés and bringing home Russian recipes for his sisters to try.

58. Schlingensiepen, *Dietrich Bonhoeffer, 1906–1945*, 1.

59. On their arrival in Berlin the Bonhoeffers rented a house near the Tiergarten. In 1916 they bought and moved into a large house in Berlin-Grunewald (Wangenheimstrasse 14) and lived there until moving in 1935 to Berlin-Charlottenburg (Marienburger Allee, 43).

60. Schlingensiepen, *Dietrich Bonhoeffer, 1906–1945*, 12.

61. Until marriage or work caused them to move elsewhere, or, in the case of his brother Walter, until his death in May 1918 due to wounds received while marching to the front. (See Leibholz-Bonhoeffer, *The Bonhoeffers*, 18.)

62. See Sabine Leibholz-Bonhoeffer, "Childhood and Home" in *I Knew Dietrich Bonhoeffer*, eds. Wolf-Dieter Zimmermann and Ronald Gregor Smith, trans. Käthe Gregor Smith (London: Collins, 1966), 22.

63. Leibholz-Bonhoeffer, *The Bonhoeffers*, 121.

64. Leibholz-Bonhoeffer, *The Bonhoeffers*, 98.

65. Bonhoeffer, *Fiction from Tegel Prison*, 85.

66. Schlingensiepen, *Dietrich Bonhoeffer, 1906–1945*, 16, and see Leibholz-Bonhoeffer, *The Bonhoeffers*, 20.

67. See Schlingensiepen, *Dietrich Bonhoeffer, 1906–1945*, 10. Paula Bonhoeffer had, when a young woman, spent several months at Herrnhut, where the Moravian community was founded by Nikolaus von Zinzendorf in the eighteenth century. Although enthusiastically embracing Moravian ideals in her youth, she did not encourage a devout or pious atmosphere in

her family home after her marriage. (See Eberhard Bethge, *Dietrich Bonhoeffer: Theologian, Christian, Contemporary*, 21.) Bonhoeffer valued the Moravian community's book of daily devotions and used it throughout his life. (See for example Bonhoeffer, *Letters and Papers from Prison*, 342 and 353 for instances of Bonhoeffer using the Daily Texts while in prison.)

68. See Leibholz-Bonhoeffer, "Childhood and Home," 24.
69. Leibholz-Bonhoeffer, *The Bonhoeffers*, 8.
70. See Leibholz-Bonhoeffer, "Childhood and Home," 22, 24, and 30–31 respectively.
71. Leibholz-Bonhoeffer, "Childhood and Home," 30.
72. Bonhoeffer, *Fiction from Tegel Prison*, 106.
73. See Bonhoeffer, *Fiction from Tegel Prison*, 137.
74. Bonhoeffer, *Fiction from Tegel Prison*, 134.
75. See Bonhoeffer, *Fiction from Tegel Prison*, 141.
76. Bonhoeffer, *Fiction from Tegel Prison*, 135–36.
77. Bonhoeffer, *Fiction from Tegel Prison*, 135.
78. Bonhoeffer, *Fiction from Tegel Prison*, 136.
79. I return to a discussion of Frau Karoline Brake and the Word of God, preaching, and the Reich Church in a case study in the conclusion.
80. Bonhoeffer, *Fiction from Tegel Prison*, 135.
81. The description of Klara and Karoline's relationship illustrates Ruth Zerner's comment on *Novel*: "Undoubtedly, Bonhoeffer's novel conveys a conservative, fixed sense of social roles assigned to each generation and sex, stressing appropriate functions and mutual responsibilities." Ruth Zerner, "Dietrich Bonhoeffer's Prison Fiction: A Commentary," in Bonhoeffer, *Fiction from Tegel Prison: Gathering Up the Past*, 154.
82. Renate Bethge, Editor's Afterword to the German Edition of Bonhoeffer, *Fiction from Tegel Prison*, 226. Renate Bethge cites Eberhard and Renate Bethge, *Last Letters of Resistance*, 56 [trans. altered].
83. Renate Bethge, Editor's Afterword to the German Edition of Bonhoeffer, *Fiction from Tegel Prison*, 226. Renate Bethge also notes that "This keeping things to oneself is reminiscent of the 'discipline of the secret . . . whereby the mysteries of the Christian faith are protected against profanation' (letter of May 5, 1944)," 226, footnote 136.
84. It is striking that Sabine Leibholz-Bonhoeffer remembers specifically the times at which this reserve was abandoned, for example when she received a kiss from her mother on her wedding day: "When we returned home my mother greeted me and Gert with a kiss. It was only on very special occasions that we received kisses from our parents. I can count the number of times this happened." Leibholz-Bonhoeffer, *The Bonhoeffers*, 58.
85. Leibholz-Bonhoeffer, *The Bonhoeffers*, 10.
86. Renate and Eberhard Bethge, Introduction to Bonhoeffer, *Fiction from Prison: Gathering Up the Past*, 5.
87. See for example Bonhoeffer, *Fiction from Tegel Prison*, 35 and 86.
88. See Bonhoeffer, *Fiction from Tegel Prison*, 144–58, and chapter 3 of this book.
89. Bonhoeffer, *Fiction from Tegel Prison*, 84–85.
90. Bonhoeffer, *Fiction from Tegel Prison*, 136–37. See also Blackbourn, "The German bourgeoisie: An Introduction," 9, where, writing about elements of similarity between the "making" and "thinking" sections of the *Bürgertum*, he notes that "A general respect for literary, artistic, and musical culture—for the idea of it, at any rate—was also a common denominator, although it was probably stronger among the educated than the propertied middle class."
91. See Bonhoeffer, *Letters and Papers from Prison*, 82–87, particularly page 86, where Bonhoeffer comments on Ephesians 5:23: "For the husband is the head of the wife just as Christ is the head of the church, the body of which he is the Saviour." Bonhoeffer writes: "The honor that is here assigned to the husband consists not in his personal skills and capabilities but in the office given to him by his marriage. His wife ought to see him as being clothed in this honor. For himself, however, this honor entails the highest responsibility. As the head he bears the responsibility for his wife, for the marriage and the home."
92. See Bonhoeffer, *Fiction from Tegel Prison*, 137, footnote 23.
93. Bonhoeffer, *Fiction from Tegel Prison*, 86.

94. Bonhoeffer, *Fiction from Tegel Prison*, 86.
95. Bonhoeffer, *Fiction from Tegel Prison*, 86.
96. Bonhoeffer, *Fiction from Tegel Prison*, 86.
97. Bonhoeffer, *Fiction from Tegel Prison*, 82.
98. Bonhoeffer, *Letters and Papers from Prison*, 358.
99. Bonhoeffer, *Letters and Papers from Prison*, 510, translation altered, cited in Bonhoeffer, *Fiction from Tegel Prison*, 86, footnote 64.
100. The greengrocer's children in *Novel* are called Thekla and Armin. Renate Bethge and Ilse Tödt explain: "Saint Thecla, a martyr, is the main character of a late-second-century work named *The Apocryphal Acts of Paul and Thecla*. Armin [Herrmann] the Cheruskian, victor in the Battle of Teutoburg Forest in the year 9, is a stage figure in Christian Grabbe's drama Herrmannschlacht." Bonhoeffer, *Fiction from Tegel Prison*, 84–85, footnote 54.
101. Leibholz-Bonhoeffer mentions that Dietrich had even considered becoming a professional pianist, although "In the end he had the good judgment to realize that he would not be good enough at the piano to make music his profession." Leibholz-Bonhoeffer, *The Bonhoeffers*, 34.
102. Leibholz-Bonhoeffer, *The Bonhoeffers*, 98.
103. See for example "Christ, Reality, and Good" in Bonhoeffer, *Ethics*, 47–75, and the character Frau Brake's analysis of a sermon in *Novel*, in Bonhoeffer, *Fiction from Tegel Prison*, 73–80, which I discuss in the case study in the conclusion.
104. Bonhoeffer, *Fiction from Tegel Prison*, 86.
105. See Nancy Lukens, "Narratives of Creative Displacement: Bonhoeffer the Reader and the Construction of 'Unconscious Christianity' in Fiction from Tegel Prison." Paper presented at the Ninth International Bonhoeffer Congress, Rome, Italy, 6–11 June 2004, 18–19.
106. See Dietrich Bonhoeffer, *Creation and Fall: A Theological Exposition of Genesis 1-3*, DBWE vol. 3, ed. John W. de Gruchy, trans. Douglas Stephen Bax (Minneapolis: Augsburg Fortress, 1997), 98.
107. See for example Bonhoeffer, *Fiction from Tegel Prison*, 40, 171–77, 185–87.
108. Lukens, "Narratives of Creative Displacement," 6.
109. For example, the importance of both the recognition of beauty and the care for others is made evident by Hans's reaction to Franz's criticisms of a family musical evening, outlined in this chapter.
110. The footnote in Bonhoeffer, *Letters and Papers from Prison*, reads "In Tegel note 13 (NL, A 86), Bonhoeffer notes: 'Discipline—to keep life in daily relation to pain. Unfulfilled tension as blessing. Meaning of passion not only fulfillment but the very tension as well, existential suspense toward the future.'"
111. Bonhoeffer, *Letters and Papers from Prison*, 227
112. See Bonhoeffer, *Fiction from Tegel Prison*, 77.
113. See Bonhoeffer, *Fiction from Tegel Prison*, 144–59. Looking back on his youth, and his friendship with Hans Brake, Harald von Bremer says: "Our views and the concepts of honor and decency that we had learned from our parents were the same" (159). The exception to Hans and Harald's superiority is the character Paul, an older boy who is nevertheless in the same class as the others. He is presented as having a "slow way" (148) about him, and is exempt from the power struggles that plague the other students.
114. John A Moses, "Dietrich Bonhoeffer's Fiction from Tegel Prison 1943–45: His Reflections on the Dark Side of Cultural Protestantism in Nazi Germany" in *The Dark Side: Proceedings of the Seventh Australian and International Religion, Literature and the Arts Conference*, Sydney, 2002, eds. Christopher Hartney and Andrew McGarrity (Sydney: RLA Press, 2004), 98–99.
115. Moses, "Dietrich Bonhoeffer's Fiction from Tegel Prison 1943–45," 99.
116. Moses, "Dietrich Bonhoeffer's Fiction from Tegel Prison 1943–45," 99: "Where all this differed from Anglo-Saxon political culture in the same era is in the total unawareness of an instituted class struggle. Boys in British or Australian secondary boarding schools knew that there was an organised working class that had already succeeded in claiming its place in the sun and had thrown up able leaders to make that patently clear. The *Bildungsbürgertum* never

really accepted that it would be one day the same in Germany, and there is strong evidence to suggest that Bonhoeffer came later to realise this."

117. Zerner, "Dietrich Bonhoeffer's Prison Fiction: A Commentary," 153. Zerner cites Thomas I. Day, "Conviviality and Common Sense: The Meaning of Christian Community for Dietrich Bonhoeffer" (PhD dissertation, New York: Union Theological Seminary, 1975), 630.

118. See Bonhoeffer, *Fiction from Tegel Prison*, 102–8.

119. Zerner, "Dietrich Bonhoeffer's Prison Fiction: A Commentary," 154. Zerner cites Bonhoeffer, *Fiction from Prison: Gathering Up the Past*, 77

120. Sorum, "Another Look at Bonhoeffer," 474.

Chapter Two

Unconscious Christianity in Four Texts

INTRODUCTION

This chapter serves to lay a solid foundation for the analysis of unconscious Christianity that follows in chapter 3, by pinpointing when, where, and how Bonhoeffer refers to unconscious Christianity in his late writing. Here I give an overview of each text in which Bonhoeffer refers to unconscious Christianity. I also outline where necessary the different contexts in which the texts were written, to ensure that in the following analysis Bonhoeffer's thoughts on unconscious Christianity are not taken out of context. As mentioned previously, Bonhoeffer refers to unconscious Christianity for the first time in a marginal note at the end of his *Ethics* essay "Ultimate and Penultimate Things." The term reappears three times in the prison fragments: in his fiction,[1] in a letter to Bethge,[2] and in some notes Bonhoeffer made in preparation for writing an outline for a book he was planning.[3] In the case of the fiction, giving an overview of the text requires a certain amount of description of both plot and characters. However, a working knowledge of certain characters' backgrounds and motivations will prove invaluable to proposing a definition of unconscious Christianity in the following chapter. Because here and in the subsequent chapters I approach the fiction fragment as a theological text, I begin this chapter by explaining why the fiction texts should be regarded not only as useful resources for insight into Bonhoeffer's family life, but also as theological texts in their own right. Due to the fact that the four texts treated in this chapter represent different literary forms, the second part of this chapter describes Bonhoeffer's experimentation with different forms, and the strengths and weaknesses he encountered in each.

This chapter is structured in three parts, beginning with a brief explanation of which texts are referred to when discussing Bonhoeffer's fiction, and my reasons for viewing the fiction as theology. The second part addresses the question of the various literary forms explored by Bonhoeffer. In the third part I give an overview of each text in which Bonhoeffer mentions unconscious Christianity, adding contextual information where needed.

BONHOEFFER'S FICTION: THE FICTION TEXTS AND WHY THEY SHOULD BE CONSIDERED THEOLOGICAL

What Texts Make Up Bonhoeffer's Fiction?

Bonhoeffer wrote several pieces of fiction in Tegel between summer 1943 and early 1944.[4] The three surviving texts are collected in *Fiction from Tegel Prison*.[5] In this most recent English edition of Bonhoeffer's fiction, each of the three works bears a title describing its literary form: *Drama, Novel,* and *Story*.[6]

In *Drama*, we encounter two protagonists mentioned briefly in the previous chapter. The first, Heinrich, is a young man recently returned from the trenches. He had grown up by the docks, being raised in his aunt's tavern, "surrounded by sailors and prostitutes."[7] In these unpromising surroundings, Heinrich says, "Suddenly, there in the middle of hell, I met—God."[8] However, Heinrich has been embittered by his experience of war, and no longer wants to live with God. The turning point came when he awoke in a military hospital, his life having been saved. "This awakening was my end," he says. "Since then I have hated God and everybody."[9] The second character, Christoph, is the son of the doctor who saved Heinrich's life. He is part of a *bürgerlich* family, and has also served in the trenches. Christoph is dying (we assume from wounds received during the war). *Drama* presents both young men as grappling with questions of death and dying, as well as with questions about how society can best be ordered.

Bonhoeffer begins writing his play in July 1943, but in a letter written to his parents on the seventeenth of August,[10] he tells them that he has decided to abandon the draft he had been working on and concentrate his efforts instead on a novel; he has realized that his material is much better suited to narrative form. This statement confirms what is obvious to the reader of this fiction, that *Novel* is a reworking of the beginnings presented in *Drama*. However, despite their similarities, *Novel* reveals a clear change in both tone and focus. Whereas *Drama* has a somber, foreboding mood, and deals with the subjects of death and suffering, *Novel* is lighter and more playful, and although it broaches serious topics such as responsibility, misuse of power, and nationhood, it does so without the sense of threat and imminent catastrophe present in *Drama*. It is thought that Bonhoeffer stopped working on *Novel* in December 1943, and that he wrote his short story on prison life in February and March 1944.[11]

In a letter to Bethge, dated November 18, 1943, Bonhoeffer states his novel's aim:

> Then I began a bold undertaking that I have long had in mind; I began to write the story of a middle-class [*bürgerlich*] family of our time. All the countless conversations we have had along these lines and everything I myself have experienced formed the background for this—in brief, a rehabilitation of the bourgeoisie [*Bürgertum*] as we know it in our families, and precisely from a Christian perspective. The children of the two families connected by friendship grow up gradually into the responsible tasks and offices of a small town and attempt together the creation of common life, mayor, teacher, pastor, physician, engineer.[12]

As shown in the previous chapter, Bonhoeffer highlights the importance of *bürgerlich* life in his fiction, and indeed, the continuity between *Drama* and *Novel* is most clearly expressed by the social setting in which both stories take place. Some characters appear, albeit slightly changed, in both pieces of writing, and in both texts the central family is the same, albeit, again, slightly altered. The family represented in both *Drama* and *Novel* bears many similarities to Bonhoeffer's own, and is a model of the *Bürgertum* explored at length in the previous chapter. The letter to Bethge quoted above shows that this was a conscious decision on Bonhoeffer's part, and, further, that he intended in his fiction to "rehabilitate" the *bürgerlich* class to which he belonged.

In *Novel*, which was discussed above in relation to Bonhoeffer's biography, and to which I will return in more detail below, the central characters are the members of the *bürgerlich* Brake family. We see them get involved in all the things *bürgerlich* people are meant to be involved in: healthy outdoor pursuits, the cultivation of family life, reflection on societal problems, and vigorous debate about how these problems can best be resolved. The characters are all likeable people into whose comfortable world readers are invited to enter, and whose concerns we are encouraged to share.

All three of the fiction fragments feature *bürgerlich* people. In *Drama* and *Novel*, the *bürgerlich* people are portrayed in their own context, the family home. In both of these texts, the protagonists encounter people who are not part of the *Bürgertum*, and they discuss among themselves how to best relate to these others. In *Story*, set in prison, the *bürgerlich* characters are depicted as struggling to understand, and be understood by, others. *Story* takes place in a military interrogation prison, whose living conditions strikingly reflect those Bonhoeffer describes in his "Report on Prison Life after One Year in Tegel."[13] The main character, Lance Corporal Berg, tries and ultimately fails to ameliorate the living conditions of the prisoners, who suffer abuses in the corrupt prison. This text will be examined in more detail in chapter 4, where I suggest that in Lance Corporal Berg, Bonhoeffer is in fact presenting us with an example of an unconscious Christian.

Why Should the Fiction Be Considered as Theological Writing?

It is necessary to establish at this point why it is vital to view Bonhoeffer's fiction as theological in a discussion of unconscious Christianity. Establishing that the fiction is indeed theological work will show that it is as significant a resource for understanding Bonhoeffer's theological ideas as his other more readily identifiable theological writing.

Excerpts from Bonhoeffer's *Drama* and *Novel* were at first published sporadically in Germany, starting in 1948. In 1960 volume three of *Gesammelte Schriften* appeared, edited by Bethge. It contained some of the fiction,[14] along with a draft of the *Ethics* essay "History and Good." The title of the volume was *Theology and Congregation*.[15] This publishing of some fiction passages alongside an essay from *Ethics* confirms that Bethge at least thought of the fiction as theological.

However, since that first publication, Bonhoeffer's fiction has been considered primarily as autobiographical and sociological writing, addressing the theme of the family. It was only in 1978 that the first full publication of the prison fiction in German took place. In the introduction to that volume, Eberhard and Renate Bethge remark that until that point the director of the Christian Kaiser Verlag., the publishers, had "rightly resisted including these alien elements in the program of a theological publishing house."[16] The tension between Bethge's assessment of the fiction as theological, as shown by his inclusion of passages from the fiction in the third volume of *Gesammelte Schriften*, and his view that they were rightly rejected by a theological publishing house for several years, is intriguing. To categorize the fiction as non-theological is to ignore the rich theological content of *Drama*, *Novel*, and *Story*. Because Bethge pushed for the publication of the fiction, it must be concluded that his view that the fiction must be read in order to gain a fuller understanding of both Bonhoeffer's life and his theology overrode his sense that the texts would be out of place among theological publications.

Nancy Lukens recognizes that the fiction contains important theological themes. Writing about *Novel*, she notes among these themes the importance of the "Other":

> One of the major themes of this narrative, reminiscent of its theological formulation in his 1931 second dissertation *Sanctorum Communio*, [sic][17] is that of encounter with an "Other" who prods one to responsible action by setting limits to the ego and shifting the individual's perspective to that of 'I' and 'Thou' in the reality of a broken world.[18]

and more importantly for this book, unconscious Christianity itself:

While earlier published excerpts from the novel fragment have created the impression that Bonhoeffer's thought was wrapped up in single long speeches by the major, I contend that it is the four-way interaction between the major, Franz, Christoph and Renate in the last completed scene of the fragment that constructs an effective counter-narrative of "unconscious Christianity."[19]

Lukens distinguishes between the "theological formulation" of the idea of the "Other" in *Sanctorum Communio*, and the way Bonhoeffer formulates the idea in his fiction, implying that in the latter the formulation is not a theological one. She also sees unconscious Christianity as a counternarrative to the Nazi narrative of the day. I, however, go further than Lukens here, positing that the fiction does not merely contain theological ideas, but is in itself theological writing. There are several factors that confirm this.

Firstly, the fact that Bonhoeffer refers to unconscious Christianity in relation to "our theological theme," and a "very wide-reaching problem" in his letter to Bethge,[20] when he has already written about it in his fiction, shows that he is conscious of his fiction as dealing with important theological themes. Secondly, unconscious Christianity does not come to Bonhoeffer's mind to be included in *Novel* as a wholly new idea. This is clear because he has already used the term in the margin of "Ultimate and Penultimate Things." Therefore the use of the term in the fiction is considered and deliberate, showing the intention on Bonhoeffer's part to make the fiction theological. Thirdly, the fact that Bonhoeffer's letter-writing was limited at the beginning of his imprisonment means that he may have wanted to write to Bethge about theological ideas before he was able to do so, and so was inspired to write theological fiction instead of theological letters.[21] Even if the rules imposed on his letter-writing did not dictate this choice, it is perfectly legitimate to suppose that Bonhoeffer put his conviction of a need to find a new language in which to express Christ's gospel nonreligiously into practice by writing theological fiction before making this conviction explicit in his letters to Bethge.[22] Fourthly, my claim that the fiction should be treated as theological is reinforced by the fact that the poetry has already been considered theological by many Bonhoeffer scholars.[23] Lastly, Bonhoeffer described his intention in writing *Novel* to Bethge as "a rehabilitation of the bourgeoisie as we know it in our families, and precisely from a Christian perspective."[24] This cannot be considered merely as a social endeavor to help the *Bürgertum* save face after keeping silent in the face of the rise of the Nazi régime, but must be seen as a theological one. John A. Moses writes of the fiction that: "It is not because of its merit as literature that it is published but because of its incisive theological reflection on the *Bildungsbürgertum* of which social class Bonhoeffer's family was a most noble representative."[25] The discussion between Ulrich and Christoph on the rehabilitation of the responsible class and what society will be like in the future, in which reference is made to unconscious Christianity and which is at the heart of *Novel*, is deeply theological. It contains a preliminary discussion of theological questions that will later reappear in Bonhoeffer's writing, for instance in his musings on the future in his sermon for the baptism of his godson.[26]

Geffrey B. Kelly also refers to the boys' discussion in *Novel* in his article on unconscious Christianity.[27] Linking the novel fragment to Bonhoeffer's letters as he does in the following excerpt, Kelly suggests that the fiction is a theological precursor to Bonhoeffer's letters.

> The references to an "unconscious Christianity" in the prison letters come after this fragment of a novel[28] had been smuggled to the family. The letters offer Bonhoeffer an opportunity to ponder the new form that Christianity must assume if Christ is really to be confessed as Lord of the world with any credibility in the post-Hitler era and if churches are to live, like Christ, solely to be of service to others, and willing to shed their triumphalism, juridicism, and privilege seeking.[29]

For all these reasons, Bonhoeffer's fiction must be accepted as theological writing.

BONHOEFFER'S EXPERIMENTS WITH VARIOUS LITERARY FORMS

Kelly's comment, above, points to how letter-writing allows Bonhoeffer to ponder a theological question he had previously raised in his fiction. Bonhoeffer experimented with various literary forms throughout his time in prison, and each form allowed him to play with ideas in new ways. Bonhoeffer's literary prison texts can be categorized into four types of literary form: drama, novel, short story, and poetry. While he did not complete his play or his novel, he did finish his short story and several poems. While working on these various types of texts, he also wrote over a hundred letters.

The letters aside, Bonhoeffer tried his hand at different forms one after the other, never working on two at the same time. He began by trying to write a play, and quickly followed this with an attempt at writing a novel. Bonhoeffer admitted that he struggled to write his *Drama*, telling his parents: "In recent weeks I have attempted to draft a play. But in the meantime, I have realized that the material is not actually dramatic and will now attempt to transpose it into narrative form."[30] His progress with *Novel* was more successful, as he completed eight sections of it, as opposed to only three scenes of *Drama*. He then proceeded to work on a short story, which was the first piece of fiction that he completed. After writing *Story* he turned his attention to poetry, perhaps the form in which he was at his most polished. As Bernd Wannenwetsch notes: "All the poems that we have are Bonhoeffer's own approved and finished work, most of which have gone through several traceable revisions."[31]

Bonhoeffer clearly experimented with various literary forms in order to express his theological ideas in new ways that were compatible with his understanding of the world come of age. As mentioned previously, Bonhoeffer was convinced that it was necessary to find a new language in which to express the gospel of Christ, as religious language was becoming irrelevant.[32] Although Bonhoeffer does not explain his motivation, my hypothesis is that in starting to write in different literary forms, he was searching for ways in which to express his theological ideas accessibly to nonreligious and non-Christian people in the world come of age.

In embracing new forms of writing, Bonhoeffer moved away from writing theology in forms that are traditionally associated with theological content: sermons, lectures on biblical texts delivered at a theology faculty, letters to ministerial trainees, dissertations for degrees in theology, and so on.[33] These new texts were aimed at a different audience, one that was not familiar with the background knowledge needed to engage with the explicitly theological works. The contexts in which Bonhoeffer places the protagonists of his *Drama*, *Novel*, and *Story* can be equally well understood by the religious and nonreligious, by Christians and non-Christians. That Bonhoeffer was consciously stepping away from the traditional forms of theological writing in order to make his content accessible to all in the world come of age is evident in *Novel*, in which he roundly rejects the proclamation model as a useful way in which to proclaim Christ to the world in the current age.[34] Furthermore, Bonhoeffer's fiction writing allowed him to frequently portray his characters arguing against each other and provides an ideal forum in which he could present all sides of an argument, thus encouraging his readers to engage with the debate in question.

Within the three extant pieces of fiction it is possible to observe the development of Bonhoeffer's theological writing for a world come of age. As his time in Tegel progressed, he moved away from writing about a family on whom the influence of Christianity is obvious, toward describing a context in which there is no mention of any Christian influence or reference point. While both *Drama* and *Novel* contain several references to God, the Church, Christ, and Christianity, *Story*, Bonhoeffer's third fiction text, and the only one he completed, contains none of these words. This represents an extraordinary and unprecedented change in Bonhoeffer's writing, as all of his previous theological work relates explicitly to Christian themes. It is hardly likely that Bonhoeffer made such an unexpected departure from his usual writing style without reason. The timing of this writing is interesting, as he produced his first piece of fiction to contain no religious vocabulary only a couple of months before he wrote the following in the sermon for his godson's baptism: "So the words we used before must lose their power, be silenced, and we can be Christians today in only two ways, through prayer and in doing justice among human beings."[35] In *Story*, the hero, Lance Corporal Berg, fights for the just treatment of the prisoners in his care. *Story* contains no explanation of what motivates Berg in his striving for justice and his suffering for the sake of others; he is simply presented as a weak yet heroic figure, and one whom the reader is encouraged to emulate. Exploring literary forms allowed Bonhoeffer to present theological ideas in a way that allowed them to be grasped by people with little or no religious literacy.

Turning from fiction to poetry in late spring 1944, Bonhoeffer began to use Christian terms again. Using this new literary form he was able to present his theological ideas in a condensed way. This is the case for example in his poem "Christians and Heathens," which is discussed in detail in chapter 5.[36] He also began to make notes for a new book on the state of Christianity and the nature of Christian faith, the outline for which he wrote in August 1944. In this book Bonhoeffer intended to return to a traditional form of theological writing.[37]

The fact that Bonhoeffer only completed one piece of fiction, and abandoned fiction writing after July 1944,[38] suggests that he was unable to use the forms of drama, novel, and short story entirely as he wanted. His perseverance with writing poetry up until December 1944[39] indicates that he found this form more suitable for communicating his theological and personal thoughts. His plan to return to a traditional form of theological writing with his book also shows that he still thought that this literary form could be useful to some people. However, these factors do not diminish the importance of the drama, novel, and short story forms as useful forms in which Bonhoeffer was able to write theology. I suggest that all the literary forms explored by Bonhoeffer allowed him to think through theological concepts in different ways, and helped him prepare his articulation of theological ideas in his letters to Bethge.

OVERVIEW OF EACH TEXT AND ITS CONTEXT

"Ultimate and Penultimate Things"

Arriving on the 17th of November 1940 at the Benedictine monastery in Ettal, a mountainous region in Bavaria, Bonhoeffer began work on his essay "Ultimate and Penultimate Things."[40] The Old Prussian Council of Brethren had given him study leave so that he could work on his *Ethics*. His work on "Ultimate and Penultimate Things" lasted only until the 9th of December, when Bonhoeffer wrote to Bethge that he had begun work on a new section on "natural life."[41]

In "Ultimate and Penultimate Things," Bonhoeffer discusses the juxtaposition between the ultimate, "the justification of the sinner by grace alone,"[42] and the penultimate, human life in the world. For Bonhoeffer, God's word of mercy to the sinner is ultimate in two senses: qualitatively and temporally. Firstly, God's word is qualitatively ultimate because "There is no word of God that goes beyond God's grace."[43] Secondly, it is temporally ultimate because it is always preceded by something penultimate: "some action, suffering, movement, intention, defeat, recovery, pleading, hoping—in short, quite literally a span of time at whose end it stands."[44] This chronological succession from the penultimate to the ultimate shows that there is a connection between the two. Bonhoeffer states that he is writing specifically about the "penultimate in the life of a Christian"[45] and asks what the Christian's relation to the penultimate should be.

Bonhoeffer presents two extreme solutions to the question of the penultimate and the ultimate in Christian life and highlights the dangers of each solution. The first solution is radicalism. Supporters of this stance uphold the importance of the ultimate to the complete detriment of the penultimate. In Bonhoeffer's words: "Christ is the destroyer of everything penultimate, and everything penultimate is the enemy of Christ."[46] The world loses its importance, as only Christ is important. The Christian's only responsibility is toward Christ, the ultimate. Radicalism hates the world that God has created: "The radical cannot forgive God for having created what is."[47] The second solution is compromise. Proponents of compromise value the penultimate over the ultimate. There is no sense that the ultimate word of God stands in judgment over the penultimate. Instead, people see only the importance of the world God has given. Bonhoeffer attributes to this stance a hatred of the ultimate.[48]

Bonhoeffer writes that the common problem of these two stances is that they disconnect the ultimate from the penultimate, making them mutually exclusive. Both contain ideas that are "necessary and right in themselves,"[49] but due to the extreme nature of each viewpoint, these ideas become absolutized. Bonhoeffer's point is that Christian life should recognize both the penultimate and the ultimate, as both become one in Jesus Christ.[50] In Jesus Christ's incarnation, crucifixion, and resurrection, Bonhoeffer sees a pattern for Christian life: "Christian life means being human [Menschsein] in the power of Christ's becoming human, being judged and pardoned in the power of the cross, living a new life in the power of the resurrection."[51] Thus both penultimate and ultimate are to be found in Christian life: the penultimate in the "being human," and the ultimate in the "new life in the power of the resurrection."[52] Bonhoeffer is quick to note that Christian life does not sanction the penultimate, but includes it.

There is a certain circularity in the relationship between the ultimate and the penultimate. The ultimate, that is, the justification of the sinner by grace alone, is preceded by the penultimate and yet also determines the penultimate. The penultimate leads up to, and depends upon, the ultimate. In Bonhoeffer's words:

> There is no penultimate as such, as if something or other could justify itself as being in itself penultimate; but the penultimate becomes what it is only through the ultimate, that is, in the moment when it has already lost its own self-sufficiency. The penultimate does not determine the ultimate; the ultimate determines the penultimate.[53]

In the context of the Christian life, Bonhoeffer sees two things as penultimate: *"being human [Menschsein] and being good [Gutsein]."*[54] These states are not preconditions for justification, but are determined by justification and precede justification. Bonhoeffer argues that the penultimate "must be preserved for the sake of the ultimate."[55] If the penultimate is destroyed, the ultimate is hindered. This leads Bonhoeffer to argue that Christians must strive for social justice, as doing so preserves the penultimate for the sake of the ultimate. He writes: "To bring bread to the hungry is preparing the way for the coming of grace."[56] Whilst he acknowledges that Christ comes to humanity by grace, and not because of the state of preparedness in which humanity finds itself, he maintains that "The condition in which grace meets us is not irrelevant."[57] He gives the examples of slaves who are not able to hear the proclamation of the word of God. In these conditions, the word of God can't lead the slaves to justification. Bonhoeffer however disagrees with the view that social justice is a condition for justification. Rather, he thinks that social justice serves to defend the penultimate and thus guards against the hindrance of the ultimate.

Bonhoeffer expresses his concern that people might no longer be able to go to church to hear the word of God preached. This inability is due to "entirely external reasons,"[58] not because of some inner disposition. According to Bonhoeffer, the "last act of preparing the way, the last deed in the penultimate, is that I go where it has pleased God to give that word."[59] Bonhoeffer suggests that an effort must be made "to make it outwardly possible for people to hear and follow the call to where the word is proclaimed. That may mean that people must become human again before they can be addressed in this way."[60] Bonhoeffer's concerns lie in the physical reality of being able to hear the word of God, and in the dehumanizing effects of the war.

Bonhoeffer's thesis in this piece is that the penultimate and ultimate must not be torn apart. He writes:

> The ultimate and the penultimate are closely bound to one another. From this perspective the task is to strengthen the penultimate through a stronger proclamation of the ultimate and to protect the ultimate by preserving the penultimate. Alternatively, in Western Christianity today there is a broad sector of

people who certainly hold to penultimate things and are determined to go on holding to them, without clearly recognizing or decisively affirming the connection of those things with the ultimate, even though they are in no way hostile toward this ultimate.[61]

Bonhoeffer concludes the essay by stating that what is human and what is good must be claimed for Christ, for if they are left disconnected from the ultimate they will collapse. He mentions people who "no longer dare to call themselves Christians,"[62] and writes that they must be claimed as Christians. The human and the good should thus be "claimed for Jesus Christ, especially where, as an unconscious remnant, they represent a previous bond to the ultimate."[63] Furthermore, he argues that instead of encouraging people who no longer call themselves Christians to confess their lack of belief, it is in fact more Christian to claim these people as Christians. They can then be encouraged toward confessing Christ. In exhorting confessing Christians to help those who do not self-identify as Christians toward confessing Christ, Bonhoeffer echoes the views of both Rothe and Rade. It is unclear, however, whether Bonhoeffer thinks, with Rothe, that it is difficult for confessing Christians to recognize Christianity outside the Church, or whether he agrees with Rade that is it easy.

At the end of the manuscript, Bonhoeffer wrote in the margin a note that reads: "*Unbewußtes Christentum.*" Underneath, he wrote: "*Balzac. Leute des Antichristus.*"[64] Although it is probable that Bonhoeffer added these notes after having finished writing the essay, it is unlikely that the additions were made later than the end of what Isle Tödt refers to as the "interim phase" in his writing.[65] It certainly was not added after his arrest in April 1943, as he did not have access to his manuscripts while in prison. Therefore the first mention of unconscious Christianity in Bonhoeffer's work comes well before the beginning of the Tegel years.

The term "unconscious Christianity" refers to the people Bonhoeffer discusses at the end of his essay, and the meaning of the term in this context will be drawn out in the following chapter. It is probable that Bonhoeffer's note "*Balza*c" refers to Honoré de Balzac's play *Les Comédiens sans le savoir*, because of the comedy's title and content. Published in 1846, the play, part of *La Comédie Humaine*, is translated in German as *Die unfreiwilligen Komödianten*, and in English as *The Unconscious Comedians*.[66] The play consists of a series of vignettes in which the hero, Sylvestre Palafox-Castel-Gazonnal, arrived in Paris from the Pyrenees, meets various Parisian personalities during his stay in the capital. The people that Gazonnal meets all play different parts in the life of Paris, and are all more or less aware of their connections with each other and the ways in which their lives intertwine. Without being conscious of it, their lives all contribute to forming Gazonnal's picture of Paris. It is likely that Bonhoeffer sees a link between the people in Balzac's play and the people he has just described at the end of his essay. They are both part of something without being aware of it. They both play parts in a greater picture *sans le savoir*.

The editors of the German edition of *Ethics* suggest that there might be a link between certain characters in Balzac's work, whom they describe as "figures who embodied the inhuman and depraved characteristics of early capitalism"[67] and Bonhoeffer's note "people of the Antichrist." Beyond this comment, however, Bonhoeffer's mention of "people of the Anti-Christ" in this marginal note is unexplained by scholars, and speculation on its meaning is beyond the scope of this work. The only possibility to be mentioned here is that Bonhoeffer might be setting up an opposition between the people he describes at the end of "Ultimate and Penultimate Things" and the people of the Antichrist.[68]

Novel

Bonhoeffer wrote *Novel*, in which two characters discuss unconscious Christianity, after abandoning his attempt to write a play. Although Bonhoeffer does not mention unconscious Christianity in *Drama*, it is useful to know where he left this previous work, as it impacts the conversation in *Novel* in which unconscious Christianity comes up. In the last scene of the *Drama* fragment, two characters are in conversation. The first is Heinrich, who, as we have seen, has recently returned from the war, having grown up by the docks. Heinrich has encountered God, but now hates God and everyone else, after having his life saved against his will in a military hospital. The second character is Christoph, the son of a *bürgerlich* family who has also recently returned from the front. In their conversation, Bonhoeffer discusses trust and the circumstances in people's lives that lead them to be able to trust others easily or with difficulty. Through Christoph, Bonhoeffer shows the importance of trust, while through Heinrich, he points out that not everyone has a background that leads them to trust people automatically. Heinrich explains to Christoph the difference between the two of them, summing it up with the idea of having a solid foundation, or ground under one's feet. People like Christoph have this security, while people like Heinrich do not. This impacts how people from each category view their life, argues Heinrich, saying: "That's why we hate to give up our pathetic little life, not because we love it, but because it's all we have."[69] At length, Christoph says thoughtfully:

> Ground under your feet—I've never understood it like that—I think you're right—I understand—Ground under your feet—in order to be able to live, and in order to be able to die.[70]

Drama thus ends with a beginning of acceptance between the two men, between the two worldviews. As Heinrich urges him to have compassion for those he rejects as rabble, Christoph begins to see that without the "ground under his feet," on which he has been brought up, life and death are not things to simply accept, but for which, or against which, people instinctively fight. The last words of *Drama* are spoken by Heinrich:

> But how can you blame those who've been shoved out into the world without being given ground to stand on? Can you walk past them and talk past them without being moved to compassion?[71]

It is useful to bear this conversation on class and social structures in mind as we turn to a description of *Novel* and the scene in which unconscious Christianity is mentioned.

In *Novel*, we encounter three generations of the Brake family: Hans and his wife, Maria; their numerous children; and Hans's mother, Frau Karoline Brake. The action takes place in the summer, and consists of the Brake children going with a friend on a day trip. They stop at a pond in a forest to swim and have lunch, and are interrupted by a groundsman who attempts to get them to leave. The forester is interrupted, in his turn, by his employer, who welcomes the children onto his land. It turns out that the landowner, a Major von Bremer, is a childhood friend of the children's father, and the major's wife invites the whole party to tea at the family's castle. The Brake children meet the three von Bremer children, and it must be assumed that these are the people to whom Bonhoeffer refers when he writes to Bethge of "The children of two families connected by friendship" who "grow up gradually into the responsible tasks and offices of a small town."[72] During tea, Major von Bremer describes his meeting with Hans Brake, when he arrived as a new boy at the local *Gymnasium* in Hans's class, where the two boys competed for the position of class leader. The narrative then becomes stilted as Bonhoeffer has his characters discuss questions of leadership, power, and responsibility. However, the last section of *Novel* brings a certain closure to the action, as the children discover that the von Bremers have lost a son, who died "for a just cause—a victim of the abuse of power."[73] The von Bremers' dead son in *Novel* is a counterpart to the dying Christoph in *Drama*, and the mention of him at the end of *Novel* serves to echo the theme of death that runs throughout *Drama*. Bonhoeffer ends this literary fragment with the sound of three bells, Misericordia, Justitia, and Pax, rolling over the evening countryside: "Outside, the ringing of the bells ended. Then Misericordia, Justitia, Pax—one more time. Then silence, and it was evening."[74]

In *Novel*, Bonhoeffer uses the term "unconscious Christianity" in a conversation between Christoph, one of the Brake children, and his friend Ulrich, while they are sitting beside the forest pond. This dialogue echoes that between Heinrich and Christoph in *Drama*, and draws on some of the same themes, although in this instance both boys share the same views instead of arguing with each other. Their conversation begins with Ulrich telling Christoph about a recent school trip, which Christoph had not attended. Criticizing the bad behavior of some of their fellow students during the trip, the boys discuss societal class structures, ambition, Christian faith, and responsibility. This brings them to consider their own families' way of life. Christoph says:

> "But now I'm thinking about Papa and Mama. You can't really say they're Christians, at least not in the customary sense of the word. They don't go to church. They only say grace before meals because of Little Brother. And yet they're as little affected by the spirit of false ambition, careerism, titles, and medals as your mother is. They prefer a good laborer or craftsman a hundred times over some puffed-up 'Excellency.' Why is that?"
>
> Ulrich thought for a moment. "That's because, without knowing it and certainly without talking about it, in truth they still base their lives on Christianity, an unconscious Christianity."[75]

This mention of unconscious Christianity following on immediately from the boys' reflection on class structure, taken alongside the fact that the people Ulrich identifies as unconscious Christians are members of the *Bürgertum*, has bearing on how unconscious Christianity is to be defined, as will be investigated in the following chapter.

The Letter to Bethge

The final two instances in which Bonhoeffer uses the term *unconscious Christianity* are a letter to Bethge and some notes made before writing the outline for a new book. It is difficult to pin down in precisely which order Bonhoeffer wrote these texts, as they appear in *Letters and Papers from Prison* dated "postmarked 27th of July 1944"[76] and "July–August 1944"[77] respectively. The editors of the latest English edition of *Letters and Papers* have made the decision to list the letter before "Notes II," but we cannot therefore assume that the letter was written first. The context for both texts is the same, and so they can be treated together.

The letter was written just a few days after the failure of the attempt to assassinate Hitler, on the 20th of July 1944, for which Bonhoeffer and his friends had high hopes. In the weeks running up to this event, Bonhoeffer sent his first poems to Bethge, as well as several letters dealing with the theological themes of the world come of age, the challenge of living without God in the world, and God's powerlessness. The poems Bonhoeffer had sent to Bethge by this point are "The Past," "Who Am I?," and "Christians and Heathens."[78] He also wrote "Fortune and Calamity" and "Night Voices" at this time.[79]

In the only theological paragraph of the letter, Bonhoeffer relates "natural" piety to unconscious Christianity. He writes:

> Your formulation of our theological theme is very clear and simple. The question *how there can be a "natural" piety* is *at the same time the question about "unconscious Christianity"* that preoccupies me more and more. The Lutheran dogmatists distinguished a *fides directa* from a *fides reflexa*. They related that to the so-called faith of the infant at baptism. I wonder if we are not here addressing a very wide-reaching problem. More about that, hopefully, soon.[80]

This letter is one of the shortest Bonhoeffer wrote to Bethge, and he describes it as "Just a brief greeting and thanks for yours of the sixteenth."[81] The letter to which Bonhoeffer refers has been lost, but it is possible that in it Bethge either asked a question or proposed an idea about natural piety, as Bonhoeffer puts the term "natural" in quotation marks in his own letter, as if he is quoting Bethge in his response. It is also possible that Bethge mentioned the term "unconscious Christianity" to Bonhoeffer in the previous letter, and that Bonhoeffer is repeating both his friend's terms.[82] Klemens von Klemperer implies that unconscious Christianity was originally Bethge's phrase, subsequently worked upon by Bonhoeffer.[83] Although this might be the case as far as their exchange of letters is concerned, von Klemperer omits to comment on Bonhoeffer's previous use of the term. Even if in the exchange of letters between Bethge and Bonhoeffer the former first brought up unconscious Christianity, we know that Bonhoeffer already knew of it as he mentions it in "Ultimate and Penultimate Things" and in *Novel*. Another possibility is that Bonhoeffer is using quotation marks simply to show the connection between natural piety and unconscious Christianity. Whatever the reason for Bonhoeffer's choice of punctuation, it is clear that this passage is of the utmost importance. Unfortunately, Bonhoeffer does not mention unconscious Christianity in his later letters to Bethge that survive.

In the letter in question, Bonhoeffer presents unconscious Christianity as a theological theme. Unconscious Christianity is something that theologians discuss and analyze, in contrast to its representation in the fiction, where it is a concrete reality upon which people base their lives, and which dictates specific actions. Here, Bonhoeffer links unconscious Christianity to other theological questions: to natural piety, and to the difference between a *fides directa* and a *fides reflexa*. Bonhoeffer had already addressed the topic of *fides directa* in *Act and Being*, where he had written: "Classical Protestant dogmatics spoke of *fides directa* [direct faith] to describe the act of faith which, even though completed within a person's consciousness, could not be reflected upon in it."[84] *Fides reflexa*, on the other hand, is mediated by reflection within the individual's consciousness. In this letter, Bonhoeffer links unconscious Christianity to *fides directa*, implying that neither are mediated by reflection within the individual, but simply indicate the manner of being of that individual.

Bonhoeffer's use of the term "natural piety" is less clear. This is the only time the term "natural" occurs in Bonhoeffer's letters from prison. The term "piety" occurs more frequently, but he often uses it in a negative sense or to highlight something negative masquerading as true piety.[85] In *Life Together* he condemns the "pious" for seeking to form a community according to their own desires rather than attempting to base their common life on the Word of God. He uses the dialectic "emotional" versus "spiritual" to order sections of the book. Within this dialectic he uses the terms "pious" and "those who are called by Christ" in opposition to each other.[86] Similarly, in his *Ethics*, Bonhoeffer talks of two types of godlessness, "pious godlessness" and "promising godlessness," the latter being a "protest against pious godlessness insofar as that has spoiled the churches."[87] Here, however, this is not the case, and Bonhoeffer uses the term "piety" in a neutral sense to denote the quality of being reverent or obedient to God.

The fact that Bonhoeffer describes the question of unconscious Christianity, natural piety, *fides directa* and *fides reflexa* as being a potentially "very wide-reaching problem"[88] shows that he realizes that he has not yet reached a satisfactory conclusion about these issues. Because of this statement of Bonhoeffer's, the definition of unconscious Christianity that this book presents must include an appreciation of the development of his thought and the unfinished quality of his work on the matter.

"Notes II"

In the latest English critical edition of *Letters and Papers*, there are two sets of notes made by Bonhoeffer in preparation for writing his outline for a book. The editors of the DBW German edition comment that "these notes [. . .] contain key ideas and phrasing for the outline for a book, which Bonhoeffer sent to Bethge on August 3, 1944."[89] It is therefore necessary to briefly summarize not only the notes that mention unconscious Christianity, but also the section of the outline for a book to which they point. Unconscious Christianity appears in the second of Bonhoeffer's sets of notes pertaining to the book,[90] and the entirety of this second entry reads as follows:

Unconscious Christianity: Left hand doesn't know

what the right hand is doing.

Matt. 25.

Not knowing what to pray.

Motto: Jesus said to him: "What do you want me to do for you?"[91]

The first comment after the term "Unconscious Christianity" refers to Matthew 6:3, which reads, "But when you give alms, do not let your left hand know what your right hand is doing." The editors of the German DBW edition point out that in the Luther Bible, there is a cross reference from Matthew 6:3 to Matthew 25:37–40,[92] and it is therefore fair to assume that Bonhoeffer was thinking also of these verses, and referred to them with the shorthand "Matt. 25." This makes sense thematically, as Matthew 25:37–40 reads:

> Then the righteous will answer him, "Lord, when did we see you hungry and feed you, or thirsty and give you something to drink? When did we see you a stranger and invite you in, or needing clothes and clothe you? When did we see you sick or in prison and go to visit you?" The King will reply, "Truly I tell you, whatever you did for one of the least of these brothers and sisters of mine, you did for me."

This passage follows on from Jesus's parables of the ten bridesmaids with their lamps, the master who entrusts various amounts of gold to three of his servants, and the sheep and the goats. All three of these parables are about two groups of people: those accepted by the bridegroom, the master, the Son of Man, and those who are turned away. The division between those who are accepted and those who are turned away is based on the people's actions in all three parables. The virgins who took oil along with their lamps are separated from those who did not. The servants who worked to make their gold prosper are accepted but the one who did not is rejected. Those categorized as sheep who helped "the least of these brothers and sisters" are invited to inherit the kingdom prepared for them, while the "goats" who did not are banished into eternal punishment. In this last parable, the people who helped the needy are called "the righteous" by Jesus, the narrator of these stories.

In "Notes II," Bonhoeffer links the idea of unconscious Christianity to the actions performed by those called righteous by Jesus. The link is not made very explicit here, but is developed more in the outline for a book.

Bonhoeffer writes to Bethge that he intends to have three chapters within his essay (as he refers to it) as follows: "1. Taking stock of Christianity; 2. What is Christian faith, really? 3. Conclusions."[93] Bonhoeffer articulates ideas in "Notes I" and "Notes II" that form the basis for the outline. Some phrases reappear word for word in the notes and the outline.[94] In "Notes I" Bonhoeffer writes:

> Living without God
> But what if Christianity were not a religion at all? worldly nonreligious interpretation of Christian concepts.[95]

These thoughts line up with sections (b) and (c) in Bonhoeffer's outline of his first chapter:

> (b) The religionlessness of the human being come of age. "God" as working hypothesis, as stopgap for our embarrassments, has become superfluous (as indicated previously).
> (c) The Protestant church: pietism as a final attempt to preserve Protestant Christianity as religion;[96]

It is therefore legitimate to look for a development of Bonhoeffer's term "unconscious Christianity" in his chapter outlines. In the outline for the second chapter, he does not use the term again, but writes:

> Who is God? Not primarily a belief in God's omnipotence, and so on. That is not a genuine experience of God but just a prolongation of a piece of the world. Encounter with Jesus Christ. Experience that here there is a reversal of all human existence, in the very fact that Jesus only "is there for others." Only through this liberation from the self, through this "being-for-others" unto death, do omnipotence, omniscience, and omnipresence come into being. Faith is participating in this being of Jesus. (Becoming human [Menschwerdung], cross, resurrection.)[97]

A fuller analysis of this passage follows in the next chapter, but for the time being it should be noted that Bonhoeffer links unconscious Christianity with encounter with, and participation in, Christ. Implied in this encounter with and participation in Christ is a being-for-others that is based on Christ's own being-for-others. This in turn brings about a "liberation from the self," as one's existence is directed toward others rather than toward oneself. Bonhoeffer equates this participation in Christ with faith, as he does elsewhere.[98] In the following chapter we will look more closely at this seeming paradox of an unconscious Christianity, which is also faith.

SOME PRELIMINARY CONCLUSIONS

In the last two texts discussed, Bonhoeffer presents unconscious Christianity as a theological theme. He links it to righteous actions: encountering Christ, participating in Christ, being-for-others, faith, standing by God in God's suffering at the hands of the godless world, natural piety, and *fides directa*. This theoretical language used in conjunction with unconscious Christianity stands in stark contrast to the more straightforward representation of it in his fiction: It is something on which ordinary people can base their lives, and which compels them to act in certain ways. His marginal note "unconscious Christianity" used in reference to the people described at the end of "Ultimate and Penultimate Things" is also more matter-of-fact than the way in which he uses the term in the last two fragments.

Furthermore, whilst in the fiction Bonhoeffer displays confidence in his portrayal of unconscious Christianity, through his character Ulrich's assured analysis of his friend Christoph's parents,[99] in his letter to Bethge he is more circumspect, and wonders whether with this theological theme he will not in fact end up addressing "a very wide-reaching problem."[100] Both of these factors point to the fluid quality of Bonhoeffer's work on unconscious Christianity.

It is evident that there are differences between the unconscious Christianity expressed in the letter and notes of *Letters and Papers from Prison* and the unconscious Christianity described in *Novel* and referred to in "Ultimate and Penultimate Things." However, there are also similarities to be noted. For example, Hans Brake's unconscious Christianity compels him to value and respect alterity, and to teach his children to do so too. This is close to Bonhoeffer's theological theme of being-for-others. In addition, the people described at the end of "Ultimate and Penultimate Things" value the penultimate, engaging wholeheartedly with the world. This is akin to the behavior of the people in Matthew 25 to whom Bonhoeffer links unconscious Christianity in "Notes II."

This suggests that while in *Novel* and "Ultimate and Penultimate Things" there is less of an insistence on themes such as the encounter with and participation in Christ, and in "Notes II" and the letter to Bethge there is no trace of the specific religious observances and societal outlook that the boys refer to when discussing unconscious Christianity in *Novel*, there are still strong similarities between both types of unconscious Christianity that occur in Bonhoeffer's prison writings. In the following chapter these differences and similarities will be examined and analyzed in more detail.

NOTES

1. Bonhoeffer, *Fiction from Tegel Prison*, 106.
2. Bonhoeffer, *Letters and Papers from Prison*, 489.
3. Bonhoeffer, *Letters and Papers from Prison*, 491.
4. There is disagreement over the date at which Bonhoeffer wrote *Story*. The *Drama* and *Novel* can be dated thanks to references in Bonhoeffer's correspondence with Bethge and his parents. Bonhoeffer probably finished the novel fragment around the 5th of December 1943 (see Bonhoeffer, *Letters and Papers from Prison*, 600). However, such accuracy in dating *Story* is not possible. In his biography of Bonhoeffer, Eberhard Bethge suggests that Bonhoeffer wrote it during the summer of 1943 (see Eberhard Bethge, *Dietrich Bonhoeffer: theologian, Christian, contemporary*, 750), but does not mention *Story* in his section on Bonhoeffer's literary work. Confusingly, the editors of the most recent German edition of *Widerstand und Ergebung*, who include Bethge himself, date the composition of *Story* to February/March 1944. (See Bonhoeffer, *Widerstand und Ergebung*, DBW vol. 8, eds. Christian Gremmels, Eberhard Bethge, and Renate Bethge, with Ilse Tödt [Gütersloh: Chr. Kaiser & Gütersloher Verlag., 1998], 669.) Eberhard Bethge writes that Bonhoeffer's writing of 1943, which, according to

him in the first instance, would include *Story*, still belong "to the sphere of the Ethics." However, if we side with the later editors' opinion that *Story* was written the following year, it must be understood as belonging rather to the sphere of Bonhoeffer's Tegel theology. The later dating of *Story* is more likely, due to its content and the development of Bonhoeffer's thought that can be traced through his three extant fiction texts. This disagreement in dating *Story* serves to highlight its uniqueness. It does not fit into the same category as the first two fiction texts, and serves in fact as a test case in which Bonhoeffer develops his ideas on unconscious Christianity. For further discussion of this point, see chapter 4.

5. Bonhoeffer wrote a fourth fiction text, now lost, about two friends meeting after having been separated for a long time by war. A fragment of this text survives and is reproduced in Bonhoeffer, *Fiction from Tegel Prison*, 236. The fragment shows that this fourth text was intended to be a short story or a novel, rather than a play.

6. According to Eberhard Bethge the original title of the *Story* was *Farewell, Comrade* (*Leb wohl, Kamerad*), reflecting the parting good wishes between two of the main characters and the very end of the piece. It is now referred to as *Gefreiter Berg*. See Eberhard Bethge, *Dietrich Bonhoeffer: Theologian, Christian, Contemporary*, 750, and appendix I in Bonhoeffer, *Widerstand und Ergebung*, 669.

7. Bonhoeffer, *Fiction from Tegel Prison*, 40.
8. Bonhoeffer, *Fiction from Tegel Prison*, 41.
9. Bonhoeffer, *Fiction from Tegel Prison*, 42.
10. See Bonhoeffer, *Letters and Papers from Prison*, 135–36.
11. See appendix 1, in Bonhoeffer, *Letters and Papers from Prison*, 600–601.
12. Bonhoeffer, *Letters and Papers from Prison*, 181–82.
13. See Bonhoeffer, *Letters and Papers from Prison*, 343–47.
14. The fiction in this volume included two excerpts from the first two scenes and all of scene three from *Drama*, and two long dialogues with Major von Bremer from *Novel*. (See Bonhoeffer, *Fiction from Tegel Prison*, 15.)
15. The original German title is: *Theologie—Gemeinde. Vorlesungen, Briefe, Gespräche, 1927–1944*.
16. Renate and Eberhard Bethge, introduction to Bonhoeffer, *Fiction from Prison: Gathering Up the Past*, 1.
17. Lukens's footnote reads: "Dietrich Bonhoeffer, *Sanctorum Communio* (Dietrich Bonhoeffer Works, Vol. 1). Minneapolis: Fortress Press, 1998."
18. Lukens, "Narratives of Creative Displacement," 18.
19. Lukens, "Narratives of Creative Displacement," 20.
20. Bonhoeffer, *Letters and Papers from Prison*, 489.
21. Bonhoeffer and Bethge's secret correspondence began with a letter from Bonhoeffer to Bethge on the 18th of November 1943. At the beginning of his imprisonment, Bonhoeffer was allowed to write a letter to his parents every ten days. This increased to every four days, from the 30th of July 1943, and he could write alternately to his parents and his fiancée. See Bonhoeffer, *Letters and Papers from Prison*, 178, footnote 2, and 597–98.
22. See for example Bonhoeffer, *Letters and Papers from Prison*, 364 and 390.
23. See for example Bernd Wannenwetsch, "Who Is Dietrich Bonhoeffer for Us Today," introduction to *Who Am I? Bonhoeffer's Theology through His Poetry*, ed. B. Wannenwetsch (London & New York: T&T Clark, 2009), 3–4; Philip G. Ziegler, "'Voices in the Night': Human Solidarity and Eschatological Hope," in *Who Am I?* 115–45; and Floyd, "Bonhoeffer's Literary Legacy," 87. Wannenwetsch dismisses *Drama* and *Novel* as "short-lived attempts in abandoned fragments," arguing that the poetry deserves more attention than the fiction because Bonhoeffer turned to poetry writing after attempting fiction, and stayed with it for longer.
24. Bonhoeffer, *Letters and Papers from Prison*, 182. The German term translated as "bourgeoisie" here is *Bürgertum*. See Bonhoeffer, *Widerstand und Ergebung*, 189.
25. John A. Moses, book review of *Fiction from Tegel Prison* by Dietrich Bonhoeffer, *The Journal of Religious History*, vol. 26, No.3, (October 2002), 30. See also Moses's comment on the same page: "In a real sense Bonhoeffer's reflections articulate the crisis of conscience that the Bildungsbürgertum had to go through as a consequence of the advent of the Third Reich.

How could these most cultured representatives of European civilisation have tacitly endorsed such evil, as most of them did?"

26. See Bonhoeffer, *Letters and Papers from Prison*, 383–90.

27. Geffrey B. Kelly, "'Unconscious Christianity' and the 'Anonymous Christian' in the Theology of Dietrich Bonhoeffer and Karl Rahner," *Philosophy and Theology* vol. 9 (1995): 117–49.

28. Kelly refers in the previous paragraph to the discussion between Ulrich and Christoph on a new elite in Germany, mentioning unconscious Christianity.

29. Kelly, "'Unconscious Christianity' and the 'Anonymous Christian,'" 124.

30. Bonhoeffer, *Letters and Papers from Prison*, 135–36.

31. Wannenwetsch, "Who Is Dietrich Bonhoeffer for Us Today?" introduction to *Who Am I? Bonhoeffer's Theology through His Poetry*, 4.

32. See for example Bonhoeffer, *Letters and Papers from Prison*, 362.

33. Bonhoeffer was certainly aware of other writers who used fiction as theology. For example, Renate Bethge and Ilse Tödt point out that while writing his *Ethics* Bonhoeffer had used Romano Guardini's book *Religiöse Gestalten in Dostojewskijs Werk*, 2nd ed. (Leipzig: 1939). They note that in his book Guardini writes that Fyodor Dostoyevsky uses the image of the slanting rays of the setting sun to symbolize "an ultimate metaphysical closeness" (Bonhoeffer, *Fiction from Tegel Prison*, 26). Bonhoeffer echoes this symbolism in the opening scene of *Drama* to portray the reconciliation and closeness between a hunter and the deer that he has just shot. Bonhoeffer writes: "Afterward everything was completely still and the last rays of the evening sun shone (reconcilingly and) peacefully on the fallen prey and its hunter." Bonhoeffer, *Fiction from Tegel Prison*, 26. The words in parentheses are considered by the editors to have been deleted later by Bonhoeffer.

34. See Bonhoeffer, *Fiction from Tegel Prison*, 73–79. This is discussed in more detail in the conclusion.

35. Bonhoeffer, *Letters and Papers from Prison*, 389.

36. For further discussion of Bonhoeffer's poetry, see Bernd Wannenwetsch, ed., *Who Am I? Bonhoeffer's Theology through His Poetry* (London & New York: T&T Clark, 2009).

37. See Bonhoeffer, *Letters and Papers from Prison*, 499–504.

38. See Bonhoeffer, *Letters and Papers from Prison*, 457. In his letter to Bethge written on the 8th of July 1944, Bonhoeffer mentions *Novel* and the fourth fiction text: "The novel is bogged down, and the little piece intended for you isn't completely finished either."

39. He enclosed his poem "By Powers of Good" with a letter to Maria von Wedemeyer from Prinz-Albrecht-Strasse prison on the 19th of December 1944. See Bonhoeffer, *Letters and Papers from Prison*, 548–50.

40. For Ilse Tödt's dating of each essay contained in Bonhoeffer's *Ethics*, see Ilse Tödt, "Preparing the German Edition of Ethics," appendix 2 of Bonhoeffer, *Ethics*, 471.

41. See "Chronology of Ethics," appendix 1 of Bonhoeffer, *Ethics*, 454.

42. Bonhoeffer, *Ethics*, 146.

43. Bonhoeffer, *Ethics*, 149.

44. Bonhoeffer, *Ethics*, 150–51.

45. Bonhoeffer, *Ethics*, 152.

46. Bonhoeffer, *Ethics*, 153.

47. Bonhoeffer, *Ethics*, 155.

48. See Bonhoeffer, *Ethics*, 156.

49. Bonhoeffer, *Ethics*, 154.

50. See Bonhoeffer, *Ethics*, 157.

51. Bonhoeffer, *Ethics*, 159.

52. Bonhoeffer, *Ethics*, 159.

53. Bonhoeffer, *Ethics*, 159.

54. Bonhoeffer, *Ethics*, 159.

55. Bonhoeffer, *Ethics*, 160.

56. Bonhoeffer, *Ethics*, 163.

57. Bonhoeffer, *Ethics*, 162.

58. Bonhoeffer, *Ethics*, 166.

59. Bonhoeffer, *Ethics*, 166.
60. Bonhoeffer, *Ethics*, 166.
61. Bonhoeffer, *Ethics*, 169.
62. Bonhoeffer, *Ethics*, 170.
63. Bonhoeffer, *Ethics*, 169.
64. Bonhoeffer, *Ethics*, 170. See also document 1 in the appendix to this book. It should also be added that this phrase is hardly legible, and that it is therefore possible that there has been an error in reading and translating it as "People of the Antichrist."
65. April 1941 to the end of 1941. See Ilse Tödt, "Preparing the German Edition of Ethics," in Bonhoeffer, *Ethics*, 471.
66. In English it is also translated as *The Unconscious Humorists*, *Comedians without Knowing It*, *The Unconscious Mummers*, and *The Unwitting Play-Actors*.
67. Bonhoeffer, *Ethics*, 170, footnote 111.
68. It could possibly be linked to another part of his *Ethics* in which he mentions the Antichrist: "To Christ everything must return; only under Christ's protection can it live. Perhaps it is a largely unconscious knowledge that, in the hour of ultimate danger, prompts everything that wants to escape the Antichrist to seek refuge in Christ." Bonhoeffer, "Church and World I" in *Ethics*, 341–42. Here Bonhoeffer conveys a similar idea to the one he presents in "Ultimate and Penultimate Things": that which is good should be claimed for Christ. Here, he adds the idea that the good will eventually turn to Christ of its own accord, perhaps due to its "unconscious knowledge" that Christ will provide refuge from the Antichrist.
69. Bonhoeffer, *Fiction from Tegel Prison*, 69.
70. Bonhoeffer, *Fiction from Tegel Prison*, 70.
71. Bonhoeffer, *Fiction from Tegel Prison*, 70.
72. Bonhoeffer, *Letters and Papers from Prison*, 181–82.
73. Bonhoeffer, *Fiction from Tegel Prison*, 182.
74. Bonhoeffer, *Fiction from Tegel Prison*, 182.
75. Bonhoeffer, *Fiction from Tegel Prison*, 106.
76. See Bonhoeffer, *Letters and Papers from Prison*, 489.
77. See Bonhoeffer, *Letters and Papers from Prison*, 491.
78. "The Past" was sent on the 5th of June 1944, and the two others on the 8th of July 1944. See Bonhoeffer, *Letters and Papers from Prison*, 418–21 and 459–61.
79. These last two poems were not sent to Bethge with letters from Tegel. It is unclear how "Fortune and Calamity" reached him, but "Night Voices" was delivered to Bethge in June 1945 by Corporal Knobloch, who acted as a messenger between Bonhoeffer and the outside world during his time in Tegel.
80. Bonhoeffer, *Letters and Papers from Prison*, 489. The emphasis reflects that of the original. See the Appendix, document 3. Interestingly, in an earlier letter to Bethge, dated the 22nd of November 1943, Bonhoeffer refers to Bethge as having an "anima naturaliter Christiana." The phrase is borrowed from Tertullian, and means "a soul, Christian by nature."
81. Bonhoeffer, *Letters and Papers from Prison*, 489.
82. On the subject of Bonhoeffer and Bethge's relationship and the way in which they discussed and refined ideas in their conversations, see Bonhoeffer, *Letters and Papers from Prison*, 182, where Bonhoeffer writes: "The origin of our ideas often lay with me, but their clarification entirely with you. Only in conversation with you did I find out whether an idea was of any use. I long to read out loud to you some of what I have written. The observation of details is so much better on your part than mine." See also Bonhoeffer, *Fiction from Tegel Prison*, 105, where Bonhoeffer outlines the way in which the two boys, Ulrich and Christoph, discuss ideas: "For Ulrich it was never as easy to put his ideas into words as for Christoph, and he struggled with this. [. . .] While Christoph loved to present the same idea in ever new ways and from new perspectives, and enjoyed great ease of expression, Ulrich always formulated his ideas only once, leaving Christoph to process them, incorporate them into his thinking, and shape them into an effective message. [. . .] Others would get the impression that essentially he echoed Christoph's ideas, while in reality they were often Ulrich's ideas, observations, and feelings—briefly and awkwardly expressed—which Christoph delivered in brilliant form and with great conviction of his own." Among commentators of Bonhoeffer's fiction, Ulrich is

often regarded as representing Bethge, and Christoph as representing Bonhoeffer. However, the difference between Bonhoeffer's account of his own intellectual relationship with Bethge and his description of that between Ulrich and Christoph underlines the importance of not interpreting each character of the fiction as necessarily representing a specific person in Bonhoeffer's entourage.

83. See Klemens von Klemperer, review *Fiction from Tegel Prison* by Dietrich Bonhoeffer, *Union Seminary Quarterly Review*, 54 no 1–2 (2000), 112.

84. Dietrich Bonhoeffer, *Act and Being*, DBWE vol. 2, ed. Wayne Whitson Floyd Jr., trans. H. Martin Rumscheidt (Minneapolis: Fortress Press, 1996), 158.

85. See for example Bonhoeffer, *Letters and Papers from Prison*, 367: "By the way, do read Prov. 22: 11–12 sometime. This bars the way to all escapism in the guise of piety."

86. See Bonhoeffer, *Life Together*, 39f.

87. Bonhoeffer, *Ethics*, 124. "Pious godlessness," also called "hopeless godlessness," will be discussed further in the conclusion.

88. Bonhoeffer, *Letters and Papers from Prison*, 489.

89. The editors of the German edition are Christian Gremmels, Eberhard Bethge, Renate Bethge, with Ilse Tödt. See Bonhoeffer, *Letters and Papers from Prison*, 490, footnote 1.

90. Referred to as "Notes II."

91. Bonhoeffer, *Letters and Papers from Prison*, 491. See the appendix, document 4. Here I follow the layout as it is presented in *Letters and Papers from Prison*. It will be noted that the layout in the original is slightly different, with the phrase "Jesus sprach zu ihm:" appearing above the phrase "Motto: was willst du, daß ich dir tun soll?" with a sign in Bonhoeffer's hand perhaps indicating that it should form one long sentence.

92. See Bonhoeffer, *Letters and Papers from Prison*, 491, footnote 4.

93. Bonhoeffer, *Letters and Papers from Prison*, 499.

94. For example, "Experience of transcendence" appears in Notes I, and in the outline for chapter 2: "Jesus's 'being-for-others' is the experience of transcendence!" See Bonhoeffer, *Letters and Papers from Prison*, 490 and 501.

95. Bonhoeffer, *Letters and Papers from Prison*, 490.

96. Bonhoeffer, *Letters and Papers from Prison*, 500.

97. Bonhoeffer, *Letters and Papers from Prison*, 501.

98. See Bonhoeffer, *Letters and Papers from Prison*, 482, letter dated the 18th July 1944 where Bonhoeffer equates people's sharing in the suffering of God with faith: "The one thing they all have in common is their sharing in the suffering of God in Christ. That is their 'faith.'"

99. Bonhoeffer, *Fiction from Tegel Prison*, 106: "That's because, without knowing it and certainly without talking about it, in truth they still base their lives on Christianity, an unconscious Christianity."

100. Bonhoeffer, *Letters and Papers from Prison*, 489.

Chapter Three

Defining Unconscious Christianity

INTRODUCTION

As is now clear from the previous chapter, analyzing Bonhoeffer's references to unconscious Christianity is problematic. At least at first glance, these references seem to point to several different elements that may be contradictory. It has been shown that in *Novel* Bonhoeffer establishes a link between unconscious Christianity and the *bürgerlich* way of life. This is illustrated in the Brake parents' inheritance of certain Christian practices and suggests that unconscious Christianity is a state that comes naturally to someone with a particular type of background and upbringing. However, in "Notes II," Bonhoeffer relates unconscious Christianity to morality, linking unconscious Christianity to the passage in Matthew on the correct way to give alms, "do not let your left hand know what your right hand is doing."[1] The reference to unconscious Christianity in "Notes II" suggests that it is a state in which people act morally. These two uses of the term "unconscious Christianity" seem, if not incompatible, then at least difficult to reconcile into one unified definition. Furthermore, the marginal note at the end of "Ultimate and Penultimate Things" shows that in that instance Bonhoeffer links unconscious Christianity to claiming the "human" and the "good"[2] for Jesus Christ, and claiming as Christians "precisely such persons who no longer dare to call themselves Christians."[3] The people described at the end of "Ultimate and Penultimate Things" are not presented in the same way as the Brake parents, in that they do not practice any Christian rituals, and their social class is not highlighted in the way that the Brakes' is. However, they are still linked to unconscious Christianity.

This chapter considers the apparent tensions between Bonhoeffer's various depictions of unconscious Christianity, and asks whether one unified definition of unconscious Christianity emerges from Bonhoeffer's late writings, or whether the term has several different, and irreconcilable, meanings. I conclude that despite apparent contradictions it is possible, and indeed necessary, to see unconscious Christianity as a concept that Bonhoeffer was in the process of developing, and about which he already had some clear views. I propose a definition of unconscious Christianity that unites all the definitions arising from analyses of the pertinent texts, whilst recognizing the tensions that remain between Bonhoeffer's various accounts of it.

In the next chapter, I test my definition against Bonhoeffer's wider writings, in order to assess whether my hypothesis stands in the wider context of Bonhoeffer's late theology, and whether it is possible to see the roots of his ideas about unconscious Christianity in his earlier work.

This chapter consists of two parts. The first, longer part constructs definitions of unconscious Christianity based on an examination of each of the texts described in chapter 2. The second part will discuss these definitions and put forward an overarching definition of unconscious Christianity.

DEFINITIONS OF UNCONSCIOUS CHRISTIANITY IN EACH OF THE FOUR TEXTS

Unconscious Christianity in the Marginal Note at the End of "Ultimate and Penultimate Things"

Bonhoeffer's marginal note "*Unbewußtes Christentum*," made at the bottom of the manuscript of "Ultimate and Penultimate Things," refers to the group of people he describes at the end of the essay. As has been noted in the previous chapter, Bonhoeffer ends his text with a discussion of a specific group of people in "Western Christianity today."[4] While Bonhoeffer makes clear that these people value penultimate things, and are "determined to go on holding to them,"[5] their relationship to the ultimate is less clear. Bonhoeffer writes that they are "in no way hostile toward this ultimate,"[6] although they hold fast to the penultimate and do not fully recognize or affirm the connection between the penultimate and the ultimate.[7] This group therefore does not exclude the possibility of its engagement with the penultimate being informed by the ultimate, even if this happens unconsciously. Thus the group's way of life can be said to amount to one that values the world created by God, without being fully conscious of any reference to God or to God's ultimate word of grace.

Previously in his argument, Bonhoeffer had stated that being good and being human are addressed as the penultimate from the viewpoint of the ultimate, and can be understood only from the viewpoint of the ultimate.[8] Being human and being good both precede, and are determined by, the ultimate: This circularity of the relationship between ultimate and penultimate is central to Bonhoeffer's thesis that the ultimate and penultimate should not be torn apart. However, a new element is added to the argument at the end of the essay, as Bonhoeffer is dealing with a goodness and humanness that do not understand themselves as being in direct relationship with the ultimate. Therefore, in order to prevent this humanness and this goodness from collapsing due to a disconnect from the ultimate, Bonhoeffer calls for these penultimate things to be claimed for the ultimate, for Jesus Christ.[9]

Although Bonhoeffer does not see the human and the good in question as being the humanness and the goodness of Christ, he nevertheless argues that they should be claimed for Christ. These penultimate things should not be made into "self-sufficient values,"[10] but on the contrary should be seen as being in relationship to Christ, to the ultimate, and thus they will be kept from collapse. Bonhoeffer also makes the point that even though this humanness and goodness "cannot stand in the judgment,"[11] Jesus loves the rich young man who has striven to keep the commandments all his life.[12] This implies that Jesus can love penultimate humanness and goodness in and of itself. Furthermore, Bonhoeffer thinks that in some instances the human and the good are an "unconscious remnant" that "represent a previous bond to the ultimate."[13] Thus, according to Bonhoeffer, the human and the good sometimes testify unwittingly to a connection between the penultimate and the ultimate.

Bonhoeffer is not talking here of the human and the good as abstract concepts, but of human and good people. This is clear both in his reference to a "broad sector of people"[14] in Western Christianity, and in what follows on directly from his comments on the unconscious remnant: "It may often seem more serious to address such people simply as non-Christians and to urge them to confess their unbelief. But it would be more Christian to claim as Christians precisely such persons who no longer dare to call themselves Christians, and to help them with much patience to move toward confessing Christ."[15]

Bonhoeffer gives another reason, apart from his desire to affirm the connection between the ultimate and the penultimate, for claiming this group of people for Christ. He writes: "Whatever in the fallen world is found to be human and good belongs on the side of Jesus Christ. We truncate the gospel when we proclaim that only the broken and the evil are near to Jesus Christ and when, proclaiming the love of the father for the prodigal, we belittle the father's love for the son who stayed at home."[16] Bonhoeffer's understanding of the gospel message leads him to draw a parallel between the older son in Luke 15 and the people who value the penultimate without clearly seeing its link to the ultimate. Both the stay-at-home son in the parable and this group of people are loved by God, says Bonhoeffer, and should be recognized as such.

It is evident therefore that this text contains four elements that should be included in the definition of unconscious Christianity. Firstly, Bonhoeffer's marginal note "*Unbewußtes Christentum*" refers to a group of people located in a specific historical and geographical context: the late 1930s, early 1940s Western world. Even more specifically, the Christian Western world. These people, the unconscious Christians, are thus located within Christianity, insofar as they are located within the Western Christian cultural context. Secondly, they are good human beings. They personify "the human and the good"[17] that need to be claimed for Christ. Thirdly, they do not self-identify as Christians. Bonhoeffer uses the phrase "such persons who no longer dare to call themselves Christians,"[18] without expanding on why this might be the case. This is similar to Rothe's understanding of unconscious Christians as people who have turned away from the Church,[19] although Bonhoeffer talks of people distancing themselves from the label "Christians" rather than from the Church. Fourthly, unconscious Christians are attached to the penultimate, that is, the worldly. They value penultimate things as having their own intrinsic worth, regardless of the link between the ultimate and the penultimate. These four points lead us to a picture of unconscious Christianity in this text that includes a specific cultural context, goodness, a conscious decision not to self-identify as Christian, and a desire to hold on to the penultimate.

Before turning to unconscious Christianity in *Novel*, it is necessary to ask why unconscious Christians are choosing to no longer identify as Christians. Bonhoeffer's choice of words, "such persons who no longer dare to call themselves Christians,"[20] hints at the loss of meaning of words such as "Christianity" and "redemption," and a general reluctance among certain people to use such words, themes he develops in his writings in Tegel prison.[21] It could be that the people Bonhoeffer refers to here previously identified as Christians but no longer wish to do so, due to the loss of meaning of words like "Christian" that has come about due to the propaganda of the Nazi régime and Reich Church's involvement with it. The choice to no longer identify as Christians could equally point to the gradual alienation of society from the Church that Bonhoeffer portrays in *Novel*.[22] Bonhoeffer could also be suggesting that these people have considered self-identifying as Christian but, due to their only vague recognition and tentative affirmation of the link between the ultimate and the penultimate, have chosen not to. While Bonhoeffer echoes Rothe's view that unconscious Christians are those who have turned away from the Church, he doesn't talk about a lack of understanding on their part of what Christian faith is, as Rothe does. However, he follows Rothe's, and to a certain extent Rade's, exhortation that Christians must strive to explain Christianity to those outside the Church. In the following *Ethics* essay "Natural Life," he highlights both the morality central to Christian faith, which is crucial for Rothe, and, following Rade, explains Christian teachings pertaining to the natural. Whatever the motivation behind unconscious Christians' decision to reject self-identification as Christians, this choice has not led Bonhoeffer to reject them as Christians. On the contrary, he encourages others, who are conscious of the link between the ultimate and the penultimate, to claim unconscious Christians for Christ and "help them with much patience to move toward confessing Christ."[23] Here Bonhoeffer echoes another of Rothe's points, outlined in the introduction, that the Church must "convict our unconscious Christians of their Christianity."[24]

Unconscious Christianity in *Novel*

As outlined in the previous chapter, it is in a conversation between the two friends Ulrich Karstensen and Christoph Brake that unconscious Christianity is mentioned in *Novel*.[25] Their brief discussion of unconscious Christianity concludes their dialogue, and the content of the whole conversation provides enough material to be able to propose a definition of unconscious Christianity as used in *Novel*. In discussing the bad behavior of some of their fellow-students on a recent school outing, Ulrich notes that not all of the students act in such a way, but that: "It's always just a few big wheels and then the rest tip right over."[26] In discussing the roots of this problem, they arrive at an analysis of the particular situation of Meyer, the ringleader, that points to a more general social problem: Meyer's mother, who is a seamstress and therefore not a member of the *Bürgertum*, is so nervous of officials that she teaches her son to have a great respect for "all the official 'somebodies.'"[27] Christoph concludes, "So is it any wonder if Herr Archibald Meyer, Graduating Senior, thinks the only proper thing to do is to behave like an aspiring government official by going out drinking, picking up a girl—if possible one from a cabaret—etcetera, etcetera, and, last but not least, flunking his graduation exams and making his mother miserable?"[28]

Christoph places the responsibility for this false ambition in certain people at the feet of the upper class,[29] because the rest of the population looks up to them and wants to emulate them. The blame does not rest with Frau Meyer. She believes that her actions are "pleasing to the good Lord."[30] Bonhoeffer's choice of words here indicates that people like Frau Meyer, despite their misguided actions, are sincere in their faith. The reason that the upper class inspires such a misplaced sense of ambition in others is that it is itself decayed. The blame does not lie only with the "bunch of rotten, obsequious lackeys" who make up some of the upper class, but also the few decent members of the upper class who "withdraw into themselves because they're repulsed by this vacuous, conceited society."[31]

From this analysis, it is plain to Christoph that Germany needs a new, genuine, upper class, and that the responsibility for such a renewal lies with members of the *Bürgertum*, such as himself and his family. Ulrich cautions his friend that they may not find themselves to be immune to the "poison of ambition"[32] that they see at work in members of the lower classes. He sees the lack of false ambition to be caused by something other than class. His own mother is the widow of a church organist and choirmaster, and therefore not a member of the *Bürgertum*. Nevertheless, she does not cower before her superiors, and Ulrich describes her in these terms: "Though she's quite modest, she moves with freedom and confidence wherever she goes, without wanting to be something other than she is. [. . .] When I ask myself where she gets that freedom, there's only one clear answer—from her Christian faith."[33] Thus, for Ulrich, Christian faith is that which prevents one from having false ambition, and a false idea of oneself. Ulrich attributes contemporary social evils to the fact that most people no longer have a Christian faith, and suggests that for a renewal of the *Bürgertum* to come about, its members will have to have Christian faith. Ulrich even makes a differentiation between the need for religion and the need for, more specifically, Christian faith, when he answers Christoph's question "So you think we must have more religion if we want to be in responsible positions someday?" with "I think, Christoph—rather, I wonder . . . no, I think—we have to be Christians."[34]

Ulrich's conclusion leads to a problem: What is to be made of the current members of the *Bürgertum* who do not go to church or exhibit any inclination toward Christian faith, but who are not prey to false ambition? Christoph asks Ulrich why his own parents, who only say grace before meals because of their youngest son, are not "infected by the spirit of false ambition."[35] Ulrich answers: "That's because, without knowing it and certainly without talking about it, in truth they still base their lives on Christianity, an unconscious Christianity."[36] By having Ulrich be able to recognize unconscious Christianity in the Brake parents, Bonhoeffer echoes Rade's statement that it is possible for people to be able to recognize unconscious Christianity in others.[37]

Ulrich's recognition of unconscious Christianity in the Brake parents solves the problem of why some people who are not consciously Christian are able to avoid false ambition. It is the Brake parents' unconscious Christianity that allows them to avoid it. In this text, therefore, Christianity, whether conscious or unconscious, is portrayed as that which allows the individual to have a genuine view of herself, "without wanting to be something other than she is."[38] Unconscious Christianity is what causes the Brake parents to be immune to the temptations of careerism and titles. Christoph compares this aspect of their character and finds it to be the same as that of Ulrich's mother, who is immune because of her Christian faith.

The two boys move on quickly from the staggering revelation of unconscious Christianity to briefly pose one more question to which they have no answer. This is the question of equality and inequality between human beings. Bonhoeffer's characters do not even attempt to resolve it. They simply state that Christ "made a point of making no distinction between people,"[39] whilst noting that their experience of life is that some people should have authority while others should be in lower social positions. This conflict of ideas brings the boys to wonder whether it will indeed be the current members of the *Bürgertum* who will, helped by Christianity, bring about a renewal of their class, or whether, taking the biblical idea of equality between people, a new "genuine upper class"[40] will be formed by members of all social strata. The end of this chapter in *Novel* gives the impression that Bonhoeffer flung some difficult questions at the reader and then retreated into the next chapter, which begins with an action sequence. Despite the unsatisfactory ending to the boys' conversation, we can still draw a definition of unconscious Christianity from this text: unconscious Christianity, like conscious Christianity, frees the subject from harboring false ambition, as she does not wish to be other than what she is.

This passage suggests that at this point Bonhoeffer thought primarily of unconscious Christians as being members of the *Bürgertum*, as in the text members of the lower classes who are Christian are consciously Christian. This points to the idea that Christianity is a part of the culture that members of the *Bürgertum* have inherited from their ancestors, but of which they are no longer consciously aware. This view is similar to Rothe's idea that people outside the Church should still be considered Christians due to their participation in society and history in which God is at work. However, Rothe did not specify that this was the case only for a certain section of society. According to Bonhoeffer's fiction, while members of the lower classes may also have inherited their religious beliefs from previous generations, if they have done so, they are conscious of it. Bonhoeffer's working class character in *Drama*, Heinrich, who found God whilst living near the docks among sailors and prostitutes,[41] does not have any background of Christianity, and, indeed, seems not to have any stable background at all, which leads him to comment to Christoph[42]: "We want something much simpler, ground under our feet, so we can live. That's what I call the foundation. Can't you feel the difference? People like you have a foundation, you have ground under your feet, you have a place in the world."[43] In Bonhoeffer's *Novel*, in addition to land and status in the world, the unconscious inheritance of Christianity appears to be exclusively a commodity of the *Bürgertum*.

Unconscious Christianity in the Letter to Bethge

In this letter, Bonhoeffer links unconscious Christianity to natural piety. It has already been mentioned that the term "piety" in Bonhoeffer's writing often denotes something negative.[44] However it appears that here the term "natural" qualifies the term "piety" in the sense that, according to Bonhoeffer, piety usually points to a human desire to make oneself appear holy and indicates therefore a sinful, self-aggrandizing state. However, when used in conjunction with the term "natural," it refers instead to a natural state of spiritual awareness. The person who is naturally pious does not strive for an appearance of holiness, but lives effortlessly according to God's will. In this text therefore, Bonhoeffer suggests that unconscious Christianity be viewed in conjunction with this state of natural piety.

Although Bonhoeffer links unconscious Christianity and natural piety summarily in a single sentence, the fact that the words *"wie es eine 'natürliche' Frömmigkeit"* and *"zugleich die Frage nach dem 'unbewußten Christentum'"* are underlined shows that it was the most important part of the letter.[45]

Having stated that the question of unconscious Christianity preoccupies him, Bonhoeffer does little to clarify which aspects of the question in particular are at the forefront of his mind. The only indication of the direction of Bonhoeffer's thinking concerning unconscious Christianity at this juncture lies in the following two sentences: "The Lutheran dogmatists distinguished a *fides directa* from a *fides reflexa*. They related that to the so-called faith of the infant at baptism."[46] The distinction made in these two sentences helps us form a hypothesis of how Bonhoeffer understands unconscious Christianity at this stage of his writing.

The distinction between *fides directa* and *fides reflexa* sheds some light on the link Bonhoeffer makes between unconscious Christianity and natural piety, as he implicitly ranges *fides directa* alongside unconscious Christianity and natural piety, in opposition to *fides reflexa*. In this text Bonhoeffer is echoing a point he had already made in *Act and Being*, in which he noted that old Protestant dogmatics called *fides directa* the act of faith that is performed by the agent's consciousness, but upon which it is not possible for the agent to reflect.[47]

Bonhoeffer is therefore suggesting that unconscious Christianity should be thought of in terms of an act of faith upon which the agent cannot reflect. Bonhoeffer notes that there is a precedent in Protestant thinking that allows for an individual's obedience to God to come about without the individual having to reflect upon it. Unconscious Christianity, therefore, is characterized by acts of faith that come about naturally within an individual, without that individual being able to reflect upon them, just as the infant is incapable of reflecting upon its faith at the moment at which it is baptized.

It is important to note that in this letter, Bonhoeffer is aware that he cannot present his ideas on unconscious Christianity in a neat, concise way. On the contrary, he recognizes that by broaching these ideas, he and Bethge are "addressing a very wide-reaching problem."[48] This shows that although Bonhoeffer has by no means encapsulated what unconscious Christianity means at this stage, he is working toward defining it.

Unconscious Christianity in "Notes II"[49]

As detailed in the previous chapter, Bonhoeffer references two biblical passages in the notes in which he also mentions unconscious Christianity: Matthew 6:3 and Matthew 25. The former occurs in the Sermon on the Mount, and, more specifically, during Jesus's discussion of alms-giving. Jesus's message is that good actions, in this case alms-giving, should be so secret and hidden that even the givers of alms should not be aware of it. So oblivious must they be of their own good deeds that their left hand must not know what their right hand is doing. They should be unconscious of their righteous action.

The first few verses from Matthew 6, which surround the verse quoted by Bonhoeffer in "Notes II," present the idea that reward from God is linked to whether righteous action is carried out correctly (i.e., in a hidden and, if possible, unconscious manner) or wrongly (i.e., publicly). The latter passage, Matthew 25:37–40,[50] also contains the idea that God's reward is related to righteous action, and whether it was done consciously or unconsciously. In the few verses referred to by Bonhoeffer in "Notes II," the theme of righteous action is augmented by the idea that those who performed it were unaware that they were doing so. In these few verses the righteous ask the king, "When was it that we saw you hungry and gave you food, or thirsty and gave you something to drink?" The king has told them that they have done so, and is rewarding them accordingly, yet they themselves do not know of their righteousness.

It is obvious that in these notes Bonhoeffer links the idea of unconscious Christianity with those who are called righteous by Jesus, who have performed good actions and have either done so in secret, or are not even aware of their good actions. The view that unconscious Christians can perform good actions without being aware of it echoes Rothe's statement that people outside the institutional Church can display Christian morality, acting in ways that further the Kingdom of God. For Rothe, this group's inability to understand that morality is central to the Christian faith prevents them from seeing that their actions link them to Christianity. Bonhoeffer does not explain why unconscious Christians do not view their actions in terms of Christianity, he simply asserts that this is the case. Bonhoeffer develops this idea further in his outline for a book, for which these notes were written.

The following section, from the outline for the second chapter, is the one that gives us the most insight into Bonhoeffer's idea of unconscious Christianity during this period, although he does not use the term itself again. Bonhoeffer links Jesus's question to the blind man, "What do you want me to do for you?"[51] that he references at the end of his "Notes II," with the idea of Jesus's being-for-others in this passage. Although already cited above, it is worth reproducing the passage here for the sake of clarity.

> Who is God? Not primarily a belief in God's omnipotence, and so on. That is not a genuine experience of God but just a prolongation of a piece of the world. Encounter with Jesus Christ. Experience that here there is a reversal of all human existence, in the very fact that Jesus only "is there for others." Jesus's "being-for-others" is the experience of transcendence! Only through this liberation from the self, through this "being-for-others" unto death, do omnipotence, omniscience, and omnipresence come into being. Faith is participating in this being of Jesus. (Becoming human [Menschwerdung], cross, resurrection.) Our relationship to God is no "religious" relationship to some highest, most powerful, and best being imaginable—that is no genuine transcendence. Instead, our relationship to God is a new life in "being there for others," through participation in the being of Jesus.[52]

By reading "Notes II" as part of the basic groundwork for this section, we can see that Bonhoeffer links unconscious Christianity to an encounter with, and participation in, Jesus Christ. This link is clear in Bonhoeffer's reference to Matthew 25, as the people who are accepted by the king in that text have engaged unconsciously with Christ in their actions toward the needy, and have thus participated in Jesus's being-for-others. The unconscious Christians have encountered Jesus Christ in their participation in Jesus's being-for-others. This in turn brings about a "liberation from the self," as one's existence becomes directed toward others, rather than toward oneself. In the chapter outline, Bonhoeffer does not emphasize the unconscious, unwitting aspect of serving others as much as he does in "Notes II," but the same idea is present in the liberation from the self in order to be for others. If Jesus's being-for-others is the experience of transcendence, then the unconscious Christian's participation in the being of Jesus, that is, her participation in being-for-others, leads her to transcend herself. Through this participation in the being of Jesus, the unconscious Christian is in relationship with God. Through this being-for-others, she has faith. Indeed, Bonhoeffer equates participation in the being of Jesus with faith, as he does elsewhere.[53] By equating faith with participation in the being of Jesus, Bonhoeffer echoes the idea mentioned above, that the person who carries out righteous action without being aware of it engages with Christ.

The encounter with Christ that Bonhoeffer describes in his notes does not occur due to the individual's natural tendency toward God. The way he describes this encounter, noting that it leads to an "experience that here there is a reversal of all human existence" shows what a far cry this is from Rahner's view that humans encounter God because they tend naturally toward the divine. In fact, Bonhoeffer imagines scenarios in which the encounter takes place without the individual involved having sought any interaction with the divine. This is the case for example for Heinrich, in *Drama*.[54]

The picture of unconscious Christianity that emerges from "Notes II," read alongside the outline for a book, is one of righteous action, performed, ideally, without the subject's being aware of it. In Matthew 25, which Bonhoeffer links into his idea of unconscious Christianity, those who perform righteous actions are called righteous by Jesus, and are called to inherit the kingdom by the king. It seems therefore that Bonhoeffer thinks that those who perform righteous actions are called righteous and accepted by God. The righteous action Bonhoeffer is referring to is not performed out of piety, for the perfecting of one's own moral character, but is righteous action directed toward others. It is more than one isolated righteous action. Rather, it is a way of being, a being-for-others. Jesus Christ "is there for others,"[55] and it is possible to participate in Jesus's being, which leads to a new life of "being there for others"[56] and relationship to God. The unconscious Christian has faith, as faith is equivalent to participation in Jesus's being-for-others, but is unaware of it.

In Matthew 25, those called righteous end up consciously engaging with Jesus Christ when he addresses them and rewards them for their righteous action. Before being addressed, however, they engaged with him unconsciously, feeding and clothing others whom Jesus later claims in some sense to represent him. It is fair to assume, therefore, that unconscious Christians engage unconsciously with Jesus in their being-for-others. It is unclear whether Bonhoeffer expects unconscious Christians to engage consciously with Jesus at some point in the future, as the righteous do in Matthew 25.

Despite this uncertainty, however, it is possible to posit a basic definition of unconscious Christianity as used in "Notes II": It is a participation in Jesus's being-for-others that denies the self, and is recognized by God as righteous. This participation can begin unconsciously (Matthew 25:37–40), or can become unconscious (Matthew 6:3).

PRESENTING A DEFINITION OF UNCONSCIOUS CHRISTIANITY

Having proposed definitions for unconscious Christianity as used in each of the texts in which Bonhoeffer mentions it, this section brings them all together in order to ascertain whether or not a coherent definition of unconscious Christianity emerges from these writings.

The main points made so far are, briefly, the following: The analysis of "Ultimate and Penultimate Things" demonstrates that Bonhoeffer uses the term "unconscious Christianity" to refer to a specific group of people defined in space and time, who are good, who do not self-identify as Christians, and who are attached to the penultimate. *Novel* shows that Bonhoeffer thinks of unconscious Christianity as freeing the individual from harboring false ambition and wanting to be other than what he is. *Novel* also indicates that Bonhoeffer thinks of unconscious Christianity as being peculiar to members of the *Bürgertum*. He contrasts Christians from the lower classes who are conscious of their Christianity, and members of the *Bürgertum* who have inherited a cultural form of Christianity, suggesting that the *Bürgertum* is somehow unconscious of its Christianity because it is part and parcel of its cultural heritage. Examination of the letter to Bethge reveals that unconscious Christianity is manifested in an individual by acts of faith that come about naturally within her, and upon which she cannot reflect. Finally, analyzing the notes made by Bonhoeffer in preparation for writing a book shows that unconscious Christians deny themselves and participate in Jesus's being-for-others. This is either done in secret, or the unconscious Christians are unaware of it. Being-for-others, which Bonhoeffer equates with faith, is an unconscious engagement with Jesus. By linking unconscious Christianity to Matthew 25, Bonhoeffer suggests that unconscious Christians are recognized as righteous by God.

In order to reflect the fact that when Bonhoeffer writes about unconscious Christianity he is writing about real people who are unconscious Christians, and not merely about an abstract concept, the following section will take the form of a series of questions pertaining to unconscious Christians. In answering questions pertaining to concrete unconscious Christians, I will gradually construct a complete definition of the abstract concept of unconscious Christianity.

Who Are Unconscious Christians?

Bonhoeffer's idea of who is an unconscious Christian broadens as he develops his thoughts on this question. At first he considers unconscious Christians to be specific to the Western world and to the time period in which he lives, and likely to be members of his own class, the *Bürgertum*. However, as he continues to engage with the topic, he broadens his view to include people who act in a certain way, selflessly being for others, without reference to their social class or geographical and temporal location. This development can be traced through all four texts in which Bonhoeffer refers to unconscious Christianity, and shows that his thinking on the subject was not static.

One aspect of the unconscious Christian's identity, however, that remains unchanged throughout Bonhoeffer's reflection is that the unconscious Christian does not self-identify as a Christian. This is a given in all four of the texts under discussion, and is most explicitly expressed in "Ultimate and Penultimate Things." In *Novel* it is not stated whether the Brake parents self-identify as Christians, but it is more likely that they don't, as their son does not identify them as such. In the letter to Bethge, unconscious Christians are linked to people with a *fides directa*, who perform acts of faith without reflecting upon them. Because of the lack of awareness of their acts of faith, it is assumed that unconscious Christians following the description in the letter do not self-identify as Christians either. According to "Notes II," unconscious Christians deny themselves and participate in Jesus's being-for-others without knowing it. It follows that they, too, do not self-identify as Christians.

Another characteristic expressed in "Ultimate and Penultimate Things" is that the unconscious Christian values the penultimate, that is, the worldly. At first glance, this seems to be the only point in these particular texts at which Bonhoeffer describes a desire to hold on to the worldly, but in fact the people he describes elsewhere as unconscious Christians also share this trait. Hans Brake, described in *Novel* as basing his life on an unconscious Christianity,[57] values the worldly, the immanent. He instils in his children a love of nature and a respect for social structures that inspire them to consider how they can be, in turn, responsible stewards of nature and society.[58] Indeed, what stands out in Bonhoeffer's young protagonists is their sense of responsibility for maintaining social order in the face of corruption and abuse of power. Bonhoeffer's characters thus display care for the penultimate, the worldly, while only occasionally thinking about the ultimate.[59] The care for the penultimate is not evident in unconscious Christianity as depicted in the letter, but in his last text mentioning unconscious Christianity, Bonhoeffer portrays unconscious Christians as caring for strangers and people who need food, drink, and clothes. This displays a concern for the worldly, the penultimate, that is the same as that expressed in "Ultimate and Penultimate Things." Interestingly, one of the few details that Rahner gives about how an anonymous Christian might behave is a "devotion to his material duties."[60] This ties in well with Bonhoeffer's vision of the unconscious Christian valuing the penultimate. Both thinkers recognize concrete involvement with the world as part of the profile, as it were, of an anonymous or unconscious Christian.

Part of the unconscious Christian's makeup that is only made explicit in "Ultimate and Penultimate Things" is goodness. In "Ultimate and Penultimate Things" Bonhoeffer refers to the people to whom he links unconscious Christianity as "the human and the good."[61] He does not refer to the unconscious Christians in *Novel* as good, but in portraying Hans Brake as valuing the penultimate he is depicting him as being like the good people described in "Ultimate and Penultimate Things." Likewise, the people alluded to in "Notes II" also are shown as valuing the penultimate, caring for the hungry and naked people in the penultimate. This counts them among the good people. The letter to Bethge is the only text in which goodness and unconscious Christianity are not linked.

From these four texts there emerges a picture of the unconscious Christian as a good person who cares about and feels a sense of responsibility for the penultimate and who does not self-identify as Christian. The characteristic of the unconscious Christian that changes as Bonhoeffer develops his concept is that she no longer necessarily belongs to the *bürgerlich* class in the 1930s–1940s Western world, but might come from different types of backgrounds.

What Makes Someone an Unconscious Christian?

Another element in the makeup of the unconscious Christian that emerged from analyzing *Novel* is that of being free from wanting to be other than what one is. Unconscious Christians are preserved from false ambition. According to *Novel*, it is Christian faith that causes the individual to be immune to false ideas of what he should be. But how does this Christian faith come about? Elsewhere, Bonhoeffer writes: "Christianity arises out of the encounter with a concrete human being: Jesus."[62] It can therefore be assumed that encounter with Jesus is at the root of becoming an unconscious Christian. However, as will be discussed below, the precise causal relationship between the encounter with Christ and the actions carried out by the unconscious Christian is somewhat unclear.

In *Novel*, those who are content with who they are also endeavor to preserve the penultimate, and do not self-identify as Christian. So far the analysis shows that the definitions of unconscious Christianity taken from the various texts in which it is mentioned can be seen to be compatible, except for the issue of class described above.

What Is the Causal Relationship between the Unconscious Christian's Encounter with Christ, the Actions They Carry Out, and Their Righteousness in God's Sight?

The people depicted in Matthew 25:37–40, referred to by Bonhoeffer in his "Notes II," don't know how they have engaged with Jesus; he has to explain to them that they have already encountered him, in the form of the hungry and cold, whom they have fed and clothed. Through their selfless action they have participated in Jesus's being-for-others. In the four texts under discussion in this chapter, Bonhoeffer does not make clear whether the unconscious Christian feeds the hungry, and then, because of this act of faith, encounters Christ, or on the other hand, encounters Christ in the hungry, and therefore feeds the hungry.[63] Regardless of this, the encounter of the unconscious Christian with Christ leaves her changed, but without her knowing it. There is no knowledge of having been changed; like the people in Matthew 25, the unconscious Christian does not know that her act of faith, upon which she cannot in any case reflect, has been caused by, or has led her to, an encounter with Christ. However, a change has occurred, and the change is that the unconscious Christian is now considered by God to be among the righteous. Matthew 25 makes clear that those who have acted in the selfless serving of others are righteous, and will be rewarded with eternal life. According to

Bonhoeffer, the pronouncement of righteousness upon the people in Matthew 25 is shared by unconscious Christians, as he links them to this passage.

There is, therefore, a causal link between unconscious Christianity (more specifically here the encounter with Christ, participation in Jesus's being-for-others, and selfless action) and being recognized as righteous by God, which indicates that unconscious Christianity is not regarded as a neutral state by God. This factor can be added to the developing definition of unconscious Christianity, and is compatible with all the elements of the definition gathered so far.

How Do the Acts upon Which the Subject Cannot Reflect and the Participation in Jesus's Being-for-Others Fit In with Other Traits of the Unconscious Christian?

Hans Brake offers a good illustration of selfless being-for-others. In *Novel*, we learn that as a teenager, during a school sports day, Hans willingly selected a faulty pole to use in the pole-vault contest, so that his rival would not have to use it. Bonhoeffer portrays this decision as one taken on the spur of the moment, that Hans would not have had time to reflect upon. This action therefore fulfils two of Bonhoeffer's criteria for an action that is proper to the unconscious Christian: It is an act upon which the subject cannot reflect, and it is a selfless act, conforming to Jesus's example of being-for-others. In Hans Brake, therefore, we have all the facets of unconscious Christianity that we have gleaned from Bonhoeffer's late writing united in one person. He belongs to the time period and location that Bonhoeffer refers to in "Ultimate and Penultimate Things" in conjunction with unconscious Christianity and he is part of the specific social class that Bonhoeffer at first sees as being the most likely to produce unconscious Christians. He does not self-identify as Christian, but is recognized as such by his son's friend. He values the penultimate, which can be seen in the conduct he teaches his children. He perceives himself as he truly is and is thus free from false ambition. As this trait is presented in *Novel* as going hand-in-hand with Christian faith, we can infer that Hans has Christian faith, even if this is unconscious. He acts selflessly, participating in Jesus's being-for-others, and performs acts of faith upon which he cannot reflect.

It's worth noting that Rahner includes something that seems to be similar to Bonhoeffer's notion of participating in Jesus's being-for-others in his description of the anonymous Christian. Rahner notes in this very brief description that the anonymous Christian "lives the duty of each day in the quiet sincerity of patience, in devotion to his material duties and the demands made upon him by the persons under his care."[64] I've already pointed out the connection between the "material duties" that Rahner mentions and Bonhoeffer's comments on valuing the penultimate. Now we're looking at the connection between participating in Jesus's being-for-others, in Bonhoeffer, and the devotion to the demands made upon one by the people in one's care, in Rahner. Both ideas point to self-giving service to others. On a more fundamental level, both of these actions are connected to an encounter with Christ. As we have seen, there is no clear causal link between the unconscious Christian's encounter with Christ and the selfless actions through which she participates in Jesus's being-for-others, but they are certainly linked in some way. For Rahner the link between faith, albeit a faith that is not made explicit, and this care for others is clearly causal. First, the individual accepts the revelation of God, even though this might be in a way that does not lead to a conscious affirmation of faith. Then, because of this acceptance of God's self-communication, which Rahner equates with faith,[65] the individual undertakes the actions just described, which include care for others. For both theologians, then, encounter with Christ is intimately connected with how we approach our relationship to others. While for Bonhoeffer, this connection is not fully explained, for Rahner it is clear that once we have encountered Christ we relate differently to other human beings.

To return to Bonhoeffer and his example of an unconscious Christian, the only things that can't be ascertained from reading *Novel* is that Hans Brake has encountered God, and that he is recognized as righteous by God. These are elements that occur later in Bonhoeffer's development of unconscious Christianity than the writing of *Novel*, and it is therefore not surprising that Bonhoeffer does not articulate them explicitly in his description of Hans.

CONCLUDING COMMENTS

It is clear that Bonhoeffer developed his thinking on unconscious Christianity over the course of several years, and at various points during this period he highlighted different elements of it. The most obvious change in his thought on the topic is his view that unconscious Christians emerge from *bürgerlich* society, which he does not refer to again after writing *Novel*. In addition, Bonhoeffer never wrote at length on unconscious Christianity, as he did on other theological concepts, in his theological letters to Bethge. This is another indicator that he was still struggling to formulate his ideas during the last months of his life.[66] His writing on unconscious Christianity moves from an emphasis similar to Rothe and Rade's on why good people who no longer dare to self-identify as Christians should be claimed for Christ, through a detailed description of such a person in the character of Hans Brake, to making a link between unconscious Christianity and natural piety, and finally to an association of unconscious Christians with the biblical characters of Matthew 25:37–40. Bonhoeffer's work on unconscious Christianity is wide-ranging, encompassing four different types of text, and its contents seem scattered and disparate.

Nevertheless, apart from his abandoning of the idea that unconscious Christians must belong to a specific social class and cultural context, Bonhoeffer does not give conflicting accounts of unconscious Christianity. A clear picture of unconscious Christianity emerges from these texts, and includes all the definitions listed above. By integrating these definitions and taking into consideration the answers to the questions posed in this section, I propose the following definition of unconscious Christianity.

Unconscious Christianity refers to the whole body of good people who have encountered Christ without being aware of it and do not self-identify as Christians. In addition, they may fulfill any of these six criteria: (1) to have faith without knowing it, (2) to be selfless and participate in Jesus's being-for-others, (3) to not seek to be other than what they are, (4) to value the penultimate, (5) to perform acts of faith without reflecting on them, (6) to be a member of the *Bürgertum*. Because of the link between "Notes II" and Matthew 25, it seems that as he further develops his ideas on unconscious Christianity Bonhoeffer suggests that unconscious Christians are recognized as righteous by God.

NOTES

1. Matthew 6:3.
2. Bonhoeffer, *Ethics*, 169.
3. Bonhoeffer, *Ethics*, 170.
4. Bonhoeffer, *Ethics*, 169.
5. Bonhoeffer, *Ethics*, 169.
6. Bonhoeffer, *Ethics*, 169.
7. See Bonhoeffer, *Ethics*, 169, and chapter 2 of this book.
8. See Bonhoeffer, *Ethics*, 159, and chapter 2 of this book.
9. Bonhoeffer, *Ethics*, 169.
10. Bonhoeffer, *Ethics*, 169.
11. Bonhoeffer, *Ethics*, 169.
12. See Mark 10:17–22, and Bonhoeffer, *Ethics*, 169.
13. Bonhoeffer, *Ethics*, 169. The idea that the human and the good are in some instances an unconscious remnant representing a previous bond to the ultimate is confirmed by the German original: "Nicht soll das Menschliche und Gute für sich einen Wert bekommen, sondern es soll und darf für Jesus Christus in Anspruch genommen werden, besonders dort, wo es als unbewußter Rest einer vormaligen Bindung an das Letzte dasteht." Dietrich Bonhoeffer, *Ethik*, DBW vol. 6, eds. Ilse Tödt, Heinz Eduard Tödt, Ernst Feil, and Clifford Green (Munich: Christian Kaiser Verlag., 1992), 162.
14. Bonhoeffer, *Ethics*, 169.
15. Bonhoeffer, *Ethics*, 169–70.
16. Bonhoeffer, *Ethics*, 169.
17. Bonhoeffer, *Ethics*, 169.
18. Bonhoeffer, *Ethics*, 170.
19. See the introduction to this book.
20. Bonhoeffer, *Ethics*, 170.

21. See for example Bonhoeffer, *Letters and Papers from Prison*, 389, and Bonhoeffer, *Fiction from Tegel Prison*, 50. Wannenwetsch comments on Bonhoeffer's sensitivity to the abuse of words, pointing out that over the course of writing letters from prison, Bonhoeffer starts to put certain key words in quotation marks. Wannenwetsch offers this explanation: "These familiar terms he no longer considered to be safe—it dawned on Bonhoeffer that he witnessed a time of transition that rendered ambiguous any previous meaning these terms may have had." Bernd Wannenwetsch, "'Christians and Pagans,' towards a Trans-Religious Second Naiveté or How to Be a Christological Creature" in *Who Am I? Bonhoeffer's Theology through His Poetry*, 178.

22. See for example Bonhoeffer, *Fiction from Tegel Prison*, 74.
23. Bonhoeffer, *Ethics*, 170.
24. Rothe, "Zur Orientierung über die gegenwärtige Aufgabe der deutsch-evangelischen Kirche," 67. For a discussion of Rade's qualified agreement with Rothe on this point, see the introduction to this book.
25. Bonhoeffer, *Fiction from Tegel Prison*, 106, and chapter 2 of this book.
26. Bonhoeffer, *Fiction from Tegel Prison*, 102.
27. Bonhoeffer, *Fiction from Tegel Prison*, 102.
28. Bonhoeffer, *Fiction from Tegel Prison*, 103.
29. Here Bonhoeffer does not use the term *Bürgertum*, but *Schicht*. "Die tonangebenden Schichten, die sogenannte Oberschicht," Dietrich Bonhoeffer, *Fragmente aus Tegel, Drama und Roman*, eds. Renate and Eberhard Bethge (Munich: Chr. Kaiser Verlag., 1978), 96.
30. Bonhoeffer, *Fiction from Tegel Prison*, 103.
31. Bonhoeffer, *Fiction from Tegel Prison*, 103.
32. Bonhoeffer, *Fiction from Tegel Prison*, 104.
33. Bonhoeffer, *Fiction from Tegel Prison*, 104.
34. Bonhoeffer, *Fiction from Tegel Prison*, 105–6.
35. Bonhoeffer, *Fiction from Tegel Prison*, 106.
36. Bonhoeffer, *Fiction from Tegel Prison*, 106.
37. See the introduction to this book.
38. Bonhoeffer, *Fiction from Tegel Prison*, 104.
39. Bonhoeffer, *Fiction from Tegel Prison*, 107.
40. Bonhoeffer, *Fiction from Tegel Prison*, 103.
41. Bonhoeffer, *Fiction from Tegel Prison*, 41.
42. The character Christoph in Drama is very similar to the Christoph in *Novel*.
43. Bonhoeffer, *Fiction from Tegel Prison*, 68.
44. See chapter 2 of this book.
45. See Bonhoeffer's letter in the Appendix, document 3, and Bonhoeffer, *Letters and Papers from Prison*, 489: "The question how there can be a 'natural' piety is at the same time the question about 'unconscious Christianity' that preoccupies me more and more." The original reads: "Die Frage, wie es eine 'natürliche' Frömmigkeit geben kann, ist zugleich die Frage nach dem 'unbewußten Christentum,' die mich mehr und mehr beschäftigt." (Dietrich Bonhoeffer, *Widerstand und Ergebung*, 545.)
46. Bonhoeffer, *Letters and Papers from Prison*, 489.
47. Dietrich Bonhoeffer, *Act and Being*, 158: "Classical Protestant dogmatics spoke of *fides directa* to describe the act of faith which, even though completed within a person's consciousness, could not be reflected in it. The act of faith rests on the objectivity of the event of revelation in Word and sacrament. Clinging to Christ need not become self-conscious; rather, it is wholly taken up by completion of the act itself. Human beings are in Christ, and as there is no sin and death in Christ, human beings do not see their sin or death, not do they see themselves or their own faith. They see only Christ and their Lord and God." The idea that it is indeed an act of faith is found in the original German: "*Fides directa* nannte die altprotestantische Dogmatik den wohl vom Bewußtsein der Person vollzogenen, aber nicht in ihm reflektierbaren Glaubensakt." Dietrich Bonhoeffer, *Akt und Sein*, ed. Hans-Richard Reuter (Munich: Chr. Kaiser Verlag., 1988), 158.
48. Bonhoeffer, *Letters and Papers from Prison*, 489.

49. As clarified in the previous chapter, Bonhoeffer mentions unconscious Christianity in his second batch of notes, labeled "Notes II" in *Letters and Papers from Prison*. "Notes II" is directly preceded by "Notes I," and both contain ideas for Bonhoeffer's outline for a book.

50. For my argument as to why we can assume that Bonhoeffer refers to these verses in particular when writing "Matthew 25" in his notes, see chapter 2 of this book.

51. See Mark 10:51.

52. Bonhoeffer, *Letters and Papers from Prison*, 501.

53. See Bonhoeffer, *Letters and Papers from Prison*, 482, letter dated the 18th July 1944 where Bonhoeffer equates people's sharing in the suffering of God with faith: "The one thing they all have in common is their sharing in the suffering of God in Christ. That is their 'faith'."

54. See Bonhoeffer, *Fiction from Tegel Prison*, 40–41.

55. Bonhoeffer, *Letters and Papers from Prison*, 501.

56. Bonhoeffer, *Letters and Papers from Prison*, 501.

57. Bonhoeffer, *Fiction from Tegel Prison*, 106.

58. See Bonhoeffer, *Fiction from Tegel Prison*, 98 and 172.

59. Of the younger generation of the family, only Klara, the younger Brake daughter, is presented as following any Christian practice, reading a chapter of the Bible every morning. See Bonhoeffer, *Fiction from Tegel Prison*, 134.

60. Rahner, *Theological Investigations*, 394.

61. Bonhoeffer, *Ethics*, 169.

62. Bonhoeffer, *Letters and Papers from Prison*, 490.

63. Due to the sharp focus of this chapter on a few selected texts it is not possible to ascertain here whether, according to Bonhoeffer, the act of faith is the cause of the encounter with Christ, or vice versa, or whether the two do not have a causal link at all. The following two chapters will consider a wider range of texts and will propose an interpretation of Bonhoeffer's view on the link between the encounter with Christ and the act of faith.

64. Rahner, *Theological Investigations*, 394.

65. See Rahner, *Theological Investigations*, 394.

66. Of course, it is possible that he did write to Bethge about unconscious Christianity in the "September Correspondence." If this was indeed the case, Bonhoeffer may have reached firm conclusions about unconscious Christianity in the autumn of 1944.

Part II

Situating Unconscious Christianity within Bonhoeffer's Theology

Chapter Four

Unconscious Christianity in Context

Within Bonhoeffer's Late Theology and Secondary Literature

INTRODUCTION

Having constructed a working definition of unconscious Christianity, we can now turn to some important questions that it raises. Can the other prison texts help to substantiate the definition of unconscious Christianity suggested above, or do they raise problems for it? Can anything be added to our understanding of unconscious Christianity by taking into consideration Bonhoeffer's other prison writings?

In this chapter, the focus will widen a little in order to place Bonhoeffer's thoughts on unconscious Christianity in the context of the other late writings, and to assess whether my definition of unconscious Christianity fits in with the rest of the prison theology. This chapter will show, by examining unconscious Christianity alongside other major ideas Bonhoeffer developed in prison, that the various elements of unconscious Christianity highlighted by Bonhoeffer at different points in time do not clash with any of the other central ideas discussed. This chapter also discusses Bonhoeffer scholarship pertaining to unconscious Christianity, and looks at the definition of unconscious Christianity proposed here in the context of this secondary literature.

This chapter consists of two sections. The first section examines my definition of unconscious Christianity alongside the more well-known ideas from Bonhoeffer's prison writings. In this section I argue that unconscious Christianity and other ideas occurring in the late theology are complementary concepts, the correct grasp of each adding depth to the understanding of the other. I have chosen two central concepts for this comparison, the world come of age and religionless Christianity. The reasons for this choice are twofold. Firstly, I have chosen these two concepts for theological reasons. The world come of age is the pivotal concept upon which the rest of the Tegel theology turns and thus must be considered in any discussion of concepts from the prison period. The concept of the world come of age encompasses all the following ideas found in the prison texts: the concept of God as a stopgap,[1] Bonhoeffer's rejection of the religious *a priori*,[2] the idea that humanity no longer needs God to appear as a *deus ex machina*,[3] or to refer to a "working hypothesis: God,"[4] and the thought that humanity is called to live *etsi deus non daretur*.[5] Religionless Christianity is perhaps the most well-known idea from this time in Bonhoeffer's life, and it is also the concept that is the most likely to be confused with unconscious Christianity. It therefore also deserves particular attention in this work. Secondly, there is the practical consideration that it is not possible to compare unconscious Christianity with all the ideas to be found in the Tegel fragments, and I therefore address the two that are most pertinent to understanding unconscious Christianity. Some preliminary conclusions will show in what way a grasp of unconscious Christianity adds to an understanding of the prison texts.

In the second section I compare my definition of unconscious Christianity with Bonhoeffer scholarship on the subject, drawing attention to how this definition ties in with some of what has already been written on the subject, while also offering a new, more detailed and well-rounded approach to unconscious Christianity.

UNCONSCIOUS CHRISTIANITY AND THE TEGEL THEOLOGY

The World Come of Age

Before considering the relationship between unconscious Christianity and the world come of age, a recapitulation of what Bonhoeffer meant by "world come of age" is useful here.[6] The phrase "world that has come of age" first appears in a letter to Bethge, in June 1944.[7] It is the central concept on which hang all the other theological ideas that von Klemperer describes as "among the most radical, if not revolutionary, in modern theology."[8] The phrase itself is borrowed from the nineteenth-century German philosopher Wilhelm Dilthey's work, *Weltanschauung und Analyse des Menschen seit Renaissance und Reformation*, which Bonhoeffer had been reading in prison.[9] Dilthey describes the historical development of human knowledge, and in parallel, the secularization of reason that has taken place slowly since the late medieval Renaissance of the thirteenth century. Dilthey uses the term "adulthood" to describe the status of humanity having reached autonomy from God. Ernst Feil points out that it is likely that Bonhoeffer's use of the image of adulthood to describe the human state of autonomy from God comes from his reading of Dilthey.[10]

According to Ralf K. Wüstenberg, it is due to his study of Dilthey that Bonhoeffer's view of human autonomy changed from a negative view to a positive one in the period between writing *Ethics* and *Letters and Papers*.[11] Indeed, by the time of his prison writing, it is rather the religious atmosphere in which the West has been steeped for centuries that Bonhoeffer views negatively. Here God is only perceived as providing an explanation to questions that are beyond human knowledge. As human knowledge increases, so the space that God may occupy diminishes. By this time in his theological development Bonhoeffer sees humanity's lack of autonomy from God, relying on God to explain the inexplicable, as a state to be avoided. In the letter to Bethge dated the 8th of June, Bonhoeffer writes that in the twentieth century, in the world come of age, the emancipation of humanity from its need for God as the answer to the unknowable has reached its completion: "Human beings have learned to manage all important issues by themselves, without recourse to 'Working hypothesis: God.'"[12]

Wüstenberg draws attention to the importance of Bonhoeffer's change in methodology to mirror that of Dilthey, as Bonhoeffer begins to articulate themes such as the critique of religion in a historical framework. This new historical approach, Wüstenberg suggests, brings Bonhoeffer to affirm that the era of religion is now over:

> The age when we could tell people that [who Christ is for us today] with words—whether with theological or with pious words—is past, as is the age of inwardness and of conscience, and that means the age of religion altogether. We are approaching a completely religionless age; people as they are now simply cannot be religious anymore.[13]

This quote shows that Bonhoeffer links together the ideas of religion, inwardness, and conscience, indicating that religion promotes the separation of the individual from the world. Christiane Tietz picks up on this in her comments on Bonhoeffer's definition of religion. Tietz identifies four characteristics pertaining to the "religion" that Bonhoeffer identifies as being on the wane, "metaphysics, inner life, individualism, and partiality":

> Metaphysics had determined God as the highest, omnipotent, world-removed being that serves as an explanation when human beings are unable to explain certain realities within the world, and which intervenes in the world from outside, when human beings stumble on their limitations and no longer know how to help themselves. When the religious, metaphysical God is located in human limitations, it is in religion's interest to strengthen the boundaries of human beings—not just their epistemological boundaries but also their interior boundaries where they don't know how to go on, their inner life. The religious thesis is that only with God can human beings cope with their questions arising

at these boundaries, with the so-called ultimate questions about suffering, guilt, and death. This, however, renders religion essentially something oriented toward individualism—that is, the personal concerns of individuals for their inner well-being and the salvation of their souls. All three characteristics—metaphysics, inner life, and individualism—have the common feature that through them religion becomes something partial, something that affects only a part of human life but never the human being in his or her entirety.[14]

Tietz pinpoints the important fact that for Bonhoeffer, these four characteristics of religion are not necessary for humanity in a basic sense. They were, at one point in human history and in the European context, part of how Christianity was expressed. However, they are not fundamentally required for Christianity to continue to be expressed, but were merely "but a historically determined and transitory human expression."[15] In the current age, Christians no longer need to live behind the barrier of religion that separates them from the world, but can and must live fully in the world.

Wüstenberg explains that, according to Dilthey, there can be no theoretical knowledge beyond that which life itself can show. Knowledge of the nature of humanity must base itself on real human life, as it is presented to us in history. He writes: "To have knowledge of humanity means to have knowledge of human life depicted in history."[16] This brief outline of Dilthey's thought and its influence on Bonhoeffer reveals one of the reasons for Bonhoeffer's emphasis on daily, practical life in his prison writing, outlined for example in his thoughts on marriage.[17] Only life in the world can be a source of knowledge about humanity and God. As Wüstenberg points out: "Interpreting in a nonreligious way means interpreting Christianity not through religion but in terms of *life*."[18] Bonhoeffer uses Dilthey's methodology to seriously rethink Christianity based on the idea of life without God as a given.

Bonhoeffer thus accepts the world come of age as a nonnegotiable reality. The world is increasingly detached from God; it is, to use one of Bonhoeffer's images mentioned above, like a man who has reached adulthood.[19] It is important to note that for Bonhoeffer the world's coming of age should not be seen as the triumph of secular society successfully separating itself from God, but on the contrary, as the continuation of human history in which God is intimately involved. Bonhoeffer's rejection of God as a working hypothesis, and of the religious *a priori*,[20] and his assertion that in the world come of age humanity has outgrown its need for a God as a *deus ex machina*,[21] stands in opposition to Rahner's view that humanity has a constant "tendency towards God, which is on occasion quite implicit and incoherent and yet always completely permeates man's being and existence."[22] For Rahner, humans will also tend toward God; this tendency is an integral part of being human. For Bonhoeffer, it is simply not the case that humans have an in-built tendency toward God. This is not to say, however, that in the world come of age God is absent, or can't be experienced by humans. God is present, but this presence will be experienced in new ways.

Tom Greggs highlights Bonhoeffer's view of God's continuous action in the world, even the world come of age, as follows: "It is not that sociologically speaking the world has come of age by its own secularity; it is rather that theologically speaking one must speak of 'a world that has come of age *by Jesus Christ*.'"[23] Bonhoeffer insists that Christianity must take this world come of age seriously, without trying to persuade it to remain within the old way of life, unable to "live without 'God' as its guardian."[24] At the same time, Christianity must present to the world a Christ who wants to be at the center of human life. Bonhoeffer is led to wonder how Christians can communicate the truth about God in the emancipated world in which they live:

> For today I'll just say this: if one wants to speak of God "nonreligiously," then one must speak in such a way that the godlessness of the world is not covered up in any way, but rather precisely to uncover it and surprise the world by letting light shine on it. The world come of age is more god-less and perhaps just because of that closer to God than the world not yet come of age.[25]

This shows that far from being intimidated by the world come of age, Bonhoeffer sees in it a hope for a new, "closer" relationship between God and humanity. According to Bonhoeffer, in unveiling the "godlessness"[26] of the world, humanity can see clearly that God as a working hypothesis has disappeared. This way of understanding God no longer has a place in the world come of age, and therefore, if there is a God, God must be in the center of human existence.

UNCONSCIOUS CHRISTIANITY AND THE WORLD COME OF AGE

To serve as a reminder, here is the definition of unconscious Christianity arrived at the end of the previous chapter: Unconscious Christianity refers to the whole body of good people who have encountered Christ without being aware of it and do not self-identify as Christians. In addition, they may fulfill any of these six criteria: (1) to have faith without knowing it, (2) to be selfless and participate in Jesus's being-for-others, (3) to not seek to be other than what they are, (4) to value the penultimate, (5) to perform acts of faith without reflecting on them, and (6) to be a member of the *Bürgertum*. Also, due to his linking Matthew 25 to unconscious Christianity, Bonhoeffer seems to arrive at the suggestion that unconscious Christians are recognized as righteous by God.

Does the idea of the world come of age substantiate this definition of unconscious Christianity? And does such an understanding of unconscious

Christianity add depth to the concept of the world come of age? Considering unconscious Christianity as a serious theological idea in Bonhoeffer's theology enables us to see that the world come of age allows for a broader understanding of Christianity, and for a wider range of ways in which people can be Christians, than was the case in the world before it came of age. Unconscious Christianity appears as an additional category of valid Christian expression in the late theology, alongside religionless Christianity. Greggs argues that the world come of age does not indicate the triumph of the secular over Christianity, but indicates rather the rejection of false ideas of God, which allows a flourishing of new forms of true Christianity.[27] Following Greggs, it is possible to include unconscious Christianity as one of these new forms of true Christianity. These new forms of Christianity are such that they can exist in a world come of age without attempting to conceal its maturity and autonomy from God.

It should be noted at this point that while unconscious Christianity is treated here as a new form of Christian expression that is possible in the new context of the world come of age, Bonhoeffer also associates it with Christians living in the world before it came of age. This is evidenced in his linking unconscious Christianity with the people described in Matthew 25. The people referred to in Matthew's gospel are portrayed as encountering Christ in those whom they serve, and only afterward learning about Christ's identity. Their starting point is the same as that of the unconscious Christians Bonhoeffer imagines living in the world come of age. Their daily lives unfold in a social context that bears no reference to Christ; they are autonomous from Christ. This connection between the people in Matthew 25 who live in a pre-Christian society, and those living in the post-Christian world come of age, is important, as it highlights the idea that unconscious Christians do not need to live in a Christian context or Christian society, but that it is possible for people to be unconscious Christians outside institutional and societal Christian structures. However, while Bonhoeffer links the people in Matthew 25 with unconscious Christians in the world come of age, he sees unconscious Christianity as a result of the world come of age.

According to Bonhoeffer, before the world's coming of age, humanity in general was not autonomous and thus was unable to act under the guidance of its own free responsible choice.[28] Bethge cites Kant's description of immaturity in the opening comments of *Was ist Aufklärung?*: "The Enlightenment is the emergence of man from immaturity that he himself is responsible for. Immaturity is the incapacity to use one's own intelligence without the guidance of another person."[29] In the pre-enlightened West, the only form of Christianity possible, according to the historical development model that Bonhoeffer borrows from Dilthey, is conscious Christianity. In this framework, God is the "other person" under whose guidance human beings act. Where this conscious obedience to God's guidance is only intermittent rather than constant, God becomes the stopgap God that Bonhoeffer alludes to in his letters, to whom the individual turns when his own knowledge and resources run out.[30]

The fact that unconscious Christianity only comes about in humanity in general in a world come of age highlights the way in which Bonhoeffer views the coming of age of the world as a tipping point, after which Christianity can evolve into new, hitherto unimagined forms. Although, of course, some of the features of unconscious Christianity contained in my definition could have been present in humanity before the coming of age of the world, it is the ability to do without reference to God that indicates that unconscious Christianity is a product of the world come of age.

Most scholars agree that Bonhoeffer viewed the world come of age not as a threat but as brought about through Christ.[31] Klemens von Klemperer agrees with this assessment in his review of Bonhoeffer's fiction, writing:

> Bonhoeffer's radicalism lay in his theology and is reflected in his "literary" work. Of course he was deeply concerned with secularization and with what he called the "world come of age." But there was no note of lamentation in his thinking about this modern condition. It was a reality which had to be faced. While in his letters to Eberhard Bethge he went as far as to propose the wildly revolutionary concept of "religionless Christianity," in his novel it is Ulrich—that is Eberhard Bethge—who launches the concept of "unconscious Christianity." Its connotation is perhaps less paradoxical, less shocking than Bonhoeffer's "religionless Christianity," and as a matter of fact, it reflects very appropriately Bethge's temperament compared with that of his friend. It eases the believer's sensibilities into the perception of modernity, without shock, as though the condition in question had always existed and had always been underlying the mysteries of the Christian faith.[32]

Although I agree with von Klemperer's view of Bonhoeffer's approach to the world come of age, I think that his analysis of Bonhoeffer's account of unconscious Christianity fails to credit the radical nature of Bonhoeffer's thought on unconscious Christianity and misunderstands Bonhoeffer's presentation of it in *Novel*. His view that Bonhoeffer writes of unconscious Christianity in such a way that it is made to seem as if it had "always existed" is also open to question. The way in which the characters discuss the idea of unconscious Christianity in *Novel* shows that it is a new way of thinking about people's relationship with the divine. Even though the characters described as unconscious Christians may have been unconscious Christians for some time, unconscious Christianity is not a state that would have been possible, generally speaking, in the Western world before it came of age. Then, most people consciously defined themselves as Christians. While it is true that Bonhoeffer aligns unconscious Christianity with the *fides directa* of an infant at baptism, infancy was the only state at which the average Western individual would have had a *fides directa* rather than a *fides reflexa*. It is therefore important to recognize that in referring to unconscious Christianity in *Novel* Bonhoeffer is suggesting a new way of being Christian that is made possible in the world come of age. What von Klemperer correctly draws attention to, however, is the pastoral aspect of the concept of unconscious Christianity, helping the believer to accept that Christianity may take different forms in the world come of age.

Story: Bonhoeffer's Illustration of Unconscious Christianity in the World Come of Age

An example of what unconscious Christianity looks like in the world come of age is the central character of *Story*, Lance Corporal Berg. Looking to this character is in keeping with the idea explored previously[33] that Bonhoeffer thought of unconscious Christianity in terms of people rather than only in abstraction.

Story is the only fiction text in which Bonhoeffer doesn't mention God, Christ, religion, or the Church. It is, on the surface, a much simpler tale than those related in *Drama* and *Novel*, and is a shorter text. Although it precedes Bonhoeffer's theological letters, *Story* illustrates his conviction that in the world come of age, people cannot be told with theological or pious words who Christ is,[34] and so instead he shows his readers what participating in the life of Christ looks like with words that they will understand.

Considered without reference to unconscious Christianity, Lance Corporal Berg comes across simply as a man who is doing the best he can in a difficult situation. Read as the embodiment of the phrase Bonhoeffer jotted down in the margin of "Ultimate and Penultimate Things," and the theological ideas that he would articulate just weeks later in his letter to Bethge and the notes for his book, Berg is the unconscious Christian acting in a world come of age.[35] *Story* is Bonhoeffer's first effort at speaking entirely nonreligiously of God, uncovering the godlessness of the world, and proclaiming its coming of age.

Written in February and March 1944,[36] just before the first theological letter to Bethge, *Story* is part of a different movement to *Drama* and *Novel* and is less concerned about rehabilitating the *Bürgertum* than the other two pieces are. This piece should be read as a preliminary working out of the theological ideas that Bonhoeffer is about to discuss in his letters. Through Lance Corporal Berg, Bonhoeffer portrays a life of participation in Christ's being-for-others, which, as noted above, is an attribute of the unconscious Christian. Bonhoeffer emphasizes Berg's participation in Christ's being by attributing physical marks of suffering to him, as well as highlighting the tender care he extends toward the prisoners he works with. It is clear from Bonhoeffer's description of him that Berg is someone who acts in a Christ-like way, embodying the being-for-others that Bonhoeffer attributes to Christ and unconscious Christians.[37]

In contrast to Berg, Sergeant Major Meier,[38] who is in charge of the prison, is shown to be corrupt and aggressive. Through him and other characters involved in the running of the prison, Bonhoeffer shows the godlessness of the world. There is a complete absence of reference to God or Christian morality in how the prison is managed. For example, the facial wounds that Berg received while fighting at the front cause him to have to eat through a straw, and he is despised by the corrupt prison officers for this, among his other physical impairments. The officers soon begin to circulate rumors that visitors to the prison have asked for Berg to be removed from duty, as his appearance is too upsetting. The prisoners, on the other hand, when questioned by a guard, are extremely positive about Berg.[39] Berg is finally dismissed from the prison. The reader knows that this is because the Sergeant Major is worried that Berg will upset the cozy lifestyle he has set up for himself, by attempting to reform prison life, make it more fair, and expose the corruption and bribery that underlie Meier's relationships with his staff.[40] Berg's efforts in this direction are feared by the Sergeant Major and his corrupt aide.[41] As in Bonhoeffer's writing, God is pushed out of the world and onto the cross,[42] so Berg is pushed out of his work in the prison.

Berg represents Bonhoeffer's first formal attempts to describe the unconscious Christian in the world come of age. Berg sees through Meier's attempts to bribe him, and realizes that the sergeant major is unsettled by him, using his damaged face as an excuse to dismiss him.[43] He encounters Christ in the prisoners, for whom he tries to negotiate better prison food. He does not apparently self-identify as Christian. He values the penultimate. This valuing of the penultimate is conveyed by his desire to return to the front and fight, engaging in the reality of the world rather than attempting to eschew it by remaining in safety behind the lines.[44] It is true that Berg could be read as a religionless Christian, but his lack of private acts of worship signals that Bonhoeffer meant to portray him as an unconscious Christian as opposed to a religionless Christian.[45]

What this text shows is that it is entirely possible to be an unconscious Christian in a world come of age. Bonhoeffer uses Berg as a test case to demonstrate this. In *Story* Bonhoeffer works through the ways in which Berg's qualities as an unconscious Christian affect Berg in a world whose godlessness is uncovered, but wherein God is still present. Berg practices a form of Christian expression that has substantial consequences for his life. His uncompromising commitment to sharing God's sufferings in the world, here illustrated by his striving for the rights of the suffering prisoners and ultimately suffering rejection himself, defines him. As a character he is by no means out of place in the story that Bonhoeffer is telling, and in this, the only complete piece of fiction we have from Bonhoeffer, he convincingly represents the life of an unconscious Christian in the world come of age.

I have shown here that far from containing mutually exclusive points, the concepts of the world come of age and unconscious Christianity sit well together. Understanding the world come of age as a non-threatening context in which Christianity can flourish in new ways allows unconscious Christianity to be seen as an example of such flourishing. Moreover, a proper understanding of unconscious Christianity is impossible without first grasping Bonhoeffer's idea that the world come of age is a new situation in which humanity finds itself. Here God is not at the borders of existence but at the center of life. Defining unconscious Christianity as I suggest allows an appreciation of the world come of age as a new context full of possibilities for the evolution of Christianity. Thus the world come of age adds credence to the definition of unconscious Christianity that I propose, while that very definition of unconscious Christianity engenders a deeper understanding of the world come of age.

Religionless Christianity

Does the idea of religionless Christianity substantiate or hinder that of unconscious Christianity? Does unconscious Christianity add depth to religionless Christianity? To answer these questions, and in order to prevent a misunderstanding of Bonhoeffer's idea of religionless Christianity, I begin by outlining the concept.[46] As religionless Christianity is sometimes viewed as implying a rejection of theology as well as a rejection of the established institution of the Church, it is important to note that Bonhoeffer's idea of religionless Christianity is based on his Christocentric theology. Greggs writes that Bonhoeffer advocates a religionlessness *"theologically understood* through the Bible and in the incarnation of the Word of God" that presents "Christianity with the *necessity* of religionlessness."[47] For Bonhoeffer, therefore, religionless Christianity does not cut itself off from Christian theology.

In what is considered to be Bonhoeffer's first theological letter to Bethge, dated the 30th of April 1944, he discusses the question of religionless Christianity. In this letter, there is a suggestion that there can be several definitions of the term "religious." Bonhoeffer writes: "Even those who honestly describe themselves as 'religious' aren't really practicing that at all; they presumably mean something quite different by 'religious.'"[48] Bonhoeffer's use of the term "religious" in the first part of this sentence is positive. He is not referring here to the negative religious habit of wanting God to be a problem solver.[49] In this instance, the term "religious" indicates observing Christian ritual and practice: going to church, reading the Bible, praying, and so on, as described in his book *Life Together*. The people he is talking about here, who "honestly describe themselves as 'religious,'" must be doing something else, as he states that they are "not really practicing that [religion] at all." So what are they doing? Are they, like Berg in *Story*, a suffering presence striving for justice? The willingness shown by Bonhoeffer to enlarge the meaning of "religious" to include acts that are not traditional Christian practice points toward his willingness to rethink his understanding of Christianity itself, as indicated in this letter. He writes: "If religion is only the garb in which Christianity is clothed—and this garb has looked very different in different ages—what then is religionless Christianity?"[50] The question arises because he is devoured by other questions, "What is Christianity?" and "Who is Christ actually for us today?" whilst at the same time recognizing that "we are approaching a completely religionless age."[51] With his concept of religionless Christianity, Bonhoeffer introduces a way of being Christian that is the reverse of what he says religious people do: to turn to God as the *deus ex machina* who will make everything right.[52]

The religionless Christian does not call on God to be a problem solver, or to appear at the eleventh hour to put things right when she can't do so herself. In practice, the religionless Christian continues to pray, worship God with her fellow religionless Christians, and keep the mystery of faith alive, practicing what Bonhoeffer calls arcane discipline.[53] According to Bonhoeffer, until such a time as people are called again to speak the word of God to the world, "the Christian cause will be a quiet and hidden one."[54] Thus, Bonhoeffer's exhortations to Christians to pray and do justice among human beings[55] represent two sides of the same coin, as Wüstenberg writes:

> At the same time, worship and prayer in "secret" ought always to be followed by responsible action in the world. If the discipline of the secret was one side of the dialectic, the other was Bonhoeffer's nonreligious interpretation of Christianity. He proposed, thus, a dynamic dialectic of dogmatics and ethics, of indicative and imperative, of faith and deed. You cannot, he argued, have one without the other.[56]

There is thus a dual emphasis in religionless Christianity on private prayer and just action.

In the framework of religionless Christianity, the Christian is placed in the same context as the non-Christian: Both refuse the religiosity of a world not yet come of age, both are emancipated human creatures, in a world come of age, and both have the possibility of seeing in this world come of age the presence of God at the center of life. Bonhoeffer develops the idea of nonreligious interpretation of biblical concepts alongside that of religionless Christianity. The nonreligious interpretation of biblical concepts entails making the gospels understandable and pertinent to those without any religious literacy.[57]

The necessity of religionlessness that Greggs alludes to is partly due, according to Bonhoeffer, to the Church's behavior during the years preceding the war. Because it has not fulfilled its mandate toward the rest of the world (i.e., preaching the Word of God to the world) but has instead strived to simply perpetuate itself, the Church can no longer expect to be granted space in the world.[58] The religionless Christian participates fully in the world, recognizing that God participates fully in the world as well, and is not confined to the borders of human experience. In his *Ethics*, Bonhoeffer already saw the possibility of unity between the world and God, a unity that has its roots in Jesus Christ:

> Because in Jesus Christ God and humanity became one, so through Christ what is "Christian" and what is "worldly" become one in the action of the Christian.[59]

Thus, the activity of Christians has its source in this reconciliation, in Christ, of God with the world, and there is no more static separation between that which is "Christian" and that which is "worldly." Thanks to this reconciliation, it is possible for the Christian to live in the world come of age, while still living according to the will of God, as Christian action is also action that belongs to the world. The religionless Christian is someone who is consciously attempting to be a disciple of God in the world come of age.

Greggs makes the perceptive and important point that Bonhoeffer's religionless Christianity is anti-fundamentalist in nature.[60] Fundamentalism, he writes, "attempts to reassert the God of power and seeks to win back space into which the world has encroached."[61] Bonhoeffer's religionless Christianity, on the other hand, seeks no such outcome. Instead of trying to claw back space for God in the world over against the world, it accepts the world itself as a space in which God is present, and in which God is a weak and suffering God.[62] I explore Bonhoeffer's idea of the weak and suffering God further in the following section, as I turn to a comparison of the concepts of religionless Christianity and unconscious Christianity.

Unconscious Christianity and Religionless Christianity

Unconscious Christianity shares some elements with religionless Christianity. Unconscious Christians do not go to church, and do not possess the religious habit of turning to God as a *deus ex machina*. Two characters referred to in the fiction as unconscious Christians do say grace before meals, a practice that could be called "religious," but they only do so because of their young son. The fact that they say grace because of their son indicates that they are not doing so because of their own need to turn to God, but rather because of a desire to instill in their son certain types of behavior, analyzed further in the section on *Bürgertum* in this book.[63] Unconscious Christians, like religionless Christians, do not want God to be a problem solver or stopgap in their lives. However, these similarities stem from different motivations: For the religionless Christian, it makes no sense to think of God as a *deus ex machina*, as such a perception does not tally with her view of reality and the place of God in the world. As for the unconscious Christian, it simply does not occur to him to perceive God as a stopgap, as he has no conscious need or desire for God, or in some cases, has consciously turned his back on Christianity. Thus, outwardly, religionless Christians and unconscious Christians can display similar behavior in terms of their rejection of religion, but they do so for different reasons.

Both groups engage with God, one consciously, the other unconsciously. They also share a common approach to interaction with the other, seeking to alleviate the suffering of others. Again, this common action is not based on the same convictions; while the people in Matthew 25 to whom Bonhoeffer refers in relation to unconscious Christianity have no stated motivation for their actions, religionless Christians seek to share God's suffering in the world[64] and relieve the suffering of others because of their conscious desire to imitate Christ's being-for-others.

By looking at Bonhoeffer's comments on his poem "Christians and Heathens," we will see what he considers to be true Christianity, and how both unconscious Christians and religionless Christians fulfill the criteria he sets down for being Christian, albeit for different reasons. This also highlights the similarities between unconscious Christians and conscious Christians. In a letter to Bethge dated the 18th of July 1944,[65] Bonhoeffer comments on the poem "Christians and Heathens" and writes of the difference between these two groups of people. Wannenwetsch argues that when Bonhoeffer refers to heathens here, he means "religious people," the "pious." He points out that the poem "does not address the problem of the relationship of Christianity to any concrete non-Christian religion but rather how Christianity relates to the *homo religiosus*—humankind in their notorious transcendental striving."[66] I agree with Wannenwetsch's analysis and consider the heathens that Bonhoeffer discusses in this letter to be those who refuse to be freed from their religiosity. They do not want to acknowledge a God who suffers in the world, who is weak. They prefer to continue to call upon an almighty God, who does not let Godself be dragged into the world. They refuse to suffer alongside God in the world, and it is this rejection of suffering that differentiates them from Christians. Bonhoeffer writes, referring to his poem "Christians and Heathens":

> The poem "Christians and Heathens" includes a thought that you will recognize here, "Christians stand by God in God's own pain"—that distinguishes Christians from heathens. "Could you not stay awake with me one hour?"

Jesus asks in Gethsemane. That is the opposite of everything a religious person expects from God. The human being is called upon to share in God's suffering at the hands of a godless world.[67]

During this period, Bonhoeffer redefines Christianity in the light of the world come of age. In the same letter he explains what he believes it means to be a Christian:

> Being a Christian does not mean being religious in a certain way, making oneself into something or other (a sinner, penitent, or saint) according to some method or other. Instead it means being human, not a certain type of human being, but the human being Christ creates in us. It is not a religious act that makes someone a Christian, but rather sharing in God's suffering in the worldly life.[68]

Both religionless Christians and unconscious Christians "share in God's suffering in the worldly life," and therefore are true Christians.

It should be noted that the identification of both religionless and unconscious Christians as Christians as opposed to heathens, arrived at by examining the poem "Christians and Heathens" and Bonhoeffer's comments on it, is not meant to be understood in terms of salvation, but rather in terms of what it "looks like" to be Christian. The closing stanza of the poem makes it clear that God's response to all people is the same:

> God goes to all people in their need,
> fills body and soul with God's own bread,
> goes for Christians and heathens to Calvary's death
> and forgives them both.[69]

Therefore, while Bonhoeffer is redefining Christianity in the new context of the world come of age and drawing clear distinctions between how Christians and heathens behave in the world, he is by no means drawing parallel distinctions about the salvation of people within these two groups. As Greggs helpfully points out, Bonhoeffer's theology, based squarely as it is on the incarnation, crucifixion, and resurrection of Christ, draws us away from an anthropocentric account of salvation and toward a God-centered view of salvation, in which God, not humanity, is the central actor.[70]

An understanding of unconscious Christianity sheds light on the concept of religionless Christianity because it shows that religionless Christianity is not the only valid form of Christian expression that Bonhoeffer envisages in the world come of age. Although Bonhoeffer places great responsibility on the shoulders of the religionless Christians, saying that they must keep alive the mysteries of the faith, do justice, and pray, they are not the only Christians to be found in Germany after the war. They are not solely responsible for the survival of the Christian faith, because this burden is shared with the unconscious Christians. The latter do not of course realize this, but I think that part of what is discernible in Bonhoeffer's writing about both unconscious and religionless Christians is a pastoral concern for those who will keep the Church alive after the war. What Bonhoeffer is saying is that religionless Christians can turn to those good people that surround them in their workplaces, families, and towns. They can see them as participating in the suffering of the world, as they themselves are, and for this reason, as sharing their own faith.

In addition to the fact that, for Bonhoeffer, both religionless Christianity and unconscious Christianity are valid forms of Christian expression, it should be stressed that they are *equally* valid. There is no hierarchy here. Although this is never stated explicitly in Bonhoeffer's texts, there is no evidence to suggest that he thought of these types of Christianity as being set within a hierarchical framework. On the contrary, his portrayal of unconscious Christians in *Novel*, as well as his depiction, in the same text, of people who choose to abandon the Church and those who choose to stay within it as equally justified, show that he viewed all these categories of Christian expression as equally defensible. For Bonhoeffer, an unconscious Christian, a religionless Christian, or a churchgoing Christian all embody different, and equally valid, forms of Christian expression, and cannot be rated as superior or inferior to each other. This stands in contrast to Rahner's view of anonymous Christianity in relation to other types of Christianity. In Rahner's schema, as was noted in the introduction, it is to be hoped that each anonymous Christian will progress eventually toward being a part of the "community of the Eucharist."[71] He writes,

> This name [anonymous Christian] implicitly signifies that this fundamental actuation of a man, like all actuations, cannot and does not want to stop in its anonymous state but strives toward an explicit expression, toward its full name. An unfavourable historical environment may impose limitations on the explicitness of this expression so that this actuation may not exceed the explicit appearance of a loving humaneness, but it will not act against this tendency whenever a new and higher stage of explicitness is presented to it right up to the ultimate perfection of a consciously accepted profession of Church membership.[72]

For Bonhoeffer, progression from one manner of being Christian to another is unnecessary. This is a vital difference between Rahner's anonymous Christian and Bonhoeffer's unconscious Christian.

Looking at unconscious Christianity alongside religionless Christianity shows that the two forms of Christian expression are complementary concepts, and that the definition of unconscious Christianity suggested here fits in with the concept of religionless Christianity without being hindered by it.

UNCONSCIOUS CHRISTIANITY AND BONHOEFFER SCHOLARSHIP

Having demonstrated that the new definition of unconscious Christianity that I propose fits well within the Tegel theology, I will now compare it to what other Bonhoeffer scholars have written on the subject. Only a handful of scholars have written about Bonhoeffer's comments concerning unconscious Christianity. Of those few, some have concentrated on one particular text in which unconscious Christianity is mentioned, while others have focused on one aspect of what they think unconscious Christianity is. None offer a systematic discussion of unconscious Christianity in Bonhoeffer's texts on the subject.[73] I begin by addressing the work of Eberhard Bethge, who was the first to mention unconscious Christianity in Bonhoeffer's work.

Eberhard Bethge

Bethge first discusses unconscious Christianity in 1970 in relation to the concept of the world come of age. Bethge notes that the phrase "world come of age" appeared in Bonhoeffer's writing on the 8th of June 1944, adding that it then became a dominating idea within Bonhoeffer's theology.[74] He highlights the fact that when talking about the world come of age, Bonhoeffer is making a "theological statement."[75] This is because, Bethge writes, "the recognition of the world's coming of age is, with Bonhoeffer, neither philosophy nor phenomenology, but the knowledge of God, i.e. 'theology,' and that is a knowledge that seeks to follow God where he has already preceded us."[76] Bonhoeffer's understanding of the maturity of the world in terms of his Christology ("It was the crucified Christ who, for him, makes possible 'true worldliness,' 'genuine this-worldliness' and 'coming of age,' judging and renewing it."[77]) sets him apart from other Christians, whom he criticizes,[78] who fear the increasing autonomy of the world as they perceive it as a turning away from God.

Bethge writes that just as Bonhoeffer's statement concerning the world come of age is a theological one, so also his statement concerning unconscious Christianity is theological.[79] Although Bethge does not expand more on the topic of unconscious Christianity, his comment is invaluable as it shows that he categorizes Bonhoeffer's writing about unconscious Christianity alongside his work on the world come of age as theological writing. Bethge refers here to the statement Bonhoeffer makes in his letter about unconscious Christianity,[80] rather than any of the other three instances in which the phrase appears, but nevertheless Bethge's judgment gives credence to the claim that unconscious Christianity is a theological theme that must be taken seriously in Bonhoeffer's late writing.

Ruth Zerner

It was eleven years before unconscious Christianity was mentioned again in Bonhoeffer scholarship. When Ruth Zerner did so, in 1981, she did not follow Bethge's lead in the matter. In her insightful commentary on the prison fiction, Zerner departs from Bethge's view of unconscious Christianity, claiming that it is a concept through which Bonhoeffer "fitted the nonreligious among his family and friends into his Christian world view."[81] Viewing unconscious Christianity as a means of integrating these nonreligious people into his own Christian worldview, Zerner discards it as an "uneasy and fragile" synthesis, suggesting instead that a more successful term might be "unconscious Judaism," which would serve to unite Christians and secularists.[82]

Zerner considers the introduction of unconscious Christianity as an important aspect of Bonhoeffer's fiction.[83] Although she views the fiction as valuable because of the "original, flexible, and challenging theological thinking that followed,"[84] she writes that the prison narratives "experimented with nonreligious language for such religious concepts as sacrifice and reconciliation."[85] As this book makes clear, the fact that Bonhoeffer experimented with nonreligious language for religious concepts shows that the fiction texts are theological in themselves. I disagree with Zerner's analysis that they are merely "modest but necessary detours in a journey consummated by the fresh, tempting, and transforming theological insights of his spring and summer 1944 correspondence."[86]

John de Gruchy

For John de Gruchy, writing in 1987, it is necessary to understand Bonhoeffer's idea of the world come of age in order to grasp what he writes about unconscious Christianity. To set the scene, de Gruchy argues that for Bonhoeffer, the question of ecclesiology is always present, and that therefore:

> For him it was impossible to think of Jesus Christ without also thinking of the church. The church in a world come of age would need to regain its position at the centre of the world, not in a spirit of triumphalism, but in openness to secular people and a willingness to engage with them in the struggles and issues which shape life in society. This meant becoming a "church for others" in conforming with Jesus Christ, rather than following a path of self-preservation, concrete "righteous actions" rather than repeating worn-out cliches or enunciating principles.[87]

According to de Gruchy, Bonhoeffer considers that those committed to righteous action, rather than to preserving the Church as it was in the past, form the Church in the world come of age. In the context of the true Church in the world come of age, de Gruchy turns to the question of unconscious Christianity.

> It is in this context that we can understand Bonhoeffer's cryptic remarks about "unconscious Christianity" [. . .] Here we find continuity between his concern for non-religious "good people" (*Ethics*), typified by his own family and his friends in the conspiracy, and the development of a "non-religious interpretation of Christianity."[88]

For de Gruchy, unconscious Christianity forms the link between the question relating to the good people discussed in Bonhoeffer's *Ethics* essay "Ultimate and Penultimate Things" and his fiction fragment *Novel*, and the need to talk about Christianity in nonreligious language, illustrated by his completed fiction piece *Story*. De Gruchy thinks that it is in the context of the Church evolving to be relevant in the world come of age that unconscious Christianity can be understood as this link. Because of this, it can be assumed that it is now the duty of the Church to present the gospel in such a way as to allow the unconscious Christians, who are the good people, to consciously engage with Christ and thus become part of the Church. Whether they already formed part of the Church when they engaged with Christ unconsciously is not explicitly dealt with here.[89] However, in the discussion of arcane discipline that follows on from the passages quoted above, de Gruchy argues that Bonhoeffer was advocating a type of arcane discipline that would be appropriate for his own era. He writes: "Only in such a way could the faith be preserved from profanation and cheap grace be avoided."[90] It is therefore unlikely that he would go so far as to suggest that unconscious Christians formed part of the Church, but he does see Bonhoeffer's concern about unconscious Christians, the good people, as being in part the cause of his sense of urgency in developing a nonreligious interpretation of Christianity.

Geffrey B. Kelly

Geffrey B. Kelly discusses Bonhoeffer's unconscious Christianity alongside Karl Rahner's concept of the anonymous Christian in an article written in 1995.[91] He argues that both concepts "symbolize the deeper, more hidden, reality of God that each intuited or extrapolated from their respective Christian worldviews."[92] There are three salient points to be taken from Kelly's article. Firstly, Kelly thinks Bonhoeffer was able to intuit unconscious Christianity thanks to his "ethical bearings,"[93] but that while Bonhoeffer's concept of unconscious Christianity remained a mere intuition, Rahner's theory of the anonymous Christian adds theological coherence to Bonhoeffer's idea. Therefore, Kelly sees Bonhoeffer's concept of unconscious Christianity to be lacking in theological coherence. Secondly, Kelly argues that Bonhoeffer thinks there is an "authentic faith that justifies" to be found outside the

Christian world. Referring to Bonhoeffer's desire to go to India and meet Gandhi, Kelly writes: "But India did represent for him a non-Christian world graced with the indefinable essence of what he knew in his heart to be the authentic faith that justifies."[94] Here Kelly states that Bonhoeffer thought that there was justification, and faith, to be found outside of the Christian world. That is not to say, however, that Bonhoeffer thought justification could occur without Christ. As Kelly notes, Bonhoeffer wrote in 1931: "If we cannot perceive the presence of Christ in our personal life, then we would like to find it in India."[95] Thirdly, Kelly agrees with Zerner that Bonhoeffer "includes the non-religious members of his family among the 'unconscious Christians.'"[96]

Even though Kelly thinks that Bonhoeffer's concept of unconscious Christianity is not fully theologically coherent, he points to Bonhoeffer's use of Matthew 25 in relation to unconscious Christianity, and writes that the reference to the incognito of Christ contained in Matthew 25 "is the constant spark that fires Bonhoeffer's theological imagination in formulating a form of Christian faith for which even the non-religious and non-Christian are gifted."[97] The unconscious Christian's form of Christian faith, writes Kelly, provides the Church with a way out of its *extra ecclesiam nulla salus* problem. Kelly highlights Bonhoeffer's conviction that faith must be something people stake their lives on, rather than a question of obligation or rationality.[98] This ties in with Kelly's point about Bonhoeffer's view of his fellow resistance members:

> Frankly, as far as he [Bonhoeffer] was concerned, the non-religious members of the German resistance movement were acting more "Christianly" than the Christian believers, proud of their fidelity in church attendance but captive to the Hitlerian ideology to the very end.[99]

Kelly sees the connection between unconscious Christianity and Matthew 25 as "made more emphatically when Bonhoeffer, in his *Ethics*, indicts the Christian churches for having denied Christ."[100] He also sees the influence of unconscious Christianity in "After 10 Years,"[101] and describes Bonhoeffer in this text as offering "a refreshing description of just what constitutes the Christian in those turbulent times."[102] Bonhoeffer wrote "After 10 Years" for three friends who were also part of the German Resistance: his brother-in-law Hans von Dohnanyi, Eberhard Bethge, and Hans Oster. It is interesting that Bonhoeffer should write a theological text for Oster and von Dohnanyi, as they did not identify as Christians. "After 10 Years" can perhaps be understood in the same way as "Natural Life" and the missing chapter on "Good," as Bonhoeffer's attempt at portraying Christians as not so very different from those who have chosen to distance themselves from Christianity and "no longer dare to call themselves Christians."[103]

Kelly discerns an important aspect of unconscious Christianity when discussing the terms "unconscious Christianity" and "anonymous Christian" and their "provisional and intermediate"[104] nature. Given current interfaith conversations, he writes: "The terms may yet evolve into more explicit affirmations of the basic goodness and divine grace that exist outside the social unities of Christianity."[105] Kelly implies here that the terms already affirm "the basic goodness and divine grace that exist outside the social unities of Christianity," and that they might do so more explicitly in the future. He thus confirms the idea that there is a strong link in Bonhoeffer's writing between basic goodness and unconscious Christianity. Indeed, Kelly echoes here Bonhoeffer's link between unconscious Christianity and the closing section of "Ultimate and Penultimate Things." Here, as shown in chapter 2, Bonhoeffer states that there is good "in the fallen world" that should be "claimed for Christ."[106] The question of the good and Christ's relationship to good people is the one that pushes Bonhoeffer to develop his concept of unconscious Christianity.

Kelly sees the upshot of unconscious Christianity as being a "Christic embrace of people as they are in their creation by our common Father God and in their own uniquely gifted relationship to God, however unrelated to Christian denominations."[107] In this form of Christianity, there will also be a "more honest, open dialogue with non-Christians and non-believers."[108] However, Kelly reminds us of the provisional nature of the terms *unconscious Christianity* and *anonymous Christian*, and the potentially damaging way in which they can be understood:

> For most non-Christians the terms "anonymous Christian" or "unconscious Christian" ring with all the tinkle of telling a nice African American that a kind act on his part was "very white of him." Or like telling a Torah-observing Jew that she is really a "Christian." Christians may need to hear themselves called "anonymous Jews" or "unconscious Moslems" to get the drift of how limited even these helpful theological concepts are for the practical social application of one's Christian outreach to all people.[109]

Kelly's warning about the dangers of the idea of unconscious Christianity are important to any discussion of unconscious Christianity.

Nancy Lukens

Almost another decade elapses before Nancy Lukens approaches the question of unconscious Christianity. She does so from a literary, rather than theological, perspective in her text "Narratives of Creative Displacement: Bonhoeffer the Reader and the Construction of 'Unconscious Christianity' in *Fiction from Tegel Prison*" written in 2004.[110] The paper's title indicates that

Lukens does not intend to look to all the available texts on unconscious Christianity in her investigation of the subject.

While Zerner sees Bonhoeffer's prison writing as revealing a "complex polyphony of responses: self-scrutiny and self-confrontation, retrogression and artistic re-creation of past experiences, and the desire to bear witness to suffering,"[111] Nancy Lukens views it as an effort to provide a counternarrative to Nazi ideology. Lukens contends that Bonhoeffer's depiction of unconscious Christianity within his fiction is connected to his "critical reception of literature."[112] In order to draw parallels between the two, she asks questions such as: "What does Bonhoeffer's preference for the worldliness and religious tolerance of medieval epics such as *Parzival* over Schiller's idealist dramas,[113] for example, have to do with the substance of Christian humanist values depicted in his own realistic fiction from Tegel?"[114] Lukens also sees strong links between Bonhoeffer's concept of unconscious Christianity and his "project of reconsidering the fundamental values of Christian humanism for contemporary culture and education."[115] According to Lukens, unconscious Christianity lies at the very heart of Bonhoeffer's attempts at fiction:

> Bonhoeffer's foray into writing fiction, which he describes as an attempt to "rehabilitate middle-class life . . . specifically from a Christian perspective," reflects his consciousness, as a theologian and pastor deeply involved in political resistance that the middle-class in Germany had failed to articulate Christian humanist values by defending the victims of Nazi oppression. My sense is that—far from indulging in a primarily nostalgic or inward look at his past—Bonhoeffer's intent in trying his hand at fiction was to give imaginative shape to what he called "unconscious Christianity" in the "world come of age."[116]

However, beyond describing unconscious Christianity as the impetus for Bonhoeffer's fiction writing, Lukens does not go on to give a detailed explanation of what unconscious Christianity is. She borrows the idea of cultural studies theorist James Clifford that culture cannot be studied from the outside looking in, but rather that "culture IS travel itself, is boundary-crossing."[117] Lukens suggests that we should view Bonhoeffer as a "travelling reader,"[118] not viewing culture from the outside, but participating in culture by crossing boundaries in his physical and literary travels. Because of his identity as a "travelling reader," influenced by writers from many different time periods and cultural contexts, Bonhoeffer was able, in his fiction, to provide a construction of unconscious Christianity that served as a counternarrative to the dominant Nazi culture and ideology.

Lukens writes that "it is the four-way interaction between the major, Franz, Christoph and Renate in the last completed scene of the fragment that constructs an effective counter-narrative of 'unconscious Christianity.'"[119] For Lukens, Bonhoeffer's portrayal of an interaction between four of the major characters in *Novel* is in itself a counter-example of what political debate should look like. There is a frank exchange of views, and each character involved listens to the others carefully. Although the characters come to an uneasy agreement that different generations have had to face different challenges, that each generation adapts to meet its own challenge, and that therefore each generation thinks differently, there is no final unanimous agreement. Lukens points to the fact that Christoph and Renate are torn apart by the former's harsh words about some people being born to be slaves.[120] The younger generation must learn to come to terms with conflicting world views, and to recognize the barrier that is alterity.

Unconscious Christianity for Lukens then, regardless of what other theological meaning it may contain, is in itself a discourse, or forms part of a discourse, that conflicts with Nazi ideology. According to Lukens, the object of writing the fiction and giving voice to unconscious Christianity in a world come of age was "to help those [he] hoped would survive [him] find a language to help understand the abuse of power, chaos and destruction around them, a language of compassion, dialogue, life for others and affirmation of the world as it is, grounded in the reality of faith."[121]

Reinhold Bernhardt

Bernhardt draws out four main points about unconscious Christianity in his 2010 article "Christentum ohne Christusglaube: Die Rede von 'unbewusstem Christentum' und 'latenter Kirche' im 19. und 20. Jahrhundert." First of all he sets the context of Bonhoeffer's writing on unconscious Christianity as that of being surrounded by his fellow-prisoners and prison guards as the bombs fell on Berlin, and of observing in these men a belief in "anything 'supernatural.'"[122] This, writes Bernhardt, causes Bonhoeffer to reflect on the question of "natural piety," which he links to unconscious Christianity.[123] Secondly, he points to the difference between, on the one hand Bonhoeffer's differentiation between Christianity or faith in Christ, and religion, and on the other liberal theologians' differentiation between Church and Christendom. Bernhardt comments that according to Bonhoeffer, biblical and theological concepts should be communicated nonreligiously, so as to ensure that nonreligious people can grasp them, and practicing the Christian faith should consist in "being-for-others."[124] In referring to the idea of being-for-others, Bernhardt introduces his third point, which is that, according to Bonhoeffer, taking part in God's suffering in the world determines who is a Christian. Citing Bonhoeffer's letter to Bethge in which he describes what being a Christian means,[125] Bernhardt adds:

> Taking part in the suffering of God in worldly life determines being a Christian. His experience in the resistance against the National-Socialist regime showed Bonhoeffer that unbelievers also partake of this suffering and devote

their lives to the fight against its cause. They can be closer to Christ than "religious" Christians.[126]

Thus, notes Bernhardt, it is not necessary to have a conscious faith in Christ in order to be a Christian. People can engage with God without knowing that they do so. Bernhardt links the idea that it is possible to engage with God without even being aware of God's presence with Bonhoeffer's earlier writing in *Ethics* on the idea of "promising godlessness."[127]

Returning to his assessment of unconscious Christianity in Bonhoeffer, Bernhardt draws on the idea of promising godlessness to highlight his fourth point that neither an experience of God's presence, nor the ability to reflect on such an experience, are necessary for God to be present:

> Bonhoeffer uses the dialectic of the nearness of God and the distance or absence of God to express that the presence of God does not depend on the sensation or experience of this presence, and certainly not on the reflective recording of such an experience.[128]

Although these points are all accurate, Bernhardt only draws on half of the texts in which Bonhoeffer mentions unconscious Christianity, and therefore the picture he presents is somewhat narrow. His conclusion reflects the insufficiency of his text selection, as he depends on a very early text relating to unconscious Christianity to support his opinion, appearing to ignore Bonhoeffer's later work on the issue.

Bernhardt concludes that according to Bonhoeffer, unconscious Christians must necessarily be brought to realize their Christianity, and turn into conscious Christians. To consolidate his view, Bernhardt cites the end of Bonhoeffer's *Ethics* essay "Ultimate and Penultimate Things," writing:

> It would be more Christian to "claim as Christian precisely such persons who no longer dare to call themselves Christians, and to help them with much patience move toward confessing Christ" than to "address such people as non-Christians and urge them to confess their unbelief."[129]

Bernhardt's conclusion does not take sufficiently into consideration the later fragments relating to unconscious Christianity, and relies too heavily on one text that is, furthermore, an early one in Bonhoeffer's thoughts on the subject. Such an opinion is untenable if the later writings are viewed as equally valid, which I hold them to be.

Ferdinand Schlingensiepen

Ferdinand Schlingensiepen adds his voice to the conversation on unconscious Christianity in 2011. Like Bernhardt, Schlingensiepen's presentation of unconscious Christianity in Bonhoeffer's writing is rendered narrow by his decision not to deal with all the available texts. This omission is a consciously made one, however, as Schlingensiepen's intention is to examine unconscious Christianity and "lived faith" in the fiction from Tegel.[130] He pays detailed attention to Bonhoeffer's fiction, and finds in it two indications of how to understand Bonhoeffer's concept of unconscious Christianity. He sees *Novel* as a text in which unconscious Christianity is contrasted with lived faith, and is exemplified in living people.[131]

Firstly, he posits that each expression of unconscious Christianity is based on the sort of "quiet ideal" personified by the young characters' ancestor, a cathedral provost called Josias Brake. He bases this on the story that Bonhoeffer relates about Josias Brake, who had been banned from his pulpit during the Enlightenment. Refusing to respect the ban, and continuing to serve his congregation, Josias Brake had finally been put in prison. He was eventually released due to the pressure put on the authorities by his congregation, only to die at the altar during his first service back at his post. Schlingensiepen picks up on how the young generation of the Brake family relate to the story of their ancestor, and quotes Bonhoeffer:

> The children knew this story from childhood and revered the picture of their ancestor almost like a little icon of a saint. Even when, as they grew older, they grew away from the church, this did not change. The old pastor was a quiet ideal in their hearts.[132]

Added to the idea that each form of unconscious Christianity that Bonhoeffer presents is based on such examples as that of Josias Brake,[133] Schlingensiepen suggests that unconscious Christians are those who grow up in contact with people who embody a lived faith. Someone who embodies lived faith is the young Brakes' grandmother, Frau Karoline Brake. Schlingensiepen illustrates his point by describing a scene in Bonhoeffer's *Novel* in which Frau Brake comforts her grandson after he witnesses a bird knock her baby out of its nest. Upon his asking her why a bird would do such a thing, she gives him a thoughtful response instead of a "dishonest morality lesson."[134] She explains to her grandson the way in which she thinks God cares for God's creation, both innocent animals and human beings. According to Schlingensiepen, conversations with people embodying a lived faith lay the ground for a relationship with the Christian faith that it is impossible to lose, even if this faith later turns into unconscious Christianity.

Both ideas that Schlingensiepen puts forward about unconscious Christianity emphasize the importance of the surroundings in which unconscious Christians grow up. The people that influence them and the examples from which they learn are a central feature of their type of Christianity.[135] In chapter 3, I showed that social context was important in Bonhoeffer's understanding of unconscious Christians, but that it was not the only element that he thought contributed to people being unconscious Christians. Although Schlingensiepen offers a detailed view of the fiction, and contributes to the understanding of unconscious Christianity, his approach, like Bernhardt's, is too narrow to present a full picture of what Bonhoeffer meant by unconscious Christianity.

Ilse Tödt

In her article "Wir leben im Vorletzten: Bonhoeffer und das unbewusste Christentum,"[136] also written in 2011, Tödt sets Bonhoeffer's concept of unconscious Christianity in opposition to the type of Christianity practiced by the Berneuchen movement, to which the von Wedemeyer family were attached.[137] Tödt contrasts the Berneuchen movement's emphasis on the spiritual life with Bonhoeffer's conviction that Christians must live in the world and not seek to escape into a spiritualized way of life. Tödt draws on Bonhoeffer's *Ethics* essay "Ultimate and Penultimate Things" to show how Bonhoeffer understands the relationship between the ultimate and the penultimate, and states that the ultimate only ever takes form in the penultimate as a "being there for others."[138] This implies active involvement in the world, rather than distancing oneself from the world.

Tödt argues that according to Bonhoeffer, human beings existing in the penultimate are able to love God, but this love occurs without the individual being aware of it. An individual's awareness of his love of God can only occur after the fact.[139] Furthermore, she writes: "Bonhoeffer knows that if Christianity occurs in one's own life, if at all, then it is *to me* unconscious Christianity."[140] The individual is unable to reflect on his Christianity, and can only reflect on his love of God with hindsight.

Tödt's presentation of unconscious Christianity is problematic as it does not sit well alongside the other theological ideas that Bonhoeffer developed in prison. Her depiction of unconscious Christianity contains accurate accounts of one of the elements that make up the concept in Bonhoeffer's theology: that it is possible to be Christian without knowing it. However, she does not outline any of the other elements that go to make up the concept, and goes too far in her claims about Bonhoeffer's opinion of Christianity in general.

The New Definition of *Unconscious Christianity* and Bonhoeffer Scholarship

None of these approaches to unconscious Christianity provide a complete account of unconscious Christianity in Bonhoeffer's theology. De Gruchy and Kelly, and to a lesser extent Bernhardt and Schlingensiepen, highlight the connection between unconscious Christianity and good people in Bonhoeffer's work, which was discussed in relation to "Ultimate and Penultimate Things" in chapters 2 and 3. This appraisal of the scholarship also demonstrates how the question has been approached from both a theological and a literary angle.

However, the strongest point to emerge from this overview is that there has not as yet been a systematic study of unconscious Christianity based on all the available texts and the contexts in which they were written. Several analyses fall short due to the narrow range of texts on which they are based.

The definition of unconscious Christianity that I propose sits well with some of the views outlined above, but finds itself at odds with others. Despite contrasting opinions on what unconscious Christianity is, the definition I propose is confirmed by what others have written.

It was noted previously that Ruth Zerner views Bonhoeffer's use of unconscious Christianity as a way in which to integrate his nonreligious family and friends into his Christian view of the world. Rejecting the usefulness of such a term, Zerner proposes instead the phrase "unconscious Judaism," which, she argues, would be more useful to unite Christians and secularists.

While Zerner makes a good case for unconscious Judaism, arguing that it would avoid forcing the Jewish scriptures into Christian categories, and provide a "bridge opening the road to deepening Jewish-Christian understanding,"[141] her suggestion that it would "not be out of keeping with Bonhoeffer's inclinations"[142] shows that she has not taken into account the Christological underpinning of Bonhoeffer's concept. By not taking into account the fact that Bonhoeffer links unconscious Christianity with Matthew 25, which shows that unconscious Christianity has to do with engaging with Christ, Zerner lessens the import of unconscious Christianity as a concept based on Bonhoeffer's understanding of Christ as the son of God. Zerner's choice of language here is also problematic, as she describes the synthesis that Bonhoeffer attempts through unconscious Christianity as being between "nonreligious" people and his "Christian worldview."[143] As has already been shown above, Bonhoeffer has no problem with reconciling nonreligious people with a Christian worldview. Nonreligious people can be Christians, and religionless Christians are merely those who practice Christianity having put aside the "garb" of religion.[144] A more difficult gap to bridge is that between people who purposefully don't self-identify as Christian and a Christian worldview. This is the synthesis, I argue, that Bonhoeffer is attempting with his concept of unconscious Christianity and his ideas concerning good people.

Both Kelly and de Gruchy highlight the link between unconscious Christianity and Bonhoeffer's concern about Christ's relationship to good people. De Gruchy points out that the good people Bonhoeffer was thinking about were, concretely, his family and friends. Although Zerner agrees that Bonhoeffer was considering his family and friends when thinking about unconscious Christianity, her take on his experiment with unconscious Christianity is somewhat more negative. Regardless of Zerner's views on the success of his venture, both she and de Gruchy agree that the family and friends whom Bonhoeffer was seeking to describe as unconscious Christians did not self-identify as Christians. This accords with my assessment that Bonhoeffer considered unconscious Christians to not self-identify as Christians throughout his development of the concept.

In contrast to Zerner, Kelly recognizes the importance of the link that Bonhoeffer makes between unconscious Christianity and Matthew 25 for keeping in view the Christological grounding of his concept. He draws attention to the way in which this link impacts the question of salvation in the Church's discourse, writing:

> The reference to Matt. 25 is crucial for unpacking the mode of being Christian that opens a route out of the "*extra ecclesiam nulla salus*" corner into which the Christian Church had backed itself. The reference to the incognito of Jesus Christ is the constant spark that fires Bonhoeffer's theological imagination in formulating a form of Christian faith for which even the non-religious and non-Christian are gifted.[145]

Kelly thus confirms the view that unconscious Christians are recognized as righteous by God, like the people in Matthew 25 who are described as receiving eternal life.[146] By saying that this new mode of being Christian articulated by Bonhoeffer provides a solution to the "*extra ecclesiam nulla salus*" problem faced by the Church, he implies that unconscious Christians are saved. Arguing that in "After 10 Years" Bonhoeffer gives a "refreshing" description of what Christianity actually is,[147] Kelly goes on to note of this text:

> Bonhoeffer's essay has the additional merit of bringing out important implications of what he meant by an "unconscious Christianity" and what Rahner developed in his theology of "anonymous Christianity." Both concepts constitute a call to Christians to be attuned to the word of God that might never reach beyond the tacit dimension of all knowing and loving. In a world in which that word has become enfleshed in Jesus the Christ and enfleshed anew in all those who cry out in their hunger, thirst, homelessness, imprisonment, and suffering, Christians are called to affirm the presence of God and God's Son and their Spirit in all creatures. Christians are those who are enabled by God to recognize the Spirit outpoured in a world that is bigger than its explicitly Christian dimension but nonetheless ever graced by God's presence.[148]

"After 10 Years" was written at Christmas 1942, two years after "Ultimate and Penultimate Things," and a few months before *Novel*. It is therefore interesting that Kelly sees in this piece "implications of what he meant by 'unconscious Christianity,'" as if Bonhoeffer's developing ideas on unconscious Christianity can be perceived in this text. Kelly's assessment of "After 10 Years" echoes my thought that even though he mentioned it only a few times, Bonhoeffer was thinking about unconscious Christianity over a long period of time.

In the above paragraph it seems as though Kelly broadens his definition of unconscious Christianity from referring to those who act in the same way as the people in Matthew 25, including unconscious Christians in his description of Christians generally. By leading on to a description of Christians as those who are "enabled by God to recognize the Spirit outpoured in a world that is bigger than its explicitly Christian dimension but nonetheless ever graced by God's presence," he implies that unconscious Christians fulfill this criterion also, suggesting that they somehow recognize the Spirit at work in the world. While this recognition of the Spirit outpoured in the world cannot be attributed to unconscious Christians, as the very name Bonhoeffer gives to this group shows that they are not conscious of God's presence or of engagement with God, it could be attributed to religionless Christians, who are consciously Christian. The latter group, due to their denial of the religious habit outlined earlier in this chapter, and because they see God as inhabiting the center of existence instead of being confined to the outer reaches of experience, can recognize that the world is "ever graced by God's presence," and can readily admit the existence of unconscious Christians. While Kelly refers to unconscious Christianity and religionless Christianity as "kindred concepts,"[149] here he goes too far in commingling them.

Kelly addresses the idea that unconscious Christians are those who engage with Christ by being for others, and his description of unconscious Christianity as being a "Christic embrace of people"[150] confirms the idea put forward in my definition that when an unconscious Christian feeds the hungry, there is more going on than simply a human act. By describing it as a "Christic embrace" rather than a human one, Kelly emphasizes Bonhoeffer's idea that there is an engagement with Christ happening in the selfless act of helping the other individual. Kelly's choice of language also points to Bonhoeffer's idea that the unconscious Christian participates in Jesus's being-for-others, and thus when she engages with others, she engages with them in a Christ-like manner, gathering them into, as Kelly terms it, the "Christic embrace."

Kelly also confirms the idea contained within my definition of unconscious Christianity that unconscious Christians perform acts of faith, even if they cannot reflect upon them. By writing that Bonhoeffer was "formulating a form of Christian faith" when writing about unconscious Christianity,[151] Kelly allows unconscious Christianity to be understood as a form of Christian faith. The fact that he follows this comment immediately with the phrase "for which even the non-religious and the non-Christian are gifted," confuses the issue somewhat. It is impossible to say that people can be unconscious Christians and at the same time non-Christian. Perhaps it would be better to qualify Kelly's statement, changing it to: *for which even the non-religious and those who do not self-identify as Christians are gifted.*

Kelly's point that Bonhoeffer thought there could be faith and justification outside the Christian West and its religious traditions, but not without the presence of Christ, echoes my definition of unconscious Christianity, which can do without the conscious adherence to Christianity, but nevertheless includes engagement with Christ, even though this engagement is unconscious.

We have already seen that in her article on the penultimate and unconscious Christianity Tödt accurately notes that it is possible for people to be Christians without being aware of it. However, she attributes this aspect of unconscious Christianity to Christianity in general, writing that any Christian individual cannot reflect on her own Christian faith in the penultimate.[152] This does not fit, for example, with the concept of religionless Christianity. Religionless Christians, as shown previously, are aware of their Christian faith, but choose to distance themselves from what Bonhoeffer calls religiosity. Tödt focuses too exclusively on the distinction between being unconsciously Christian in the world and consciously trying to follow a specific spiritual practice slightly apart from the world, as illustrated by the Berneuchen movement. The result of this focus is that she does not consider how unconscious Christianity, as she portrays it, would impact on Bonhoeffer's view of Christianity in general. It is possibly a problem of clarity that leads Tödt's readers to think that she is describing Christianity in general in the penultimate, when she might in fact intend to portray only unconscious Christianity. However, as it is, Tödt appears not to recognize that Bonhoeffer does not view Christianity as a whole in the way which she describes, as his other prison texts plainly evidence.

While Tödt sees unconscious Christianity as being placed in contrast to a pietistic emphasis on the spiritual life withdrawn from the world, Lukens views it as one of the driving forces behind Bonhoeffer's fiction writing. I agree with Lukens that one of Bonhoeffer's aims in writing his fiction was to give "imaginative shape to what he called 'unconscious Christianity' in the 'world come of age,'"[153] but in my view unconscious Christianity must be seen as more than a counternarrative to the dominant Nazi narrative of the day. While it is certainly true that Bonhoeffer was providing a counternarrative to the prevailing culture in his fiction, unconscious Christianity is not reducible to a discourse, but must be understood as designating a specific group of people. The pastoral aspect of Bonhoeffer's writing about unconscious Christianity that was highlighted at the end of the previous section chimes in well with what Lukens says about Bonhoeffer aiming to find a "language of compassion, dialogue, life for others and affirmation of the world as it is, grounded in the reality of faith"[154] for those who would live after him. However, while her examination of the topic notes the centrality of the concepts of alterity and being-for-others in Bonhoeffer's thought, it does not reflect the idea that unconscious Christians engage with Christ, which is central to a proper understanding of unconscious Christianity.

CONCLUDING COMMENTS

In the few scholarly articles written on the topic of unconscious Christianity, there is no hint that unconscious Christianity might not be compatible with the world come of age, or with religionless Christianity. Most see the idea of unconscious Christianity as fitting in with those of the world come of age and religionless Christianity (see Bethge and de Gruchy, and Kelly respectively), making distinctions between each of the three concepts.[155]

Bethge makes a crucial point when he says that Bonhoeffer's statements about the world come of age and unconscious Christianity are theological statements. Following his lead, my definition of unconscious Christianity takes seriously Bonhoeffer's theological intentions when using this term. The points that I include in my definition of unconscious Christianity and that do not occur in any of the current scholarship are threefold. Firstly, unconscious Christians are free from false ambition, not seeking to be other than what they are. Secondly, they value the penultimate. Thirdly, in the early phases of his development of the concept Bonhoeffer thought unconscious Christians were likely to be members of the *Bürgertum*.

This could be attributed to the fact that unconscious Christianity has not been widely treated so far in Bonhoeffer scholarship, and also to the fact there has as yet been no attempt at a systematic and detailed appraisal of the idea. This section shows that my definition finds confirmation in the little that has been written so far in this field, whilst at the same time adding new ideas that have not yet been considered. The new definition brings together aspects of unconscious Christianity that have not been treated together before, thus revealing unconscious Christianity to be a complex and developing concept in Bonhoeffer's theology, worthy of greater attention in the scholarly community.

NOTES

1. See Bonhoeffer, *Letters and Papers from Prison*, 405.
2. See Bonhoeffer, *Letters and Papers from Prison*, 362–63.
3. See Bonhoeffer, *Letters and Papers from Prison*, 366.
4. See Bonhoeffer, *Letters and Papers from Prison*, 425–26.
5. See Bonhoeffer, *Letters and Papers from Prison*, 476. For more detail on how these ideas come under the concept of the world come of age, see Peter Selby, "Christianity in a World Come of Age" in *The Cambridge Companion to Dietrich Bonhoeffer*, 233–39, John de

Gruchy, Editor's Introduction to the English edition of Bonhoeffer, *Letters and Papers from Prison*, 23–24, and Arnaud Corbic, *Dietrich Bonhoeffer: Résistant et prophète d'un christianisme non religieux, 1906-1945* (Paris: Albin Michel, 2002), 76–78.

6. For a fully detailed explanation of the concept of the world come of age in Bonhoeffer's theology, see Ernst Feil, *The Theology of Dietrich Bonhoeffer*, tr. Martin Rumsheidt. (Minneapolis: Fortress Press, 2007), 99–159. See also Clifford J. Green, *Bonhoeffer: A Theology of Sociality*, revised edition (Grand Rapids, MI & Cambridge, UK: W. B. Eerdmans, 1999), 247–58; Peter Selby, "Christianity in a World Come of Age," Corbic, *Dietrich Bonhoeffer*, 71–76; Ralph K. Wüstenberg, "'Religionless Christianity': Dietrich Bonhoeffer's Tegel Theology" in *Bonhoeffer for a New Day: Theology in a Time of Transition: Papers Presented at the Seventh International Bonhoeffer Congress, Cape Town, 1996*, ed. John W. de Gruchy (Grand Rapids, MI & Cambridge, UK: William. B. Eerdmans, 1997), 57–71; and Tom Greggs, "Religionless Christianity in a Complexly Religious and Secular World" in *Religion, Religionlessness and Contemporary Western Culture*, eds. Stephen Plant and Ralf K. Wüstenberg (Frankfurt Am Main: Peter Lang, 2008), 111–25.

7. Bonhoeffer, *Letters and Papers from Prison*, 426, letter dated the 8th of June 1944.

8. Von Klemperer, review *Fiction from Tegel Prison*, 111.

9. Feil notes that Bonhoeffer requested a copy of *Weltanschauung und Analyse des Menschen seit Renaissance und Reformation* shortly after his birthday in 1944. See Feil, *The Theology of Dietrich Bonhoeffer*, 178.

10. Feil, *The Theology of Dietrich Bonhoeffer*, 180. For Bonhoeffer's use of the term "adult" in this context, see Bonhoeffer, *Letters and Papers from Prison*, 427.

11. Ralf K. Wüstenberg, *Bonhoeffer and Beyond: Promoting a Dialogue between Religion and Politics* (Frankfurt am Main: Peter Lang, 2008), 16.

12. Bonhoeffer, *Letters and Papers from Prison*, 425–26.

13. Bonhoeffer, *Letters and Papers from Prison*, 362, letter dated the 30th April 1944.

14. Tietz, *Theologian of Resistance*, 101.

15. Tietz, *Theologian of Resistance*, 101.

16. Wüstenberg, "'Religionless Christianity': Dietrich Bonhoeffer's Tegel Theology," 69.

17. See Feil, *The Theology of Dietrich Bonhoeffer*, 153, where he refers to the sermon for the Bethges' wedding (see Bonhoeffer, *Letters and Papers from Prison*, 82–87), writing: "The affirmation of the earth which marriage represents, an affirmation to which God adds his own 'yes' occupied him again in his 'Wedding Sermon from a Prison Cell.'"

18. Wüstenberg, "'Religionless Christianity': Dietrich Bonhoeffer's Tegel Theology," 70.

19. See Bonhoeffer, *Letters and Papers from Prison*, 427.

20. See Bonhoeffer, *Letters and Papers from Prison*, 362, footnote 11. The editors note that Bonhoeffer's doctoral supervisor, Reinhold Seeberg, "defined the 'religious a priori' (in his Christliche Dogmatik, 1:103) as a 'purely formal, primeval endowment of the created spirit or ego that renders it capable of, and in need of, the direct awareness of the absolute Spirit.'" The editors cite Reinhold Seeberg, *Christliche Dogmatik*, 1 (Erlangen: Deichert, 1924), 103.

21. See Bonhoeffer, *Letters and Papers from Prison*, 450.

22. Rahner, *Theological Investigations*, 392–93.

23. Greggs, "Religionless Christianity in a Complexly Religious and Secular World," 120. Greggs cites Bonhoeffer, *Letters and Papers from Prison*, ed. Eberhard Bethge (London: SCM, 1999), 342, emphasis Greggs's. The letter he refers to is dated the 30th of June 1944.

24. Bonhoeffer, *Letters and Papers from Prison*, 426–27.

25. Bonhoeffer, *Letters and Papers from Prison*, 482, letter dated the 18th of July 1944.

26. For "godlessness" of the world, see Bonhoeffer, *Letters and Papers from Prison*, 482, letter dated the 18th July of 1944, cited above. For "without God" see Bonhoeffer, *Letters and Papers from Prison*, 479, letter dated the 16th of July 1944: "Before God, and with God, we live without God." Godlessness will be discussed further in the conclusion.

27. See Greggs, "Religionless Christianity in a Complexly Religious and Secular World," 124.

28. It is of course impossible to claim that there were no unconscious Christians in the world before it came of age, but here the discussion is focused on Western society in general.

29. Eberhard Bethge, *Dietrich Bonhoeffer: Theologian, Christian, Contemporary*, 770. Bethge writes that in using the phrase "world come of age," Bonhoeffer "is thinking of Kant's formula" quoted above. He continues: "But Bonhoeffer now takes Kant's irrevocable description of maturity as an essential element of his *theologia crucis*." Bethge cites the introductory statement of Immanuel Kant's *Was ist Aufklärung?* (1784).
30. See for example Bonhoeffer, *Letters and Papers from Prison*, 405.
31. See Greggs, "Religionless Christianity in a complexly religious and secular world," 120.
32. Von Klemperer, review *Fiction from Tegel Prison*, 112.
33. See chapter 3 of this book.
34. See the introduction to this book.
35. It could also be possible to read Berg as a religionless Christian. While Bonhoeffer makes it clear that he fulfils some of the aspects of the definition of unconscious Christianity, he does not explicitly self-identify as non-Christian. If he were a religionless Christian, the reader might expect him to attempt to put his faith into nonreligious words or actions and privately practice arcane discipline. This could in fact be the case, without Bonhoeffer making it explicit. However due to the strong similarities between the prison in *Story* and Bonhoeffer's description of prison life in "Report on Prison Life after One Year in Tegel" (Bonhoeffer, *Letters and Papers from Prison*, 343–47), and the fact that Bonhoeffer knew some compassionate and trustworthy prison guards (Corporal Linke, Corporal Holzendorf, and Corporal Knobloch; see Eberhard Bethge, *Dietrich Bonhoeffer: theologian, Christian, contemporary*, 751), who helped him communicate secretly with Eberhard Bethge and Maria von Wedemeyer, it is likely that Berg is modeled in part on the guards, and therefore represents the population that Bonhoeffer was thinking of when he was mulling over the link between Christ and good people. As has been noted, unconscious Christianity is the concept that Bonhoeffer uses to make sense of this link, and I think it is therefore fair to assume that Berg is an unconscious Christian.
36. See Bonhoeffer, *Letters and Papers from Prison*, 601. For a discussion of the confusion over the dating of this piece, see the discussion on the fiction texts and why they should be considered theological in chapter 2, and chapter 2, note 4.
37. Bonhoeffer, *Letters and Papers from Prison*, 501.
38. In both *Novel* and *Story*, the immoral character is called Meier, or Meyer. See Bonhoeffer, *Fiction from Tegel Prison*, 102 and 183.
39. Bonhoeffer, *Fiction from Tegel Prison*, 192.
40. See Bonhoeffer, *Fiction from Tegel Prison*, 183.
41. Bonhoeffer, *Fiction from Tegel Prison*, 193.
42. Bonhoeffer, *Letters and Papers from Prison*, 479.
43. Bonhoeffer, *Fiction from Tegel Prison*, 194.
44. In *Story*, because of the way characters who have been to the front are portrayed as brave, honest, with a deep sense of honor, and those who have not are depicted as base, duplicitous, and violent, participating in the war at the front symbolizes two important ideas. Firstly, it symbolizes choosing to participate in God's suffering in the world and secondly, it symbolizes the willingness to take on guilt.
45. A full description of religionless Christianity and a comparison between it and unconscious Christianity is presented in the following two sections.
46. For a fully detailed explanation of the concept of religionless Christianity in Bonhoeffer's theology, see Feil, *The Theology of Dietrich Bonhoeffer*, 192–202; Wüstenberg, "'Religionless Christianity': Dietrich Bonhoeffer's Tegel Theology"; Green, *Bonhoeffer: A Theology of Sociality*, 269–82; Corbic, *Dietrich Bonhoeffer*, 61–67; and Tom Greggs, *Theology against Religion: Constructive Dialogues with Bonhoeffer and Barth* (London & New York: T&T Clark, 2011), chapter 3.
47. Greggs, "Religionless Christianity in a Complexly Religious and Secular World," 120.
48. Bonhoeffer, *Letters and Papers from Prison*, 36
49. Bonhoeffer, *Letters and Papers from Prison*, 362.
50. Bonhoeffer, *Letters and Papers from Prison*, 363.
51. Bonhoeffer, *Letters and Papers from Prison*, 362.
52. See Bonhoeffer, *Letters and Papers from Prison*, 366.

53. Bonhoeffer, *Letters and Papers from Prison*, 373.
54. Bonhoeffer, *Letters and Papers from Prison*, 390.
55. See Bonhoeffer, *Letters and Papers from Prison*, 389.
56. Wüstenberg, "'Religionless Christianity': Dietrich Bonhoeffer's Tegel Theology," 61.
57. See Bonhoeffer, *Letters and Papers from Prison*, 372.
58. See Bonhoeffer, *Letters and Papers from Prison*, 389: "Our church has been fighting during these years only for its self-preservation, as if that were an end in itself. It has become incapable of bringing the word of reconciliation and redemption to humankind and to the world. So the words we used before must lose their power, be silenced, and we can be Christians today in only two ways. Through prayer and in doing justice among human beings."
59. Bonhoeffer, *Ethics*, 252–53.
60. See Greggs, *Theology against Religion*, 67–69. Greggs notes that applying the term 'anti-fundamentalist' to Bonhoeffer's work is somewhat anachronistic, but that it is nevertheless an important parallel to make.
61. Greggs, *Theology against Religion*, 68.
62. For a fuller discussion of this point, see Greggs, *Theology against Religion*, chapter 3.
63. See chapter 1 of this book.
64. See Bonhoeffer's comments about his poem "Christians and Heathens" in his letter to Bethge dated the 18th of July 1944. (Bonhoeffer, *Letters and Papers from Prison*, 480–82).
65. Bonhoeffer, *Letters and Papers from Prison*, 480–82.
66. Wannenwetsch, "'Christians and Pagans,' towards a Trans-Religious Second Naiveté or How to be a Chirstological Creature," 178–79.
67. Bonhoeffer, *Letters and Papers from Prison*, 480.
68. Bonhoeffer, *Letters and Papers from Prison*, 480.
69. Bonhoeffer, *Letters and Papers from Prison*, 461.
70. For Greggs's discussion of this shift from an anthropocentric to a God-centered account of salvation, and how this enables us to move away from a dangerous binary of those who are included and those who are excluded from God's salvific work, see Greggs, *Theology against Religion*, 99–111.
71. Rahner, *Theological Investigations*, 391.
72. Rahner, *Theological Investigations*, 395.
73. Ernst Feil is not included in the list below, due to the fact that he scarcely mentions unconscious Christianity. However it is worth noting that Feil makes a passing reference to it in his discussion of *actus directus* and *actus reflexus* in Bonhoeffer's thought, writing: "The problem of 'unconscious Christianity' raised in that same letter [letter postmarked 27th of July 1944], had already occupied him in *Ethics*." Ernst Feil, *The Theology of Dietrich Bonhoeffer*, 28. Feil then gives references to the places in *Ethics* where he thinks Bonhoeffer is occupied with unconscious Christianity. These include the section in "History and Good" in which Bonhoeffer writes: "The activity of Christians does not spring from bitter resignation over the incurable rift between vitality and self-denial, between 'worldly' and 'Christian,' between an 'autonomous ethic' and the 'ethics of Jesus,' but from the joy over the already accomplished reconciliation of the world with God, from the peace of the already accomplished work of salvation in Jesus Christ, from the all-encompassing life that is Jesus Christ. Because in Jesus Christ God and humanity became one, so through Christ what is 'Christian' and what is 'worldly' become one in the action of the Christian" (Bonhoeffer, *Ethics*, 252–53). However, despite stating that Bonhoeffer had been occupied with the concept of unconscious Christianity while writing *Ethics*, Feil does not attempt to define unconscious Christianity.
74. See Eberhard Bethge, *Dietrich Bonhoeffer: Theologian, Christian, Contemporary*, 770. See also Bonhoeffer, *Letters and Papers from Prison*, 424–31.
75. See Eberhard Bethge, *Dietrich Bonhoeffer: Theologian, Christian, Contemporary*, 771.
76. Eberhard Bethge, *Dietrich Bonhoeffer: Theologian, Christian, Contemporary*, 771.
77. Eberhard Bethge, *Dietrich Bonhoeffer: Theologian, Christian, Contemporary*, 770.
78. See Bonhoeffer, *Letters and Papers from Prison*, 427.
79. Eberhard Bethge, *Dietrich Bonhoeffer: Theologian, Christian, Contemporary*, 771: "Bonhoeffer's statement about the world come of age is first and last a theological statement. It is, moreover, the same with his statement concerning 'unconscious Christianity.'"

80. Letter postmarked 27th of July 1944. See Bonhoeffer, *Letters and Papers from Prison*, 489–90.
81. Zerner, "Dietrich Bonhoeffer's Prison Fiction: A Commentary," 155.
82. Zerner, "Dietrich Bonhoeffer's Prison Fiction: A Commentary," 155.
83. Zerner, "Dietrich Bonhoeffer's Prison Fiction: A Commentary," 166.
84. Zerner, "Dietrich Bonhoeffer's Prison Fiction: A Commentary," 166.
85. Zerner, "Dietrich Bonhoeffer's Prison Fiction: A Commentary," 166.
86. Zerner, "Dietrich Bonhoeffer's Prison Fiction: A Commentary," 166.
87. John W. de Gruchy, *Witness to Jesus Christ*, (London: Collins, 1988), 39–40.
88. De Gruchy, *Witness to Jesus Christ*, 40.
89. It should be noted that in the above excerpt, de Gruchy equates good people with nonreligious people. However, because he says that these people are "typified by his [Bonhoeffer's] own family and friends," and in the fiction Bonhoeffer portrays these very people as unconscious Christians, it is legitimate to equate the good people with unconscious Christians in the commentary on this passage.
90. De Gruchy, *Witness to Jesus Christ*, 40.
91. See Geffrey B. Kelly, "'Unconscious Christianity' and the 'Anonymous Christian.'" For my discussion of the relationship between Bonhoeffer's unconscious Christianity and Rahner's anonymous Christian, see the conclusion to this book.
92. Kelly, "'Unconscious Christianity' and the 'Anonymous Christian,'" 118.
93. Kelly, "'Unconscious Christianity' and the 'Anonymous Christian,'" 119.
94. Kelly, "'Unconscious Christianity' and the 'Anonymous Christian,'" 122. The East would not have been subject to these cultural structures, which might explain why Bonhoeffer perceived Gandhi as somehow engaging with Christ, even before Bonhoeffer has formulated the idea of unconscious Christianity.
95. Kelly, "'Unconscious Christianity' and the 'Anonymous Christian,'" 121–22. Kelly quotes Dietrich Bonhoeffer, *Gesammelte Schriften, 1*, ed. Eberhard Bethge (Munich: Christian Kaiser Verlag., 1958), 61, letter from Bonhoeffer to Rössler, 1931.
96. Kelly, "'Unconscious Christianity' and the 'Anonymous Christian,'" 124.
97. Kelly, "'Unconscious Christianity' and the 'Anonymous Christian,'" 125.
98. Kelly, "'Unconscious Christianity' and the 'Anonymous Christian,'" 125.
99. Kelly, "'Unconscious Christianity' and the 'Anonymous Christian,'" 119.
100. Kelly, "'Unconscious Christianity' and the 'Anonymous Christian,'" 139. This is particularly striking in the first two points of Bonhoeffer's confession of the Church's sin, in "Guilt Justification, Renewal" (in Bonhoeffer, *Ethics*, 134–45). While unconscious Christians serve Christ through their actions, Bonhoeffer writes that the Church "confesses that it has not professed openly and clearly enough its message of the one God, revealed for all times in Jesus Christ and tolerating no other gods besides. The church confesses its timidity, its deviations, its dangerous concessions. It has often disavowed its duties as sentinel and comforter. Through this is has often withheld the compassion that it owes to the despised and rejected." Bonhoeffer, *Ethics*, 138.
101. "After 10 Years" was written at Christmas 1942, but repeats some ideas already occurring in "Ethics as Formation," written in autumn 1940. (See Ilse Tödt's "Preparing the German Edition of Ethics," in Bonhoeffer, *Ethics*, 471.) Tödt dates the writing of "Ultimate and Penultimate Things" in November–December 1940, after that of "Ethics as Formation." It is therefore interesting that Kelly sees in the ideas that originated in "Ethics as Formation" hints of unconscious Christianity. Bonhoeffer would then have started thinking about unconscious Christianity in autumn 1940, and continued to do so until the end of his life.
102. Kelly, "'Unconscious Christianity' and the 'Anonymous Christian,'" 144.
103. Bonhoeffer, *Ethics*, 170. Interestingly, Bonhoeffer uses the phrase "ground under our feet," that appears in "After 10 Years," in his play written over a year later. In the latter, he portrays the difference between a young man who is a member of the *Bürgertum* and a young working-class man. The former has "ground" under his feet, whereas the latter does not. In "After 10 Years," Bonhoeffer notes that in his current era people have exceedingly little "ground" under their feet. (See Bonhoeffer, *Letters and Papers from Prison*, 38, and Bonhoeffer, *Fiction from Tegel Prison*, 68, and chapter 3 of this book.)

104. Kelly, "'Unconscious Christianity' and the 'Anonymous Christian,'" 146.
105. Kelly, "'Unconscious Christianity' and the 'Anonymous Christian,'" 146.
106. Bonhoeffer, *Ethics*, 169.
107. Kelly, "'Unconscious Christianity' and the 'Anonymous Christian,'" 145.
108. Kelly, "'Unconscious Christianity' and the 'Anonymous Christian,'" 145.
109. Kelly, "'Unconscious Christianity' and the 'Anonymous Christian,'" 147.
110. Nancy Lukens, "Narratives of Creative Displacement: Bonhoeffer the Reader and the Construction of 'Unconscious Christianity' in *Fiction from Tegel Prison*," paper presented at the Ninth International Bonhoeffer Congress, Rome, Italy, 6–11 June 2004.
111. Zerner, "Dietrich Bonhoeffer's Prison Fiction: A Commentary," 164.
112. Lukens, "Narratives of Creative Displacement," 3.
113. Lukens references Bonhoeffer's letter to Bethge dated the 9th of March 1944.
114. Lukens, "Narratives of Creative Displacement," 3.
115. Lukens, "Narratives of Creative Displacement," 12–13.
116. Lukens, "Narratives of Creative Displacement," 3. Here Lukens references Bonhoeffer's letter to Bethge dated the 18th of November 1943.
117. Lukens, "Narratives of Creative Displacement," 13. See James Clifford, "Traveling Cultures," in *Cultural Studies*, eds. Lawrence Grossberg, Cary Nelson, and Paula Treichler (New York and London: Routledge, 1992), 96–116.
118. Lukens, "Narratives of Creative Displacement," 14.
119. Lukens, "Narratives of Creative Displacement," 20. Renate is Major von Bremer's daughter.
120. Bonhoeffer, *Fiction from Tegel Prison*, 173 and 177.
121. Lukens, "Narratives of Creative Displacement," 22.
122. Bonhoeffer, *Letters and Papers from Prison*, 322.
123. Bonhoeffer, *Letters and Papers from Prison*, 489.
124. Bernhardt, "Christentum ohne Christusglaube," 16. Being-for-others (in German, the phrase is "Dasein-für-andere") is an idea that occurs in Bonhoeffer's late theology. The idea appears for the first time in "The Concrete Commandment and the Divine Mandates" in *Ethics*, written in early 1943: "To live as a human being before God, in the light of God's becoming human, can only mean to be there not for oneself, but for God and for other human beings" (Bonhoeffer, *Ethics*, 400). See also Bonhoeffer, *Letters and Papers from Prison*, 501. For a detailed discussion of Bonhoeffer's concept of being-for-others, see Charles Marsh, *Reclaiming Dietrich Bonhoeffer: The Promise of His Theology* (New York & Oxford: Oxford University Press, 1994), 150–57.
125. See Bonhoeffer, *Letters and Papers from Prison*, 480: "Being a Christian does not mean being religious in a certain way, making oneself into something or other (a sinner, penitent, or saint) according to some method or other. Instead it means being human, not a certain type of human being, but the human being Christ creates in us."
126. Bernhardt, "Christentum ohne Christusglaube," 17. The original reads: "Das Teilnehmen am Leiden Gottes im weltlichen Leben macht das Christsein aus. Seine Erfahrung im Widerstand gegen das NS-Regime hatte Bonhoeffer aber gezeigt, dass auch Nichglaubende an diesem Leiden teilnehmen und ihr Leben für die Bekämpfung seiner Ursachen einsetzen. Sie können Christus näher sein als 'religiöse' Christen."
127. See Bonhoeffer, *Ethics*, 124. In "Heritage and Decay" Bonhoeffer defines promising godlessness as "the protest against pious godlessness insofar as that has spoiled the churches. It thus preserves in a sure though negative way the heritage of a genuine faith in God and of a genuine church." For further discussion of promising godlessness, see the conclusion to this book.
128. Bernhardt, "Christentum ohne Christusglaube," 16. The original reads: "Bonhoeffer gebraucht die Dialektik von Gottnähe und Gottferne bzw. Gottlosigkeit, um auszudrücken, dass die Anwesenheit Gottes nicht von der Warhnehmung und Erfahrung dieser Anwesenheit abhängt und schon gar nicht von der reflexiven Erfassung einer solchen Erfahrung."
129. Bernhardt, "Christentum ohne Christusglaube," 17. The original reads: "Es sei christlicher, einen Menschen, 'der es selbst nicht mehr wagen würde, sich einen Christen zu nennen, als Christen in Anspruch zu nehmen und ihm mit viel Geduld zum Bekenntnis zu Christus zu

helfen' als ihn 'als Nicht-Christen anzusprechen und ihn zum Bekenntnis seines Unglaubens zu drängen.'" Bernhardt cites Bonhoeffer, *Ethik*, 169–70.

130. Ferdinand Schlingensiepen, "Die Darstellung von gelebtem Glauben und unbewusstem Christentum." "Gelebter Glaube" is translated here as "lived faith."

131. See Schlingensiepen, "Die Darstellung von gelebtem Glauben und unbewusstem Christentum," 268. Here he also mistakenly writes that *Novel* is the first instance in which Bonhoeffer uses the term "unconscious Christianity."

132. Schlingensiepen, "Die Darstellung von gelebtem Glauben und unbewusstem Christentum," 261. Schlingensiepen cites Bonhoeffer, *Fiction from Tegel Prison*, 91. Translation by the author; the original reads: "Diese Geschichte kannten die Kinder von klein auf, und sie verehrten das Bild ihres Vorfahren fast wie ein kleines Heiligenbild. Auch als sich die Älteren mehr von der Kirche entfernten, änderte sich daran nichts. Der alte Pfarrer als ein stilles Ideal in ihren Herzen." It is worth noting that the translation of this passage in Bonhoeffer, *Fiction from Tegel Prison*, reads: "They kept the old pastor quietly alive as an ideal in their hearts" (88), which alters the meaning of the original somewhat.

133. Schlingensiepen, "Die Darstellung von gelebtem Glauben und unbewusstem Christentum," 261.

134. Bonhoeffer, *Fiction from Tegel Prison*, 95.

135. See Schlingensiepen, "Die Darstellung von gelebtem Glauben und unbewusstem Christentum," 265, for another example of the same idea. Schlingensiepen refers to the way in which the *Novel* character Ulrich is influenced by his mother's piety, even though he has not taken it on fully as his own. Because of the influence of his mother's faith on Ulrich, he is able to see and pick apart the weak points made in his friend's argument about Christianity and society.

136. Ilse Tödt, "Wir leben im Vorletzten: Bonhoeffer und das unbewusste Christentum," in *Dietrich Bonhoeffers Christentum*, eds. Florian Schmitz and Christiane Tietz (Gütersloh: Gütersloher Verlag., 2011), 324–37. All translations relating to Tödt's article are by Duncan Greenland and the author.

137. Bonhoeffer became engaged to Maria von Wedemeyer in January 1943. Maria herself mistrusted the Berneuchen movement, and expressed her concerns about it in letters to Bonhoeffer. (See for example Ilse Tödt, "Wir leben im Vorletzten," 331–32.) The letters between von Wedemeyer and Bonhoeffer during his time in prison are collected in Dietrich Bonhoeffer, Ruth-Alice von Bismarck, Maria von Wedemeyer, and Ulrich Kabitz, *Love letters from Cell 92* (London: Fount, 1995).

138. Tödt, "Wir leben im Vorletzten," 336. The original reads: "Letztes im Vorletzten ist nur 'für andere da.'" Here Tödt references Bonhoeffer's Outline for a Book, in Bonhoeffer, *Letters and Papers from Prison*, 499–504.

139. See Tödt, "Wir leben im Vorletzten," 336.

140. Tödt, "Wir leben im Vorletzten," 336. The original reads: "Bonhoeffer weiß, dass, wenn denn überhaupt 'Christentum' im eigenen Leben vorgekommen ist, es mir 'unbewusstes Christentum' war."

141. Zerner, "Dietrich Bonhoeffer's Prison Fiction: A Commentary," 155.

142. Zerner, "Dietrich Bonhoeffer's Prison Fiction: A Commentary," 155.

143. Zerner, "Dietrich Bonhoeffer's Prison Fiction: A Commentary," 155.

144. See Bonhoeffer, *Letters and Papers from Prison*, 363.

145. Kelly, "'Unconscious Christianity' and the 'Anonymous Christian,'" 125. Kelly quotes from Dietrich Bonhoeffer, *Letters and Papers from Prison*, The Enlarged Edition, ed. Eberhard Bethge, trans. Reginald Fuller (New York: Macmillan, 1972), 382.

146. Matthew 25:46.

147. Kelly, "'Unconscious Christianity' and the 'Anonymous Christian,'" 144.

148. Kelly, "'Unconscious Christianity' and the 'Anonymous Christian,'" 145.

149. Kelly, "'Unconscious Christianity' and the 'Anonymous Christian,'" 119.

150. Kelly, "'Unconscious Christianity' and the 'Anonymous Christian,'" 145.

151. Kelly, "'Unconscious Christianity' and the 'Anonymous Christian,'" 125. Kelly quotes from Dietrich Bonhoeffer, *Letters and Papers from Prison*, The Enlarged Edition.

152. See Tödt, "Wir leben im Vorletzten," 336.

153. Lukens, "Narratives of Creative Displacement," 3.

154. Lukens, "Narratives of Creative Displacement," 22.
155. Although at times Kelly seems to confuse unconscious and religionless Christianity, this is not the norm.

Chapter Five

Unconscious Christianity as a Shift within Bonhoeffer's Theology

INTRODUCTION

In the previous chapter I looked at ways in which the concept of unconscious Christianity not only fits alongside Bonhoeffer's late theology, but also illumines it. Having established the necessity of an awareness of unconscious Christianity for a fuller understanding of the prison texts, in this chapter I investigate how unconscious Christianity relates to Bonhoeffer's earlier theology. I do not propose in this chapter to conduct a complete survey of the Bonhoeffer canon in order to establish whether there is continuity throughout the entirety of Bonhoeffer's work. Rather, I focus on whether the idea of unconscious Christianity can be perceived in Bonhoeffer's prior writing, or whether it is a product of his late theology, arguing for the latter case.

This chapter consists of four sections. The first gives an overview of the debate on the question of continuity or change in Bonhoeffer's theology, in order to have a context in which to situate the view of unconscious Christianity that I propose. In the second section I present the commonly held view that Bonhoeffer's changing personal circumstances play a major part in the development of his theological ideas. This section discusses scholarship on the impact of Bonhoeffer's life on his thought, and draws attention to specific biographical details that should be borne in mind when considering the question of whether or not unconscious Christianity represents a new departure in Bonhoeffer's theology. The second section also examines how Bonhoeffer's experience of growing up in a *bürgerlich* family influenced his concept of unconscious Christianity. I show that there is a development within his work on unconscious Christianity that reflects his move away from considering unconscious Christianity in terms of his own family and social background toward thinking of it in relation to the people surrounding him in prison. The third section addresses the change that unconscious Christianity marks in Bonhoeffer's thought, detailing how it alters, in particular, his view of the relationship between Christianity and self-identification. The fourth, longer section highlights ideas that occurred previously in Bonhoeffer's writing, and that appear again in his attempts to develop his thoughts on unconscious Christianity. In this section I show how, although some ideas related to unconscious Christianity can be found in his earlier work, the concept of unconscious Christianity only emerges in Bonhoeffer's late writings.

The chapter as a whole, therefore, shows that Bonhoeffer's work on unconscious Christianity causes a definite shift in his understanding of Christianity, but does not cause him to abandon all of his previous ideas. Rather, his work on this topic should be seen as illustrating his readiness to accept and work on new ideas, while at the same time considering how these new ideas fit in with his earlier theology and life experience.

THE ARC OF BONHOEFFER'S THEOLOGY: CONTINUITY OR CHANGE?

Since their first publication in 1951, the question of whether Bonhoeffer's prison writings are in continuity with his earlier work has been hotly debated.[1] In the previous chapter I noted Wüstenberg's opinion that Bonhoeffer's view of human autonomy changed after reading Wilhelm Dilthey. The question here, however, is not whether Bonhoeffer ever changed his view on a given subject, but rather how the prison texts should be understood as a whole within the Bonhoeffer canon.

Ferdinand Schlingensiepen gives us an insight into the first reactions to the Tegel material by quoting an early essay written in response to *Letters and Papers from Prison*:

> Anyone who knew Bonhoeffer's earlier work most likely knew him as the author of *The Cost of Discipleship* and *Life Together*. In his letters from prison, the emotional tone of those two books seems to have given way to a very different one. [. . .] To his deep unease, he was finding that the Confessing Church, in defending itself against violation by a regime of terror and lies, was leaving others threatened by that regime to their fate. . . . In this situation, it was a great discovery for Bonhoeffer to find that the only Gospel in the Bible is a Gospel turned toward the whole world. This world is, even though at enmity with God or far away from God, still the world that God loves. So there can only be a church which turns toward the world.[2]

Schlingensiepen comments on this passage: "This early review defines exactly the change in Bonhoeffer's thinking. He had not given up his stance at the front on behalf of the Church; but he no longer saw the church itself in the foreground, but rather the world that God loves."[3] Schlingensiepen agrees with this early assessment that there is both continuity and change in Bonhoeffer's theology.

Schlingensiepen's view that there is both continuity and change within Bonhoeffer's theology is predominant among Bonhoeffer scholars. Whereas some draw attention to the continuity, and some to the changes, most are agreed that Bonhoeffer's oeuvre represents a continuous development of his thought that contains changes occurring along the way. Hans-Richard Reuter is the only scholar to specifically mention unconscious Christianity in his presentation of how continuity can be traced throughout Bonhoeffer's opus. He too thinks that there is development in Bonhoeffer's thought, but that there is a constant that runs throughout this development. According to Reuter, this constant is Bonhoeffer's understanding of faith as *actus directus*, as "immediate, intentional orientation."[4] Reuter claims that Bonhoeffer's differentiation between the *actus directus* and the *actus reflexus* structures his whole theology, but that Bonhoeffer articulates this underlying principle with changing terminology throughout his life. For Reuter, faith as *actus directus* can be perceived in various points in Bonhoeffer's work, and he cites the following:

> It recurs in the "simple obedience" of the disciple in *The Cost of Discipleship*, who sees "always Christ only" and "not Christ *and* the world."[5] It is also in "the new knowledge, fully taken up into the doing, of the reconciliation accomplished in Jesus," which overcomes the splitting of knowledge into good and evil, as one of the *Ethics* fragments puts it.[6] It recurs as well in "the man of the undivided heart," who, in another sketch of the *Ethics*, is set against "the man with two souls."[7] Finally, it is in the "unconscious Christianity" of the prison correspondence, the characteristic of which is "partaking in God's suffering in the life of the world" which calls for a "non-religious interpretation of biblical concepts."[8]

The question of simple obedience in *Discipleship* is an interesting one, and is discussed later in this chapter. However, of note here is that Reuter mentions unconscious Christianity as an expression of Bonhoeffer's view of faith as *actus directus*. It has already been seen that in the letter to Bethge in which Bonhoeffer mentions unconscious Christianity, Bonhoeffer links unconscious Christianity with *fides directa*, and that the definition of the unconscious Christian to emerge from a close reading of this letter is that she has faith on which she cannot reflect. Reuter, however, does not consider unconscious Christianity quite in this light, as his understanding of the *actus directus* includes an element of intentionality, as his description of the *actus directus* as "immediate, intentional orientation"[9] shows. As has been shown, I see the unconscious Christian as someone who is unconsciously orientated toward, or engaging with, Christ, but without intending to be so. Reuter's understanding of unconscious Christianity differs slightly from that put forward here, but his statement that one of the characteristics of unconscious Christianity is that of partaking of God's suffering in the world fits with my view of unconscious Christianity. This is made clear in the definition I propose which includes the participation in Jesus's being-for-others.

Bethge, Kelly, André Dumas, and others note different stages in Bonhoeffer's life that affected the content of his theology, but they do not see these various stages as indicating serious rupture in his thought.[10] For example, Bethge offers an overview of Bonhoeffer's life and work that divides it into three sections. The first spans the years 1927 to 1933, the second 1933 to 1940, and the third 1940 to 1945. Bethge gives these three time periods the names "Foundation," "Concentration," and "Liberation,"[11] and refers to them as the

> dogmatic, the exegetical, and the ethical; or, again, the theoretical period in which he learned and taught at Berlin University, the pastoral period in which he served the Confessing Church in a preachers' seminary, and the political period in which his life became ambiguous.[12]

The stages defined by Bethge are also clear in the title of his biography of Bonhoeffer: theologian, Christian, contemporary. Leibholz-Bonhoeffer presents a helpful way of understanding how it is possible to delineate such different phases in Bonhoeffer's life without arguing that they imply abrupt changes in his life and thought. She suggests that the stages that Bethge describes should not be perceived only as succeeding each other chronologically, but also as melting into each other "in the sense that every advance to a fresh stage in life subsumed the preceding ones within itself."[13] She also notes that in applying the term "Christian" to Bonhoeffer, in conjunction with the label "contemporary," the former term must be defined as "living for others here in this world and actually committing one's life to uphold the cause of Christ."[14]

Bethge not only identifies different phases in Bonhoeffer's life, but also a change within the prison writing that takes place in April 1944. According to Bethge, whereas in 1943 Bonhoeffer's topic was the retreating world, in 1944 he wrote about the future, the future of Christianity, and the place of Christianity in the world, not only in Germany. Bethge defines the prison texts of 1943 as still belonging "to the sphere of the *Ethics*"[15] and as variations on the subject of the past. He suggests April 1944 as a turning point in Bonhoeffer's work, but does not advocate a complete division into a "before" and "after." His assessment of the question is worth noting in full:

> It is not altogether easy to decide the question of the turning-point, if only because so many elements of continuity with the past can be traced, even with *The Cost of Discipleship*. Both the latter and *Letters and Papers from Prison*

end in a remarkably similar way with the motif of *imitatio*. Moreover, many ideas of 1944 can be found already in the *Ethics* and letters of 1943, such as the love of the richness of the Old Testament and the warning against too direct an approach to the New Testament, the rejection of religious blackmail in acute distress, or the attempt to give a "non-religious interpretation" of Easter.

And yet there is much evidence that there was a decisive new start in April 1944, which does not mean, of course, that this division into periods makes what had gone before unimportant. On the contrary, it is part of the origin of the new. The bricks are there and are used. But the old arrangement of the bricks has been altered and there is, quite clearly, an extension of the theme that is equivalent to a change of theme. Bonhoeffer himself thought he was pursuing a completely new path. In the collapse of the "Christian West" he was seized by a belief in a changed face of Christianity that would be viable.[16]

This last sentence confirms that Bonhoeffer was thinking in terms of new expressions of Christianity that would be able to flourish in the "world come of age," but that might not be recognizable to people looking for familiar expressions of Christianity that had previously been viable.

One of the elements that Bethge draws attention to as being a constant throughout Bonhoeffer's thought is his Christology. He notes for example that Lutheran Kenotic Christology, "the whole fullness precisely in the total condescension, Phil. 2,"[17] is present in *Act and Being*. Bethge states that Bonhoeffer continues to refine this Christology, "in order to ground the present power of Christ even more clearly in the weakness of the human suffering of Jesus."[18] Bonhoeffer's belief that Christ is powerful in the very weakness of Jesus on the cross is clear to see in the prison texts.

John D. Godsey also emphasizes the point Bethge makes about Christology being continuously present in Bonhoeffer's writing, and while he recognizes the need to take note of the new concepts that emerge in the prison texts, he argues that Christology is "the unifying element in Bonhoeffer's theology."[19] Martin E. Marty agrees that Christology is a unifying element in Bonhoeffer's thought, although Bonhoeffer's enduring attention to Christology does not diminish the radical nature of the prison texts.[20] Marty points out that Christology is central to Bonhoeffer's theology because he derives his knowledge of God from the historical person of Jesus Christ. For Marty, the continuity between Bonhoeffer's earlier work and the Tegel period is obvious. However, he acknowledges that the view that the prison writings mark a break in Bonhoeffer's thought is not unfounded. Comparing two assessments of Bonhoeffer's work, the first seeing in it continuity and the second, discontinuity, Marty writes about the latter view: "This was a discovery or a claim that, it must be said, was plausible, because some of the late Bonhoeffer writings gave signs that this second assessment may be warranted."[21] Even Marty, a proponent of continuity within Bonhoeffer's writings, admits that it is not unreasonable to hold the view that there is discontinuity in Bonhoeffer's work.

Dumas echoes Bethge's analysis of a continuity with sections,[22] writing that although there are three distinct stages in Bonhoeffer's life, these should not be overemphasized to the detriment of the continuity within Bonhoeffer's life and work. Dumas cites Bethge's description of the three stages of Bonhoeffer's life as follows:

> In his twenties Bonhoeffer said to the theologians, your theme is the church. In his thirties he said to the church, your theme is the world. And in his forties he said to the world, your theme, which is forsakenness, is God's own theme; with his theme he is not cheating you out of the fullness of life, but opening it up to you.[23]

This analysis draws attention to the idea, discussed in more detail in the following section, that Bonhoeffer was addressing different groups of people at different points in his life, and that the changes in his audience and personal circumstances brought about changes in his theology. Despite these three well-defined stages and his assertion that the tone of Bonhoeffer's work should be perceived as "polyphonic,"[24] Dumas argues that there is no rupture in Bonhoeffer's theology. He cites Bonhoeffer's letter to Bethge in which he discusses whether or not either of them has changed, and Bonhoeffer states that he himself has not changed much.[25] Dumas notes that this letter is written only eight days before the letter usually considered to be the first theological letter from Tegel, written on the 30th of April, 1944. He declares in exasperation at the proponents of discontinuity: "This would suggest that whatever discontinuity there is must be located between 22 and 30 April 1944!"[26] Henry Mottu also balances aspects of continuity and innovation within Bonhoeffer's writing, echoing Bethge's statement that spring 1944 heralds a *"coupure sensible."*[27] He also argues that Bonhoeffer's last period of creativity, from April 1944 onward, "contains topics that had been in gestation for a long time, but which are expressed with a new audacity."[28] Perhaps Mottu thinks that the break in April 1944 enables Bonhoeffer to finally express ideas, which had been difficult to address before, in a new way. He certainly describes the letters written to Bethge from April 1944 onward as emanating a "sort of internal freedom."[29]

While the majority of scholars read the prison writings in the light of Bonhoeffer's earlier work, a minority do not. Among these are the so-called death of God theologians, who popularized Bonhoeffer's theology in the 1960s in the United States. Though the movement was short-lived, it highlighted the radical ideas present in the prison letters, such as the world come of age and religionless Christianity. Writers within the movement used these ideas to articulate their views on secularity and the impossibility of belief in

God in the world come of age. These authors drew both on Bonhoeffer's theology and his biography.[30] The death of God thinkers integrated *Letters and Papers from Prison* into their work to such an extent that it became an identifying text of the movement. However, it was the only text from the Bonhoeffer canon that they appealed to consistently, ignoring for the most part Bonhoeffer's earlier work. Their appropriation of Bonhoeffer's late theology did not extend as far as an appropriation of his understanding of reality as a reality in which God exists and participates, illustrating their readiness to be selective in their reading. However, the death of God theologians were aware that their approach to Bonhoeffer could be easily criticized, and indeed, were not above criticizing it themselves. William Hamilton, one of the central figures of the movement, wrote the semi-autobiographical essay *Thursday's Child* in which he described the contemporary American theologian and the lack of belief with which the theologian struggles. In this essay he states: "Dietrich Bonhoeffer is, of course, deeply involved in this portrait. Have we discovered this in him, and then in ourselves; or in ourselves, and then rejoiced to find it in him? I think the second is nearer the truth."[31] Hamilton sees Bonhoeffer's late texts as "the only theological words written in the recent past that can help us understand the new era into which we are moving"[32] and thinks of Bonhoeffer as "teaching a few Protestants what it means to say 'yes' to the twentieth century and still somehow to stay recognizably Protestant."[33] For the death of God theologians, Bonhoeffer's *Letters and Papers from Prison* are the defining texts of Bonhoeffer's theology.[34]

An author who is often mentioned in the same breath as the death of God movement is J. A. T. Robinson, bishop of Woolwich. His 1963 book *Honest to God* is based around the ideas of three theologians, Tillich, Bultmann, and Bonhoeffer, and calls for a rethinking of the ways in which the Church communicates Christ's Gospel to the world that takes seriously the mindset of people living in the twentieth century.[35] It brought Bonhoeffer's late theology, in particular the letters from prison, into the public eye in Britain as church groups across the country studied the bishop's text together. While Robinson does focus on the late theology, he is familiar with the early Bonhoeffer as well. He comments for instance on the relationship between Bonhoeffer's views on prayer articulated in *Life Together*, and the questions he raises in *Letters and Papers from Prison* about the place of prayer and worship in a religionless context.[36] But it is clear that for Robinson, the locus of Bonhoeffer's real prophetic challenge to the Church lies in his prison letters. Recollecting reading the letters for the first time, he writes: "One felt at once that the Church was not yet ready for what Bonhoeffer was giving us as his last will and testament before he was hanged by the S.S.: indeed, it might be understood properly only a hundred years hence. But it seemed one of those trickles that must one day split rocks."[37] In *Honest to God*, Robinson does not at all intend to address the question of continuity or change within Bonhoeffer's opus. However, he does intend to show that the late theology, and specifically the ideas of the world come of age and religionless Christianity, discussed in the previous chapter, are vital in helping the Church understand why it needs the "reluctant revolution" that Robinson calls for throughout his text. According to Robinson, Bonhoeffer's groundbreaking ideas reveal the lived reality of people in the twentieth century, who live *etsi deus non daretur*,[38] and to whom the Church must be able to speak, alongside whom Christians must be able to walk. This emphasis on the late theology as a key to beginning to think through changes in Church practice as early as 1963 is remarkable.

Hanfried Müller suggests a useful reading of Bonhoeffer's theology that uses neither the category of change nor that of continuity. Instead, Müller writes of the "movement" within Bonhoeffer's theology, and views attention to this movement as the key to understanding Bonhoeffer's thought. He writes:

> I believe that the right way to follow Bonhoeffer is to take up his development, his path, his intention and the tendency of his work: to follow him rather than stifle his vigour and vitality with a system. I think that understanding of the *whole* Bonhoeffer will come about not by systematizing everything he thought as though it were all on the same level, and thus relativizing it, but rather by taking up the *movement* of his thought in its entirety as the thing which can lead us further.[39]

In the prison texts, Müller sees contradictions with what Bonhoeffer had previously written. He cites as an example the difference between Bonhoeffer's approach to Western secularization in *Ethics* "as something threatening,"[40] and the optimism with which he treats the idea of the world come of age in *Letters and Papers*. Müller writes: "But even this contradiction is not like a clean cut between the *Ethics* and the letters; its lively force pushes ahead and impels one forward."[41] Despite the contradictions that he sees in Bonhoeffer's work, Müller argues for an analysis of Bonhoeffer's thought based on movement.

Viewing Bonhoeffer's theological development in terms of movement instead of relying on the categories of continuity and change allows for a more fluid approach to his thought. This approach fits particularly well with the definition of unconscious Christianity put forward here, which relies on the understanding that there is movement in Bonhoeffer's thoughts on unconscious Christianity as he continues to develop his ideas on the subject. The following section examines Bonhoeffer's changing personal circumstances and the ways in which they contributed to this movement within his theology, and more particularly, his development of the concept of unconscious Christianity.

HOW BONHOEFFER'S CHANGING PERSONAL CIRCUMSTANCES AFFECT HIS THEOLOGY

A central feature of Bonhoeffer's prison writing that attracts large numbers of readers to these texts is the juxtaposition of Bonhoeffer's theological reflections with his recording of personal experiences. Feil argues that personal experience shaped Bonhoeffer's theology, writing: "Bonhoeffer's thought grew out of life and his theology is an attempt to think upon faith lived out concretely."[42] For example, he credits Bonhoeffer's personal experiences as one of the causes of Bonhoeffer's world-affirming prison theology:

> Personal experiences were clearly not the least among those causes which made Bonhoeffer seek the form of faith which does not leave the world aside for reasons of religion or piety but which affirms the world and, in so doing, becomes religionless. Bonhoeffer's renewed preoccupation with the subject of the world during his incarceration arose from those experiences.[43]

I agree with Feil that Bonhoeffer's own experiences were extremely influential to the development of his theology, and it is therefore necessary to examine the changes in Bonhoeffer's personal circumstances that could have led to his developing the idea of unconscious Christianity.

Keith Clements, who also claims that a proper grasp of Bonhoeffer's life must inform any view of Bonhoeffer's theology, points out the dangers of absolutizing any one aspect of Bonhoeffer's theology that emerges from a specific period in his life. He notes the temptation of rating one text as more important than others, for example setting "*The Cost of Discipleship* with its peremptory call for obedience to Christ alone, and its sharp delimitation of the church from the world, over against the radically 'worldly' emphasis of the prison letters."[44] He draws attention to the contexts in which each text was written, stating:

> Each was addressed to a specific situation, with its own demands and responsibilities. Each took account of certain fundamental 'givens' of Christian faith. The two are not to be conflated, nor are they as antithetical as supposed.[45]

This analysis acknowledges the development of Bonhoeffer's writing and the changes that it contains, as well as the fact that, in his writing, Bonhoeffer addressed the specific contexts in which he lived and worked, and that these changed over the course of his lifetime. It is not simply that Bonhoeffer's circumstances influenced his writing without his being aware of it. He consciously responded in his theological work to the various circumstances in which he found himself. To put it another way, there are two sorts of interactions between Bonhoeffer and his changing circumstances: Firstly, the external circumstances influence him, and secondly, he acknowledges that his circumstances are changing and decides to engage with the changes taking place in a theological manner. This double interaction can be seen in the examples of Bonhoeffer's work discussed in this section.

When writing *Discipleship*, Bonhoeffer has a very clear idea of what it means to be a disciple of Christ. In *Discipleship* he describes the process by which people become disciples of Christ, writing: "Following Christ means taking certain steps."[46] This process will be discussed further on in this chapter, but of note now is that Bonhoeffer is adamant that each stage of the process must take place in a specific order, and cannot be omitted. It is an extremely prescriptive approach to the process of becoming a follower of Christ, and Bonhoeffer is careful to explain each stage of the process in detail so that there can be no misunderstanding or manipulating of the process. This extreme care taken over the description of becoming a Christian is indicative of Bonhoeffer's situation at the time of writing *Discipleship*. Writing between 1935 and 1937 in the Confessing Church seminary at Finkenwalde, Bonhoeffer is surrounded by people who have made the difficult decision of training to serve the Confessing Church, despite the potential consequences of punitive financial and political measures.[47] Taking a leading role in a project already under political threat heightens Bonhoeffer's sense of urgency. His feeling that only an extreme stance can avail against the increasing menace of Hitler's regime can be seen in a letter written to his brother, Karl-Friedrich, on the 14th of January 1935:[48]

> I think that I know that I would only achieve inward clarity and true honesty if I really began to take the Sermon on the Mount seriously. This is the only source of power which can blow up all the magic and sorcery until all that is left of the fireworks are a few charred remains. The restoration of the church will surely come only from a new kind of monasticism which has nothing in common with the old but a complete lack of compromise in a life lived in accordance with the Sermon on the Mount in the discipleship of Christ. I think that it is time to gather people together for this.[49]

It is not surprising that in his striving for the restoration of the Church, for which he was convinced that an uncompromising approach to a life of discipleship was necessary, Bonhoeffer writes didactically on how discipleship should be attained. However, Bonhoeffer's writing evolves as his circumstances change. As noted previously, Feil makes the point that the situations in which Bonhoeffer finds himself dictate what he thinks about theologically, and not vice versa. Feil draws attention to the following letter, in which Bonhoeffer reflects on whether he and Bethge have changed over the course of their lives:

I've certainly learned a good deal, but I don't think I've changed very much. There are people who change, and many who can hardly change at all. I don't think I have ever changed much, except perhaps at the time of my first impressions abroad, and under the first conscious influence of Papa's personality. It was then that a turning from the phraseological to the real ensued. As a matter of fact, I don't think you've really changed either. Self-development, of course, is a different matter. Neither of us has really experienced a break in his life. Of course, we have deliberately broken with a good deal, but that again is something quite different.[50]

Feil posits that because of the importance of reality and the need to take reality seriously in Bonhoeffer's writing, it is necessary to think of Bonhoeffer's writing from the time he describes as "a turning from the phraseological to the real" as "proceeding from then on in an unbroken development."[51] However, Feil exemplifies the difficulty of using the categories of continuity and change to describe Bonhoeffer's theology. He argues for a reading of Bonhoeffer that contains both sustained unity and progression: "In our examination of Bonhoeffer it has become more and more apparent that his theology does represent a sustained unity. In later life Bonhoeffer himself recognized this progression in his thought."[52] Yet Feil also identifies a period in Bonhoeffer's life in which Bonhoeffer views the world negatively,[53] which contrasts with his general assessment of Bonhoeffer as having a positive view of the world. Feil attempts to present continuity on this point throughout Bonhoeffer's work by stating, "Despite the manifest shift of emphasis in that work there are bases for a positive view of the world in *The Cost of Discipleship*, even though Bonhoeffer's self-critical remark is appropriate, namely, that he did not develop the matter correctly."[54] The difficulty with which Feil makes his point about continuity within Bonhoeffer's thought highlights the problematic nature of this particular debate.

Instead of trying to fit Bonhoeffer's thought into categories that do not completely accommodate it, it is more helpful to use Müller's idea of movement for thinking about Bonhoeffer's work. Not only does this negate the need, that Feil clearly feels, to show that changes can take place within a greater context of continuity, but it also reflects the idea that there is a fluid relationship between Bonhoeffer and his changing circumstances. They influence his thought; he is aware of their influence and responds to it.

Within his category of "sustained unity,"[55] Feil allows for a development of Bonhoeffer's thought during the prison period. Referring specifically to Bonhoeffer's theology of religionless Christianity and nonreligious interpretation,[56] he writes: "The 'new' insight was not new for Bonhoeffer in the sense of a break, but in the sense of a deeper experience and a deeper understanding of the ever changing historical tradition."[57] Unfortunately Feil does not mention unconscious Christianity in connection with his comments on Bonhoeffer's new insight, and it is therefore not possible to tell where he places unconscious Christianity within his understanding of development in Bonhoeffer's thought. However, his view that Bonhoeffer's life informed his theology, and that new insights brought deeper understanding rather than causing a break in his theology, echoes Bethge's assessment of the matter.

In considering the differences and similarities between Bonhoeffer's early thought and his writing on unconscious Christianity, it is essential to remember the changes in his personal circumstances during this period. Bonhoeffer's theological focus mirrors his own reality as he moves away from being surrounded by Confessing Church members and becomes increasingly involved with members of the resistance movement, who do not self-identify as Christian. In his assessment of the development of Bonhoeffer's theology, Schlingensiepen highlights the importance of the people with whom Bonhoeffer was surrounded during the war:

> The man in prison still spoke of the obedience of faith; but even in his *Ethics*, and that much more so in the letters from prison, the language had clearly changed. His vision had broadened, because in the Resistance he had come to know people who did "the right thing" without being consciously Christians, and because he was now seeing the world that he was learning to know in Tegel through the eyes of Jesus, whose cross and resurrection are the fundamental facts for every human life.[58]

Schlingensiepen asserts that the "new theology," as he calls it, could only have emerged in Tegel, and, along with Bethge, states that it revolves especially around the question "Who is Christ for us today?"[59] John de Gruchy also sees this question as central to Bonhoeffer's late theology, writing that it "sparks off his prison reflections."[60] De Gruchy notes that there is a continuity within Bonhoeffer's work relating to his understanding of revelation and reality:

> Throughout his theological development, Bonhoeffer had sought to relate a theology of revelation to reality, first focused on the church, but very soon encompassing the world as a whole, whether understood negatively (*Cost of Discipleship*) or more positively in prison.[61]

De Gruchy's analysis shows that it is possible to hold the view that there is movement within Bonhoeffer's theology.

I agree with Schlingensiepen that the people with whom Bonhoeffer lived and worked in the war years, both in the Resistance and in prison, play a central part in the shift we find occurring in his theology at this time. Because of them, Bonhoeffer begins to realize that in fact there is not a specific, prescribed way in which to describe how to become a Christian. Bonhoeffer's letter to Bethge dated the 21st of July 1944 shows that he is aware that his thoughts on the matter have evolved since writing *Discipleship*. Recounting a conversation with Jean Lasserre, in which they discussed what they wanted to do with their lives, Bonhoeffer writes:

> And he said, I want to become a saint (and I think it's possible that he did become one). This impressed me very much at the time. Nevertheless, I disagreed with him, saying something like: I want to learn to have faith. For a long time I did not understand the depth of this antithesis. I thought myself could learn to have faith by trying to live something like a saintly life. I suppose I wrote *Discipleship* at the end of this path. Today I clearly see the dangers of that book, though I still stand by it. Later on I discovered, and am still discovering to this day, that one only learns to have faith by living in the full this-worldliness of life. If one has completely renounced making something of oneself—whether it be a saint or a converted sinner of a church leader (a so-called priestly figure!), a just or an unjust person, a sick or a healthy person—then one throws oneself completely into the arms of God, and this is what I call this-worldliness: living fully in the midst of life's tasks, questions, successes and failures, experiences, and perplexities—then one takes seriously no longer one's own sufferings but rather the sufferings of God in the world.[62]

This passage shows that Bonhoeffer realizes that he had changed his view on how an individual can learn to have faith. Although he maintains a connection with his earlier work, he recognizes that his previous opinion on how an individual can become a Christian has altered.

With the notable exception of Wilhelm Dilthey, as discussed in the previous chapter, it is very unlikely that any of the books that Bonhoeffer read in prison influenced his work on unconscious Christianity. Indeed, as Bethge suggests,[63] Bonhoeffer's 1944 theology as a whole was influenced more by the experiences of the War Courts, his fellow prisoners, and even secular literature, than any theological publications he might have read in prison.[64] Interestingly, Bonhoeffer started reading Dilthey in early 1944, when he ceased to read Stifter and other nineteenth-century literature.[65] Indeed, while it is impossible to confirm this hypothesis, it may be suggested that in reading Dilthey Bonhoeffer's thoughts may have turned to other authors he had previously read who address the secularization of the West. He might have been reminded of the liberal theology of the early twentieth century, and possibly of texts like Rade's article on unconscious Christianity that he might have read during his university studies, that the rise of Barth and dialectical theology superseded. Bonhoeffer's reading of Dilthey and the possible reminders that this triggered coincides with the time at which he wrote *Story*, in which Bonhoeffer depicts for the first time an unconscious Christian who does not come from a *bürgerlich* background. As will be shown in the following section, *Story* represents a development in Bonhoeffer's thoughts on unconscious Christianity, and it is therefore possible that this development was triggered by reading Dilthey.

Bethge argues that in his later writing Bonhoeffer broadened his view of how the world and Christ relate to each other, adding: "In biographical terms the chief influences were Bonhoeffer's experience with the Confessing Church and the political conspiracy, both of which required him to develop new concepts."[66] The broadening of Bonhoeffer's focus both in terms of the relation between Christ and the world and his life experiences are reflected in his work on unconscious Christianity, as he widens his thoughts on what Christianity is to include people who do not self-identify as Christians. Despite his insistence on the overall unity of Bonhoeffer's theology, Bethge uses strong words to emphasize the change in Bonhoeffer's thought in April 1944:

> The phrase [nonreligious Christianity] was first used by Bonhoeffer when, in the last year of his life, he was moved by a new impulse to *re-examine* his theology. This new approach breathed the optimism of a *break-through* that was entirely in contrast to the situation in which he found himself at that time.[67]

And

> Bonhoeffer himself said again how much he regarded himself as being involved in a reshaping of theology.[68]

Bethge sees a link between Bonhoeffer's prison question "Who is Christ for us today?" and what Bonhoeffer was asking in 1932, in his lecture series *Creation and Fall*, relating to Christ as the center of existence.[69] Referring to the letter dated the 30th of April 1944, Bethge writes:

> [. . .] Bonhoeffer is enquiring into the way in which Christ is Lord, and not into a method whereby he can be presented today. With this kind of enquiry he took up again what he had said as early as 1932, namely that it is not a question of how we ought to proclaim the Gospels today but, in view of the historical development of the Western world, of who is its content. Given the presupposition of the presence of Christ, Bonhoeffer seeks to understand his presence today.[70]

The vital question for Bonhoeffer is still the same in 1944 as it had been at the beginning of his career: "Who is Christ for us today?" However, the way in which Bonhoeffer goes about answering the question has changed. He is committed to learning to have faith by living in the "full this-worldliness of life."[71] Bethge describes the shift between Bonhoeffer's concept of learning to have faith portrayed in *Discipleship* and that which he espouses in prison:

> Although his early Christology had to lead Bonhoeffer eventually to *The Cost of Discipleship*, the exclusive claim of Christ he had asserted there had in-

volved the risk of narrowness, and so the onesided cry of "the world for Christ" had to be counterbalanced by "Christ for the world."[72]

The emphasis that Bonhoeffer puts on learning to have faith by living life in the world rather than by following a specific pattern, such as that laid out in *Discipleship*, shows how his understanding of humanity's relationship with God has evolved between *Discipleship* and the Tegel years. There are more ways than one of having faith. There are more ways than one of being a Christian.

Development within Bonhoeffer's Work on Unconscious Christianity

Having shown how Bonhoeffer's circumstances influence his thought, attention must be drawn here to the influence Bonhoeffer's upbringing clearly had on the way in which he started writing about unconscious Christianity. The unconscious Christians portrayed in "Ultimate and Penultimate Things" and to an even greater extent in *Novel*, are people with whom he was familiar and whose cultural context he shared. The fact that in *Novel* the unconscious Christians are members of the *Bürgertum* shows how closely he associated the concept with his family and immediate cultural context. Bonhoeffer did not, of course, identify the cultural context of his family as being one of unconscious Christianity as he was growing up. However, the fact that in *Novel* it is Christoph's own parents who are portrayed as unconscious Christians could readily be seen to indicate that while in prison and thinking over his own past, Bonhoeffer concludes that the cultural atmosphere in which he grew up was informed by unconscious Christianity.

In *Novel* Bonhoeffer associates unconscious Christianity with members of the *Bürgertum*,[73] and describes the Brake children as having different values from other children, a fact that can be observed in the anecdote he includes in *Novel*, in which they make fun of other children's nicknames.[74] That the young Bonhoeffers also had different values from other children is attested to by Leibholz-Bonhoeffer's recollections of her school days, in which she pinpoints differences in behavior between herself and other members of her school, and writes of herself and her siblings: "there was something that united us, something that we owed to our parents."[75] The nickname anecdote is particularly telling when linked to unconscious Christianity as depicted in *Novel*, the main element of which is that unconscious Christians do not wish to be other than what they are. The fact that the Brake children do not go by nicknames and think such a practice foolish echoes the idea that because of the culture of unconscious Christianity in which they are being brought up they are content with who they are, not wishing to pretend that they are something else. This echoes what Bonhoeffer had written in his 1927 doctoral thesis *Sanctorum Communio*. Here Bonhoeffer argues that only when confronted with God, the divine "Thou," can the "I" truly know itself.[76] What is new in the case of unconscious Christians is that this encounter with the divine "Thou" can take place without the "I" being conscious of it.[77] Also, while unconscious Christians are immune from false ambition, they do not recognize their Christianity, indicating that they either cannot or choose not to know themselves fully.

Considering the first two of the four texts that mention unconscious Christianity, therefore, it is easy to see that Bonhoeffer is finally putting a name onto a way of living that he has known all his life. By doing so, he is giving the people who surrounded him during most of his life a spiritual dimension, and relating them to Christ in a way that they themselves would never think to do. In this sense, Bonhoeffer's work on unconscious Christianity shows a continuation with his previous life experience.

However, a change occurs between the first and second pair of texts. In the latter texts, the letter to Bethge and "Notes II," which were written within days of each other, or even possibly at the same time, Bonhoeffer introduces the ideas of an act of faith upon which the agent cannot reflect, and unconscious participation in Jesus's being-for-others. In these texts Bonhoeffer does not refer to a group of people located in a specific time, place, and cultural context, as he does in the first two texts, but points to actions that define people as unconscious Christians.

Bonhoeffer's *Story*, written in February/March 1944, illustrates the development in Bonhoeffer's thought between the first and second pair of texts that mention unconscious Christianity. There is a change of tone and pace in *Story*, compared with *Drama* and *Novel*, which conveys a greater sense of urgency to the prison narrative. Combined with Bethge's assessment that "April 1944 was clearly a milestone in Bonhoeffer's life in prison. We can see this from the change in his reading, his new manner of working, and the different tone of his letters,"[78] *Story* gains importance as the work that propelled Bonhoeffer into a new phase in his theological writing. Indeed, as I argued in the previous chapter, it is in *Story* that Bonhoeffer explores what an unconscious Christian's life would resemble in a world whose godlessness is laid bare. Lance Corporal Berg, the unconscious Christian hero of *Story*, is quite a different character from the unconscious Christian Brake parents of *Novel*. The reader knows nothing about Berg's social background or cultural context outside of the prison. The *bürgerlich* attributes that the unconscious Christians of *Novel* possessed are no longer relevant for Bonhoeffer. Berg represents a move away from an understanding of unconscious Christianity that is greatly informed by Bonhoeffer's early life experience, and a move toward an understanding of it that is influenced by the people who worked alongside Bonhoeffer in the resistance and those he met in prison.

UNCONSCIOUS CHRISTIANITY AS A NEW CONCEPT THAT REPRESENTS A SHIFT IN BONHOEFFER'S THEOLOGY

There are three facts that show that unconscious Christianity was a new concept in Bonhoeffer's thought when it appeared in the margin of "Ultimate and Penultimate Things." Firstly, the term occurs nowhere in his previous writing. Secondly, when he addresses Bethge on the matter in July 1944, he talks of a "very wide-reaching problem"[79] that is only now beginning to be addressed. Thirdly, when Bethge writes to Bonhoeffer in August 1944, he asks what further thoughts his friend has had regarding unconscious Christianity, implying that it is a new subject on which he has not yet heard many of Bonhoeffer's ideas. He also says that the matter is "so very important," conveying a sense of urgency about Bonhoeffer's development of the concept.[80] If Bonhoeffer had considered unconscious Christianity in the past, Bethge would surely have known about it.

These three facts are apparent from even a brief survey of the texts involved, and serve to show that unconscious Christianity is a new concept in Bonhoeffer's writing. However, a closer study of the texts reveals that not only is unconscious Christianity a new concept, but one that causes Bonhoeffer to reject a previously deeply held conviction: that self-identification as a "Christian," and, in some contexts, as a specific type of Christian, is a central element of Christianity.

Self-Identification in Bonhoeffer's Early Theology

In *Discipleship* it is clear that Bonhoeffer considers self-identifying as Christian to be essential for an individual to be a Christian. In a section called "The Visible Church-Community," he describes the group of people who make up the body of Christ on earth. He writes: "The body of Christ becomes visible in the church-community that gathers around word and sacrament."[81] The people making up the body of Christ on earth, therefore, are people who self-identify as Christians; otherwise they would not gather together to celebrate the Eucharist and to hear the God's word preached. Furthermore, this group "claims a *space* in this world *for its proclamation*."[82] They have a message to proclaim, the content of which is the call of Christ to discipleship, and they consciously want to be able to proclaim this to the world. The body of Christ as defined by Bonhoeffer here: "The Christian community is thus essentially the community gathered to celebrate baptism and the Lord's Supper,"[83] cannot include anyone who does not self-identify as Christian.

Further evidence of how central self-identification as Christian is to Bonhoeffer's view of Christianity in the 1930s can be found in his efforts to present the Confessing Church as the true Church in Germany. During the years of the *Kirchenkampf*, Bonhoeffer was committed to obtaining recognition for the Confessing Church in European ecumenical circles. His aim was to demonstrate that the Confessing Church represented the true German church, and that the Reich Church should not be invited to international ecumenical conferences.[84] His work to convince people to accept the Confessing Church as the true church of Germany took various forms: meeting foreign and German church leaders, speaking at conferences, and writing articles. In 1936, he wrote "On the Question of Church Communion," an article that contained the following sentence: "Whoever knowingly separates himself from the Confessing Church in Germany separates himself from salvation."[85] This article sparked a controversy that gave birth, Bethge notes, to the catchphrase: "Those without a Red Card won't go to heaven!"[86] However, the Rhineland Council of the Confessing Synod defended Bonhoeffer's stance, and promptly explained his problematic sentence in the following terms:

> Bonhoeffer's statements are based on the thesis that the call 'Here is the Church' is synonymous with the call 'Here is the Gospel'. The Rhineland Council sees in this thesis a legitimate interpretation of the reformatory concept of the Church. . . . Anyone who persistently repudiates the call 'Here is the Church, here is the Gospel' raised by the Confessing Church in 1934, and who knowingly breaks with the Confessing Church, has broken with the Gospel as it is preached.[87]

Putting Bonhoeffer's statement into context, and recalling the position that the Confessing Church had taken in 1934 in issuing the Barmen Declaration, this statement shows that Bonhoeffer was criticizing the Reich Church, which contested the Confessing Church's validity, and also all those who had abandoned the Confessing Church. This inflammatory comment is emblematic of Bonhoeffer's agenda during this period. Bonhoeffer is preoccupied with showing who is a true Christian, and who isn't, and with defining what Christianity is through new credal statements. His context dictates that he is concerned with categorizing people according to the way in which they position themselves vis-à-vis Christianity and the Church. According to Bonhoeffer, any church that knowingly fails to stand by the Confessing Church is not behaving in a responsible manner. By claiming the status of "true church" for the Confessing Church, Bonhoeffer affirms that there is no salvation outside of it.

There is a debate to be had about Bonhoeffer's views on salvation during this period, which is too wide-ranging to be addressed here. However, what needs to be noted is that at this point in his life, Bonhoeffer attaches a great deal of import to self-identification. The point he is making in his inflammatory comment about salvation is that self-identification with the Church, in this case specifically with the Confessing Church, is a vital element of Christianity. Anyone who in the context of 1930s Germany self-identifies with an opposing or even neutral body sets himself apart from salvation. In this instance, it is not merely that self-identification as Christian is crucial to the individual's Christianity, but further, that self-identification as the "correct" type of Christian is crucial to the individual's salvation.

Thus for Bonhoeffer at this time self-identification plays an important part in knowing who is in a right relationship with God, and who is not. Those who self-identify as Christians within the Reich Church, or as simply outside of the Confessing Church, have severed their relationship with God and have separated themselves from salvation. Those, on the other hand, who self-identify as Christians within the Confessing Church maintain their relationship with God, and Bonhoeffer thinks they are saved. The way in which people self-identify in terms of their Christian faith is therefore crucial for their salvation.

Self-Identification in Bonhoeffer's Late Theology

The stance described above is clearly in opposition to what Bonhoeffer writes later about unconscious Christianity, and the need for unconscious Christians to be claimed for Christ. Unconscious Christians do not self-identify as Christians in any way, and yet Bonhoeffer does not consider this to be a barrier to their being accepted as Christians. This move away from an emphasis on self-identification is a shift in Bonhoeffer's theology.

Self-identification as Christian remains a possible form of Christian expression in the prison period, as can be seen in Bonhoeffer's concept of religionless Christianity,[88] but it is no longer the only valid form of Christian expression. In developing the idea of the form of Christian expression that is unconscious Christianity, Bonhoeffer abandons the necessity of the individual's self-identification as Christian. He instead begins to consider other identifying characteristics that define the unconscious Christian as Christian, that have been outlined above in chapter 3.

CONTINUITY BETWEEN BONHOEFFER'S EARLIER WRITING AND ASPECTS OF UNCONSCIOUS CHRISTIANITY

There are some points of continuity between unconscious Christianity and Bonhoeffer's earlier writing that plainly show that Bonhoeffer develops the idea of unconscious Christianity with terms and ideas that he had already used in his letters to Bethge, and in his *Ethics*. For instance, in the outline for a book, Bonhoeffer develops his idea of unconscious Christianity alongside that of the encounter with Christ dictating a "reversal of all human existence" to the individual. The idea of the reversal demanded by the encounter with Christ can be found in his letter to Bethge dated the 18th of July, 1944, written only a few days before these notes. In this letter, Bonhoeffer writes that Jesus asking his disciples to stay awake with him in Gethsemane illustrates the fact that Christians are called to share in God's sufferings in the world. He describes Jesus's request as "the opposite of everything a religious person expects from God."[89] Bonhoeffer's use of the word *Umkehrung* in both texts,[90] which has been translated once as "reversal" and once as "opposite," highlights the link between the ideas expressed in the letter to Bethge, and the outline for a book. Here, unconscious Christianity is associated with the idea, shocking to those Bonhoeffer describes as "religious," that God is weak and endures suffering in the world, and that Christians stand by God in this suffering. It can be deduced therefore that unconscious Christianity has nothing to do with the type of religiosity that requires a strong God, who can be called upon to preserve humanity from suffering.

Similarly, the idea that "Jesus only 'is there for others'" echoes that found in the essay "The Concrete Commandment and the Divine Mandates" in *Ethics*. There, he writes:

> In becoming human, God is revealed as the one who seeks to be there not for God's own sake but "for us." To live as a human being before God, in the light of God's becoming human, can only mean to be there not for oneself, but for God and for other human beings.[91]

This reinforces the idea that unconscious Christianity has to do with being-for-others, based on Christ's being-for-others. All this evidence points toward the fact that unconscious Christianity, as presented in the notes and the outline for a book, is a concept that is linked to some of Bonhoeffer's previous ideas, although expressed in new terms.

In the following short sections, I will discuss a series of texts that show that there is continuity between some of Bonhoeffer's earlier thought and aspects of unconscious Christianity. This is not an exhaustive list of the similarities between the early and late Bonhoeffer, but serves to highlight the ways in which unconscious Christianity follows on from Bonhoeffer's earlier ideas. Comparisons between Bonhoeffer's early thought and unconscious Christianity also show that although there are similarities between the two, unconscious Christianity is not merely a repackaging of any of the concepts he had previously explored.

Bonhoeffer in 1934: Engaging with God through Selfless Deeds of Love

During his time as a pastor in London, Bonhoeffer preached a series of sermons on 1 Corinthians 13. In one of these sermons he asks: "Why must everything else come to an end, and why does only love never end?"[92] His answer to this question bears a striking resemblance to the selfless participation in Jesus's being-for-others which is a characteristic of the unconscious Christian. In the sermon, he writes:

> Because only in love does a person let go of himself or herself and give up his or her will for the other person's benefit. Because love alone comes not from my own self but from another self, from God's self. Because it is through love alone that God acts through us—whereas in everything else it is we ourselves who are at work; it is *our thoughts, our speaking, our knowledge*—but it is God's love. And what is ours comes to an end, all of it—but what is of God remains. [. . .] Everywhere [love] goes, it finds imperfection and bears witness to perfection.[93]

Bonhoeffer is clearly addressing people who self-identify as Christian, and it is impossible to guess whether at this point he thinks that God acts through someone who does not self-identify as Christian as she carries out a deed of love in the same way as God acts through a self-identifying Christian. What is clear, however, is that the deed of love provokes a giving up of the self in the individual, and enables him to participate in God's self, the origin of the deed of love.

The question of whether the individual carrying out the deed of love needs to be conscious of her connection to God in order for God to act through her is not addressed in this 1934 sermon, whereas in the case of unconscious Christianity it is clear that a person can participate in Jesus's being-for-others without realizing it. The language used in the two time periods is also different. In 1934, Bonhoeffer writes about God acting through an individual, whereas the phrases he links to unconscious Christianity include "Jesus' 'being-for-others,'" "participating in this being of Jesus," and "encounter with Jesus Christ."[94] In the former instance the individual is presented as being more passive, and in the latter, more active. Unconscious Christianity is much more than letting go of the self in order for God to act through the human being in a deed of love, but it is interesting that ten years before writing about unconscious Christianity, Bonhoeffer spoke about people engaging with God through their selfless deeds of love for one another.

"Hidden Righteousness" in Discipleship

The text that offers the most interesting insight to how Bonhoeffer thought about the unconscious or conscious nature of following Christ before he started using the term "unconscious Christianity," is the section "Hidden Righteousness" in *Discipleship*.[95] Bonhoeffer introduces this section by quoting Matthew 6:1–4, which includes the very words to which he later links unconscious Christianity.[96] In "Hidden Righteousness," he argues that the Christian should follow Christ without knowing that he is doing so:

> The only required reflection for disciples is to be completely oblivious, completely unreflective in obedience, in discipleship, in love. If you do good, *do not let your left hand know what your right hand is doing.* You should not know your own goodness. Otherwise it will really be *your* goodness, and not the goodness of Christ. The goodness of Christ, the goodness of discipleship takes place without awareness. The genuine deed of love is always a deed hidden to myself.[97]

At the end of this section Bonhoeffer adds that love for Christ, which he equates with the deed of simple obedience to Christ, entails the death of the old self. Instead of the old self, Christ lives in the loving and obedient person: "Love as the deed of simple obedience is death to the old self and the self's discovery to exist now in the righteousness of Christ and in one's brothers and sisters. Then the old self is no longer alive, but Christ is alive in the person."[98] The relationship between the human being and Christ that Bonhoeffer envisages in this text is similar to the one he describes in his "Outline for a Book."[99] As noted in chapter 3, Bonhoeffer thinks that in participating in Jesus's being-for-others, the unconscious Christian undergoes a liberation from the self, and has faith, albeit unconsciously. The disciple described in "Hidden Righteousness" has died to his old self, which can be equated to a liberation from the self, and Christ is alive in him, which can be equated to participation in Christ's being-for-others.

However, there is a significant difference between the two types of people under discussion in these two texts. In *Discipleship*, the loss of awareness of the self, which makes it possible for the disciple to perform a deed of "self-forgetting love"[100] without realizing it, comes at the end of a process that began with the disciple recognizing Christ and striving for obedience to Christ. The unconscious deed of love is the result of a conscious effort at discipleship. That the unconscious deed of love and a conscious effort to obey Christ are linked is reinforced by Bonhoeffer's choice of language: he refers to the "genuine deed of love"[101] also as "the deed of simple obedience,"[102] which presupposes a conscious desire to obey, in this instance, Christ.[103]

In *Discipleship*, Bonhoeffer outlines a sequence of events that must take place in a specific order for an individual to become a disciple. Firstly, Christ must call the individual. The response to the call of Christ cannot happen before the call itself has been given.[104] Secondly, the person called must take a "first step," which "puts the follower into the situation of being able to believe."[105] The potential disciple moves, with the first step, from a situation in which he cannot believe, into a new situation in which it is possible for him to believe. Bonhoeffer describes the call and the first step thus:

> Christ has to have called; the step can be taken only at his word. This call is his grace, which calls us out of death into the new life of obedience. [. . .] So it is,

indeed, the case that the first step of obedience is itself an act of faith in Christ's word. But it would completely misrepresent the essence of faith to conclude that that step is no longer necessary, because in that step there had already been faith. To the contrary, we must venture to state that the step of obedience must be done first, before there can be faith. The disobedient cannot have faith.[106]

This passage makes clear that obedience is vital if the individual called by Christ is to become a disciple. This obedience is consciously enacted, although at the point of taking the first step the individual does not consciously have faith in Christ. He simply knows he has received a call and is following the one who calls him: "What is said about the content of discipleship? Follow me, walk behind me! That is all."[107] It should be noted in passing that Bonhoeffer's description of the first step as an "act of faith in Christ's word" bears remarkable similarity to his thoughts about unconscious Christianity as an act of faith, akin to the *fides directa* of the infant at baptism. What distinguishes the latter is that it is in no way linked to an act of obedience to the call carried out consciously, as is the case with the former.

In respect to unconscious Christianity, Bonhoeffer does not outline a sequence of events that must take place in order for the individual to be an unconscious Christian. However, the idea that the unconscious Christian is obeying Christ is present in his work on the subject. Writing about Christ's call to his disciples to stay awake with him in Gethsemane, Bonhoeffer states that in this command Christ overturns the religious person's expectation of what God wants from them.[108] Bonhoeffer associates Christ's call in Gethsemane with the idea that Christ calls human beings to suffer in the world alongside him. As noted in chapter 4, Bonhoeffer links his poem "Christians and Heathens" to Christ's call in Gethsemane, commenting that it is the willingness to stand by God in God's own pain that distinguishes Christians from heathens, and that by this call Christ asks human beings to "share in God's sufferings at the hands of a godless world."[109] Part of the definition of unconscious Christianity that I propose is that unconscious Christians participate in Jesus's being-for-others. This being-for-others implies sharing God's suffering in the world. It is therefore possible to say that unconscious Christians, who participate in Jesus's being-for-others and share God's suffering in the world are obeying Christ's call to watch in Gethsemane. They do not do so consciously, but, like the disciples described in "Hidden Righteousness," they obey Christ's call and find themselves in a situation that Bonhoeffer describes as having faith.[110]

In *Discipleship*, the call of Christ does not cause the individual's positive response of obedience to the call; the person called can choose to ignore the call.[111] However, while not being in a causal relationship, Christ's call and the individual's decision to respond positively to that call follow on from each other in a sequence that cannot be reversed. Does Bonhoeffer have a similar prescriptive approach to unconscious Christianity? Is there a pattern that must be adhered to in order for an individual to become an unconscious Christian, as there is for an individual to enact hidden discipleship?

In *Discipleship*, Bonhoeffer envisages the deed of love carried out unconsciously as following on from a previous encounter with Christ. This pattern of encounter with Christ preceding a selfless deed of love could be applied to the unconscious Christians that Bonhoeffer describes in "Ultimate and Penultimate Things." In the essay, the unconscious Christians are those who "no longer dare to call themselves Christians," indicating that they previously had identified themselves as such, which in turn indicates that they have had an encounter with Christ.[112] The unconscious Christians of "Ultimate and Penultimate Things" share the pattern of unconscious discipleship following on from conscious discipleship with the hidden disciples described in *Discipleship*. However, there is an important difference between the two groups of people: The unconscious Christians have at some point made a conscious decision to stop identifying as Christian. The disciples in "Hidden Righteousness," on the other hand, have not made this decision, and their unconscious discipleship is a consequence of their continued effort to follow Christ.

The comparison between these two groups of people indicates that Bonhoeffer's thoughts on unconscious Christianity developed substantially between his writing "Ultimate and Penultimate Things" and his later work. The later texts do not contain the idea that a conscious self-identification as Christian must necessarily precede the state of being an unconscious Christian. Furthermore, despite similarity between the unconscious Christians depicted in "Ultimate and Penultimate Things" and the disciples described in *Discipleship*, the shift brought about in Bonhoeffer's thought by the concept of unconscious Christianity must be highlighted. Bonhoeffer now envisions a type of Christian whose engagement with Christ is completely detached from any conscious desire to follow Christ.

Unification in Christ between the Reality of God and the Reality of the World in "Christ, Reality, and Good"

In his later work on unconscious Christianity, instead of retaining the individual's self-identification as Christian as a crucial element of Christianity, Bonhoeffer presents the idea of an unconscious response to Christ in the world. The groundwork for his understanding of how a human being can unconsciously engage with Christ's suffering presence in the world, which he develops in *Letters and Papers*, can be found in *Ethics*.

In his essay "Christ, Reality, and Good,"[113] Bonhoeffer argues that because of the incarnation of Christ in the world, the reality of God and the reality of the world have become unified. He writes:

> The reality of God is not just another idea. Christian faith perceives this in the fact that the reality of God has revealed itself and witnessed to itself in the middle of the real world. *In Jesus Christ the reality of God has entered into the reality of this world.* The place where the questions about the reality of God and about the reality of the world are answered at the same time is characterized solely by the name: Jesus Christ.[114]

Bonhoeffer states that the will of God has been fulfilled in the reconciliation, in Christ, between Godself and the world. The consequence for ethics of this unification is that the individual no longer needs to ask himself, "How can I be good and do good?" but instead must simply participate in the reality of the world, which is also the reality of God. Bonhoeffer calls this the "reality of the fulfilled will of God," and goes on to write: "But to partake in this is possible only because of the fact that even I myself am already included in the fulfilment of the will of God in Christ, which means that I have been reconciled to God."[115] According to Bonhoeffer, every human being lives in the reality of a world that has been united to God. It is possible that some people will not recognize this reality, but that does not take away from the fact that the world "has no reality of its own independent of God's revelation in Christ."[116] In discussing whether there might be a part of reality that is divided from Christ, Bonhoeffer writes: "The world is not divided between Christ and the devil; it is completely the world of Christ, whether it recognizes this or not."[117]

At this time Bonhoeffer believed that only those who had faith were able to know that "God alone is the ultimate reality,"[118] and that it was only by consciously having faith in Christ that one might perceive the world as it truly is, united by Christ to the reality of God:

> There is access to this wholeness, without being torn apart by manifold influences, only through faith in Jesus Christ, "in whom the whole fullness of deity dwells bodily" (Col. 2:9; 1:19), "through whom everything is reconciled, whether on earth or in heaven" (Col. 1:20) [. . .].[119]

Only through conscious faith in Christ could an individual know the world as it really is, and thus act within the world according to the reality of the world reconciled with God.

In his later writing, Bonhoeffer develops the idea of participating in the real world according to the will of God in terms of participating in Jesus's suffering and being-for-others in the world. But when he comes to articulate this idea in new terms, he has altered his view on who is able to participate in the real world according to its reality as reconciled with God. Such a participation is no longer the exclusive action of conscious Christians; unconscious Christians are capable of it as well. It is easy to see how the radical ideas that Bonhoeffer broaches in his prison writings about unconscious Christians participating in Jesus's suffering at the hands of a godless world are different from, but at the same time are embedded in, his ideas about Christians being able to perceive the world as reconciled to God in Christ.

Christ and Good People in "Church and World I"

In the essay "Church and World I," written in the autumn of 1942, Bonhoeffer broaches the question of Christ's relationship with good people. As noted previously, it is his attempt to deal with the question of this relationship that propels Bonhoeffer toward articulating his concept of unconscious Christianity.[120] In the essay, Bonhoeffer discusses a phenomenon that he observes occurring in his time and place: People seeking to uphold justice, truth, humanity, and freedom are turning to Jesus Christ in order to find justification for these values:

> It is not Christ who has to justify himself before the world by acknowledging the values of justice, truth, and freedom. Instead, it is these values that find themselves in need of justification, and their justification is Jesus Christ alone. It is not a "Christian culture" that still has to make the name of Jesus Christ acceptable to the world; instead, the crucified Christ has become the refuge, justification, protection, and claim for these higher values and their defenders who have been made to suffer.[121]

Bonhoeffer calls the people seeking to uphold such values "good,"[122] and states that whereas in times of peace and stability it is through redemption of the "wicked" that Christ's gospel can be seen, in times of upheaval and lawlessness it is through the "good" that the gospel is best perceived.[123] He uses two of Christ's sayings to illustrate the relationship that the Christian community can have with the good people. As he had already done elsewhere,[124] he places the following sayings side by side: "Whoever is not with me is against me," and "Whoever is not against us is for us."[125] He does so in order to highlight the dangers of taking the two statements separately, which could lead to "fanaticism and sectarianism" or "the secularization and capitulation of the church" respectively.[126] Taken together, he argues, they bring to the Christian community a sharper recognition of Christ as Lord, together with a wider understanding of who falls under Christ's lordship: "The more exclusively we recognize and confess Christ as our Lord, the more will be disclosed to us the breadth of Christ's lordship."[127]

Bonhoeffer clarifies what he means by the "breadth of Christ's lordship," arguing that it is not only those who suffer explicitly for the sake of Christ that come under Christ's care, but also those who suffer for values such as truth and justice.[128] He cites the eighth beatitude[129] in order to show that "it calls those blessed who are persecuted for a just cause—and, we may now add, for a cause that is good, true, humane [. . .]."[130] He makes his point even clearer by writing:

> Jesus cares for those who suffer for a just cause even if it is not exactly for the confession of his name; he brings them under his protection, takes responsibility for them, and addresses them with his claim. Thus the person persecuted for a just cause is led to Christ. Thus it happens that such people, in the hour of their suffering and responsibility—perhaps for the first time in their lives, in a way that is strange and surprising to themselves, but nevertheless as a most deeply felt necessity—call upon Christ and confess themselves to be Christian, because it is only at that moment that an awareness of belonging to Christ dawns on them.[131]

This excerpt shows two things: that there is continuity between this essay and the texts concerning unconscious Christianity, and that in developing his thoughts on unconscious Christianity Bonhoeffer introduces a new idea that is not present in this essay about good people.

The continuity lies in the idea of the "breadth of Christ's lordship," that Christ claims for himself people who attempt to uphold a just cause and suffer in doing so, and who would not initially self-identify as Christian. The description of the good people in this essay is similar to that of the people described at the end of "Ultimate and Penultimate Things," who value the penultimate and try to preserve it. In "Ultimate and Penultimate Things" Bonhoeffer writes that those who value the penultimate should be claimed for Christ and recognized as Christians, even if they themselves "no longer dare to call themselves Christians."[132] In both texts Bonhoeffer argues that people who initially would not claim Christ for themselves are claimed by Christ, and should be recognized as such by the Christian community. Furthermore, the Christian community should itself claim these people for Christ. It is not surprising that there is continuity between "Ultimate and Penultimate Things" and "Church and World I," as they were both written in the war years before Bonhoeffer's arrest and are both part of the *Ethics*. What is perhaps more surprising, due to the difference of the contexts in which the texts were written, is the strength of the continuity between "Church and World I" and Bonhoeffer's poem "Christians and Heathens."[133] In the poem's second stanza, Bonhoeffer echoes his thoughts about good people articulated in his *Ethics* essay:

> People go to God when God's in need,
> find God poor, reviled, without shelter or bread,
> see God devoured by sin, weakness, and death.
> Christians stand by God in God's own pain.[134]

The people described here are those who suffer alongside God in the world. Because of Bonhoeffer's view of what suffering alongside God in the world involves it is possible to assert that these people are also those referred to in "Church and World I." In the second stanza of the poem, the good people first appear without a name being given to them, but by the end of the stanza they are called "Christians." Bethge comments of the second stanza of "Christians and Heathens": "This is the striking definition of what 'Christianity without religion' really is."[135]

In the poem Bonhoeffer does what, in "Church and World I," he says the Christian community should do; he claims the good people for Christ.

The second part of the above excerpt from "Church and World I," however, shows how much of a shift unconscious Christianity brings about in Bonhoeffer's theology. In this text, Bonhoeffer writes of a dawning "awareness of belonging to Christ." Furthermore, he states that the good people "confess themselves to be Christian," something that he never specifies as occurring in the case of unconscious Christians. The two points that Bonhoeffer makes here, that the good people become aware of Christ and confess themselves to be Christian are at odds with his later understanding of unconscious Christianity. The people that he describes at the end of "Ultimate and Penultimate Things," it is true, have an awareness of Christ because they "no longer dare to call themselves Christians,"[136] but in the other three instances in which he uses the term in his prison texts, there is no question of either an awareness of Christ, nor of a self-identification as Christian. The good people described in "Church and World I" experience an encounter with Christ that causes a conscious reaction on their behalf of awareness of Christ, followed by self-identification as Christian. The unconscious Christian's unconscious encounter with Christ does not trigger such a reaction.[137]

This excerpt from "Church and World I" serves a double purpose, being an illustration not only of continuity between Bonhoeffer's thoughts concerning good people and unconscious Christians, but also of the shift in focus away from self-identification as 'Christian' that unconscious Christianity brings to Bonhoeffer's theology.

Two final points about Bonhoeffer's view of good people must be made in closing this section. It was noted in chapter 3 that in Bonhoeffer's fiction, in addition to land and status in the world, the unconscious inheritance of Christianity appears to be exclusively a commodity of the *Bürgertum*. However, it is important to clarify that Bonhoeffer does not think that being a member of the *Bürgertum* automatically implies Christianity. This can be seen not only in the dialogue between Christoph and Ulrich, but also in a sentence Bonhoeffer deleted from "Church and World I":

> When we are compelled today to reflect on this very question [of the conversion of the good person to Christ], we know ourselves to be equally at odds with two fatal misrepresentations. The *first* is the understanding of bourgeois goodness as a preliminary stage of the Christian life, progress from goodness

to the Christian life taking place more or less without break. The *second* is the idealization of those biblical.[138]

For Bonhoeffer, becoming Christian cannot be seen as a point on a sliding scale, where one starts off as a good person and gradually arrives at the "Christian" point on the scale. An encounter with Christ must take place. However, in developing unconscious Christianity, he allows for the encounter with Christ to take place without the individual being aware of it. Of equal danger is the view that in order to encounter Christ everyone should attempt to become like the marginal figures in the gospel narratives, the prostitutes and tax collectors, whom Christ encounters in their sinful existence. Bonhoeffer argues that Christ also encounters good people, and claims them for himself. This point is of such import to Bonhoeffer that scholars have stated: "This theme of the good to which Christ himself lays claim, provoked not least by Bonhoeffer's own experiences in the resistance, permeates his entire work on the *Ethics*."[139] In fact, it permeates not only his work on *Ethics*, but also his development of the concept of unconscious Christianity.

CONCLUDING COMMENTS

This chapter has shown that in his working toward an understanding of unconscious Christianity, Bonhoeffer takes his theological investigation to its logical next step, pursuing his attempt to answer his question "Who is Christ for us today?"[140] He allows his theology to be influenced by the reality of the world around him, by his personal situation and the people he meets, something he had done all his life.[141] So committed is he to taking reality seriously that he is prepared to relinquish convictions he had previously held, if reality demands it. His abandoning of the idea that self-identification is a crucial component of Christianity illustrates his readiness to do this.

In developing the concept of unconscious Christianity, Bonhoeffer provides himself with a new lens through which he can look at things with which he is already familiar, and see them in a new way. For example, through the lens of unconscious Christianity, he now sees his family, and, more broadly, good people who act in specific ways within society, as unconscious Christians. He also sees the people who surround him in prison not simply as good people, but as unconscious Christians. This is evident in his portrayal of Berg as an unconscious Christian in *Story*.

Bonhoeffer's work on unconscious Christianity illustrates not only his readiness to accept new situations instead of resisting or ignoring them, but also his capacity to consider these new situations from a theological angle. In allowing his thought to evolve in order to take account of his changing circumstances theologically, he also makes use of his previous experiences and ideas, demonstrating his capacity for the articulation of new ideas alongside an effort at continuity of theological thought. Because to our knowledge Bonhoeffer did not develop unconscious Christianity beyond the few texts that we have, it is difficult to tell how he would have worked on it had he survived the war. It is possible that he would have applied his thoughts about the order of call, first step, and so on found in *Discipleship* to unconscious Christianity, arguing that the process of becoming a disciple of Christ was the same in both instances, with the sole difference that in the case of the unconscious Christian, the process is unconscious. Even if Bonhoeffer had not gone on to develop unconscious Christianity in this way, this chapter has shown that the new concept represents a shift, rather than a U-turn, in Bonhoeffer's thought. The question of self-identification as Christian, or even as a certain type of Christian, is no longer important in Bonhoeffer's understanding of Christianity, but I have shown that several ideas to be found in Bonhoeffer's earlier theology are also present in unconscious Christianity.

What this discussion brings to light is that there is a development in Bonhoeffer's thought on the subject of unconscious Christianity within his later writing. Unconscious Christianity as he conceives of it in "Ultimate and Penultimate Things" is closer to his thoughts on hidden righteousness than is the unconscious Christianity referred to in *Letters and Papers from Prison*. In the prison writing, unconscious Christianity has evolved into a state that requires no previous conscious engagement with Christ. It still necessitates engagement with Christ but this can happen without the subject being aware of it.

While this development in his ideas on unconscious Christianity cannot be used to argue the case for a radical rupture between his prison theology and previous writing, it shows how Bonhoeffer responded, in his theology, to the change in his physical surroundings. Always a "theologian of reality,"[142] Bonhoeffer could not ignore the reality of the world he was confronted by in his prison life. Ott notes that as Bonhoeffer's "context of thought" changed, so his thoughts developed:

> The earlier positions were neither forsaken later nor did they become simply available foundation-stones on which he subsequently built. Rather what was thought in the earlier stages is taken up in a later context of thought, without any binding force being retained by the formulation and shape in which earlier expression was given. The latest, for him at the end of his short life the most urgent, and therefore in a certain sense the ripest, thoughts, the *Ethics* and the sketch of the work on non-religious interpretation, of which only notes are to be found in *Letters and Papers from Prison*, remained skeletons, completely unshaped and fragmentary. As can be clearly demonstrated, he also passed through a certain development. Yet even so the thoughts of his early works remain living and appear again in later contexts in altered form but with unchanged substance. In spite then of all the external lack of unity, a clear inner "direction" is still typical of his work.[143]

The shift in his view of the relation between Christianity and conscious engagement with Christ, and the conclusion he reaches that in the case of unconscious Christianity it is possible to have the one without the other, is the result of his personal change in circumstances, and does not indicate a change of "inner direction." Bonhoeffer is content to allow his theology to be challenged and drawn into a new shape by the changing reality he faces, rather than attempting to build a rigid theological construct that is not troubled by realities external to it. Thus the continuity that permeates his theology is not contrived or forced, but organic, developing as he encounters new people and ideas. John de Gruchy sums up the fluid nature of the continuity in Bonhoeffer's theology:

> There has been considerable debate about whether the theological probings expressed in these last writings indicate a radical turning point in Bonhoeffer's theology. With some justification, the proponents of this view argue that the Bonhoeffer of the letters has finally broken with Barth's theology of the Word, and shifted his sights away from the church to the world. However, the majority of commentators claim, rightly in my view, that there is remarkable continuity in Bonhoeffer's theology from beginning to end. This does not mean that there were no important changes; clearly there were. But these were responses to changing reality worked out in relation to the foundations already laid, not radical breaks with previously held positions.[144]

The change in Bonhoeffer's idea of unconscious Christianity, from necessitating a conscious engagement with Christ to this engagement being of an unconscious nature is not in itself a "radical break with previously held positions." Engagement with Christ is still vital to unconscious Christianity. However, the consequences of this change are themselves radical. People whom Bonhoeffer would have previously considered to be outside the Church are now part of the Church. Individuals who might not want to be considered Christians are summarily named as such by Bonhoeffer. Acts of selfless love and being-for-others, with no reference to Christ, are now indicators of Christianity and of belonging in the Christian community.

As John de Gruchy rightly points out, the theological foundations on which Bonhoeffer built his view of the world did not change, but the shift in his understanding of manners of engaging with Christ, to encompass the possibility of unconscious engagement with Christ, caused him to view human beings and their relation to Christ in a wholly new way. In the conclusion, I turn to the implications that Bonhoeffer's developing ideas on unconscious Christianity have for us all.

Chapter 5

NOTES

1. For more details on the successive editions of *Widerstand und Ergebung*, and the various translations that ensued, see Martin E. Marty, *Dietrich Bonhoeffer's Letters and Papers from Prison: A Biography* (Princeton & Oxford: Princeton University Press, 2011), chapters 1 and 2.

2. Schlingensiepen, *Dietrich Bonhoeffer, 1906–1945*, 350–51. Schlingensiepen quotes from Hermann Schlingensiepen: "Zum Vermächtnis Dietrich Bonhoeffers (On the Legacy of Dietrich Bonhoeffer)," in *Die Mündige Welt*, ed. Jørgen Glenthoj, 2nd ed. (Munich: Kaiser Verlag., 1955), 96ff.

3. Schlingensiepen, *Dietrich Bonhoeffer, 1906–1945*, 351.

4. Hans-Richard Reuter, Editor's Afterword to the German Edition of Bonhoeffer, *Act and Being*, 181.

5. Here Reuter references Dietrich Bonhoeffer, *Discipleship*, eds. Geffrey B. Kelly and John D. Godsey, trans. Barbara Green and Reinhard Krauss (Minneapolis: Fortress Press, 2001), 87ff, 192, and 175ff.

6. Here Reuter references Bonhoeffer, *Ethics*, 320.

7. Here Reuter references Bonhoeffer, *Ethics*, 67.

8. Reuter, Editor's Afterword, 181. Here Reuter references Bonhoeffer, *Letters and Papers from Prison*, the letter dated the 27th of July 1944 in relation to unconscious Christianity, the letter dated 18th of July 1944 in relation to partaking in God's suffering, and the letter dated the 8th of July 1944 in relation to the nonreligious interpretation of biblical concepts.

9. Reuter, Editor's Afterword, 181.

10. See for example Geffrey B. Kelly, "Prayer and action for justice: Bonhoeffer's spirituality," in *The Cambridge Companion to Dietrich Bonhoeffer*, 246–68; and André Dumas, *Dietrich Bonhoeffer: Theologian of Reality*, trans. Robert McAfee Brown (London: SCM Press, 1971), 70.

11. Bethge attributes these names to the three time periods in a series of three lectures, of the same respective names, pertaining to Bonhoeffer's life and theology. These lectures appeared grouped together as an article in *Die Mündige Welt*, vol. IV, part of a four-volume collection of essays on Bonhoeffer edited by Bethge that was published between 1955 and 1963. This article later appeared as "The Challenge of Dietrich Bonhoeffer's Life and Theology" in *World Come of Age: A Symposium on Dietrich Bonhoeffer*, ed. Ronald Gregor Smith (London: Collins, 1967), 22–92.

12. Eberhard Bethge, "The Challenge of Dietrich Bonhoeffer's Life and Theology," 25.

13. Leibholz-Bonhoeffer, *The Bonhoeffers*, 45.

14. Leibholz-Bonhoeffer, *The Bonhoeffers*, 45.

15. Eberhard Bethge, *Dietrich Bonhoeffer: Theologian, Christian, Contemporary*, 759.

16. Eberhard Bethge, *Dietrich Bonhoeffer: Theologian, Christian, Contemporary*, 763.

17. Eberhard Bethge, *Dietrich Bonhoeffer: Theologian, Christian, Contemporary*, 793.

18. Eberhard Bethge, *Dietrich Bonhoeffer: Theologian, Christian, Contemporary*, 793.

19. John D. Godsey, *The Theology of Dietrich Bonhoeffer* (Philadelphia: Westminster Press, 1960), 262.

20. Marty, *Dietrich Bonhoeffer's Letters and Papers from Prison*, 23: "Without taking away from the radicalism of his observations and proposals, it becomes obvious that Christology remained the central theme."

21. Marty, *Dietrich Bonhoeffer's Letters and Papers from Prison*, 214–15.

22. See Dumas, *Dietrich Bonhoeffer*, 70.

23. Dumas, *Dietrich Bonhoeffer*, 70. Dumas cites Eberhard Bethge in *Die Mündige Welt*, I (Munich, Kaiser Verlag., 1955), 24.

24. Dumas, *Dietrich Bonhoeffer*, 73.

25. See Bonhoeffer, *Letters and Papers from Prison*, 357–59, letter dated the 22nd of April 1944. This letter is quoted and discussed in more detail later in this chapter.

26. Dumas, *Dietrich Bonhoeffer*, 74, footnote 83.

27. Henry Mottu, *Dietrich Bonhoeffer*, (Paris: Cerf, 2010), 52. Mottu is in fact citing and translating Eberhard Bethge, "eine spürbare Zäsur," (a noticeable caesura). See Eberhard Beth-

ge, *Dietrich Bonhoeffer, Theologe, Christ, Zeitgenossse*, (Munich: Chr. Kaiser Verlag., 1967), 959.

28. Mottu, *Dietrich Bonhoeffer*, 52–53.
29. Mottu, *Dietrich Bonhoeffer*, 53.
30. Paul van Buren was so inspired by Bonhoeffer's life story and martyrdom that he compared him to W. H. Auden's Christ-figure, the "Universal Man," and posited him as an example of what is means to be a "citizen of this modern, adult world." See Paul van Buren, *The Secular Meaning of the Gospel, Based on an Analysis of its Language* (London: SCM Press, 1963), x and 2.
31. William Hamilton, "Thursday's Child," in *Radical Theology and the Death of God*, eds. Thomas J. J. Altizer and William Hamilton (Indianapolis, New York, & Kansas City: Bobbs-Merrill, 1966), 93.
32. William Hamilton, "Dietrich Bonhoeffer," in *Radical Theology and the Death of God*, 114.
33. Hamilton, "Dietrich Bonhoeffer," in *Radical Theology and the Death of God*, 114.
34. For a fuller discussion of Bonhoeffer's theology as used by the death of God theologians, see Eleanor McLaughlin, "Dietrich Bonhoeffer and the Death of God Theologians," in *Engaging Bonhoeffer: The Impact and Influence of Bonhoeffer's Life and Thought*, ed. Matthew D. Kirkpatrick (Minneapolis: Fortress Press, 2016), 25–43.
35. J. A. T. Robinson, *Honest to God* (London: SCM Press, 1963).
36. See Robinson, *Honest to God*, 85.
37. Robinson, *Honest to God*, 23.
38. As if there were no God.
39. Hanfried Müller, "Concerning the Reception and Interpretation of Dietrich Bonhoeffer," in *World Come of Age: A Symposium on Dietrich Bonhoeffer*, 183.
40. See Müller, "Concerning the Reception and Interpretation of Dietrich Bonhoeffer," 186.
41. Müller, "Concerning the Reception and Interpretation of Dietrich Bonhoeffer," 186.
42. Feil, *The Theology of Dietrich Bonhoeffer*, 54.
43. Feil, *The Theology of Dietrich Bonhoeffer*, 54.
44. Clements, *What Freedom?* 15.
45. Clements, *What Freedom?* 15.
46. Bonhoeffer, *Discipleship*, 61.
47. For a full description of the legislation that "would ultimately bring about the destruction both from within and from without of the newly created Confessing Church," see Bethge, *Dietrich Bonhoeffer: Theologian, Christian, Contemporary*, 343. The early phases of this legislation began in 1935.
48. The context of this letter is as follows: the Old Prussian Council decided to appoint Bonhoeffer as the director of the Berlin-Brandenburg preachers' seminary on the 4th of July 1934. (See Bethge, *Dietrich Bonhoeffer: Theologian, Christian, Contemporary*, 334). Bonhoeffer was supposed to start the new job on 1 January 1935, but asked for this to be postponed in order to be able to travel to India. However, this trip never took place. In the end, the seminary at Zingsthof opened on the 26th of April 1935. (See Bethge, *Dietrich Bonhoeffer: Theologian, Christian, Contemporary*, 839.)
49. Eberhard Bethge, Renate Bethge, and Christian Gremmels, eds., *Dietrich Bonhoeffer: A Life in Pictures*, supervisor Ulrich Kabitz, designers Ingeborg Geith and Willem Weijers, trans. John Bowden (London: SCM Press, 1986), 148.
50. Bonhoeffer, *Letters and Papers from Prison*, 357–58, dated the 22nd of April 1944. It is interesting that Bonhoeffer identifies his father's personality as being a factor, along with his first experiences of traveling outside Germany, that caused him to think in terms of reality. Bonhoeffer's sense of indebtedness to his father and the way in which he was brought up can be plainly seen in both *Drama* and *Novel*. As he describes the Brake father in *Novel* as an unconscious Christian, Bonhoeffer would have been aware that he was, in a sense, describing himself as being greatly influenced by an unconscious Christian.
51. Feil, *The Theology of Dietrich Bonhoeffer*, 53.
52. Feil, *The Theology of Dietrich Bonhoeffer*, xx.

53. See Feil, *The Theology of Dietrich Bonhoeffer*, 125–26, and 135. The period in question is Bonhoeffer's time in London, 1933–1935, and during his writing of *Discipleship*, 1937. Feil writes: "The few statements about the world from his London days, made again later in sermons, reflect a predominantly negative view of the world." And: "The basic note of the understanding of the world in *The Cost of Discipleship* sounds the decline of the world and the separation of the disciples from it."

54. Feil, *The Theology of Dietrich Bonhoeffer*, 159
55. Feil, *The Theology of Dietrich Bonhoeffer*, xx.
56. See Feil, *The Theology of Dietrich Bonhoeffer*, 53.
57. Feil, *The Theology of Dietrich Bonhoeffer*, 54.
58. Schlingensiepen, *Dietrich Bonhoeffer, 1906–1945*, 351.
59. See Schlingensiepen, *Dietrich Bonhoeffer, 1906–1945*, 351. See also Bethge, *Dietrich Bonhoeffer: Theologian, Christian, Contemporary*, 767–68. I turn to Bethge's understanding of Bonhoeffer's treatment of this question further on in this chapter.
60. De Gruchy, *Witness to Jesus Christ*, 37.
61. De Gruchy, *Witness to Jesus Christ*, 37.
62. Bonhoeffer, *Letters and Papers from Prison*, 486, letter dated the 21st of July 1944. Interestingly, Mottu notes that as Bonhoeffer and Lasserre were speaking English together, some confusion may have arisen in Bonhoeffer's recollection of Lasserre's exact words. Mottu suggests that Lasserre spoke of not of "sanctity," but of "sanctification" in the Calvinist sense. Lasserre thus would simply have been referring to the idea that the consequence of Christian faith is the sanctification of the believer, agreeing with the position Bonhoeffer espouses in *Discipleship*. Mottu does not think that Lasserre could have wished to become a saint. Mottu cites, as basis for his argument, Frédéric Rognon, "Pacifisme et tyrannicide chez Jean Lasserre et Dietrich Bonhoeffer; Seconde Partie: L'Interprétation des Incidences Théologiques," in *Etudes Théologiques et religieuses* (Montpellier), tome 80, 2 (2005): 165–69. In correspondence with the author, 26th of August 2015.
63. See Bethge, *Dietrich Bonhoeffer: Theologian, Christian, Contemporary*, 747.
64. If one reviews the list of works that Bonhoeffer read in prison, taking into account Bethge's caveat that they may not all be listed, there are no works with any reference to unconscious Christianity.
65. See Bonhoeffer, *Letters and Papers from Prison*, 600.
66. Bethge, *Dietrich Bonhoeffer: Theologian, Christian, Contemporary*, 760.
67. Bethge, *Dietrich Bonhoeffer: Theologian, Christian, Contemporary*, 757. Italics mine.
68. Bethge, *Dietrich Bonhoeffer: Theologian, Christian, Contemporary*, 764. Here Bethge is commenting on the letter he received from Bonhoeffer, dated the 23rd of August 1944. In this letter Bonhoeffer says he is shocked by what he is writing in his "Outline for a Book," in the section "A Stock-Taking of Christianity": "Sometimes I am horrified by my sentences, especially in the first, critical part" (*Letters and Papers from Prison*, 518).
69. See Bethge, *Dietrich Bonhoeffer: Theologian, Christian, Contemporary*, 793 for details of Bethge's views on this link.
70. Bethge, *Dietrich Bonhoeffer: Theologian, Christian, Contemporary*, 767–68.
71. Bonhoeffer, *Letters and Papers from Prison*, 486, letter dated the 21st of July 1944.
72. Bethge, *Dietrich Bonhoeffer: Theologian, Christian, Contemporary*, 760.
73. See chapter 3 of this book.
74. See Bonhoeffer, *Fiction from Tegel Prison*, 84.
75. Leibholz-Bonhoeffer, *The Bonhoeffers*, 13.
76. Bonhoeffer, *Sanctorum Communio*, 49: "The Christian person originates only in the absolute duality of God and humanity; only in experiencing the barrier does the awareness of oneself as ethical person arise." In his later writing, Bonhoeffer writes more of the encounter with Jesus Christ than the encounter with God.
77. Bonhoeffer does not go into detail in Ulrich and Christoph's conversation in *Novel* about how the encounter with the divine "Thou" can take place without the subject being conscious of it, and how, if the "I" is unconscious of what is happening, the encounter with the divine "Thou" can constitute a real boundary to the "I." This might be simply because of the form of this piece; an in-depth theological discussion would not sit well at this juncture in the text. It

could also be, though, that Bonhoeffer himself was not ready to attempt a systematic description of unconscious Christianity, and did not himself know more than his characters say here.
78. Bethge, *Dietrich Bonhoeffer: Theologian, Christian, Contemporary*, 758.
79. Bonhoeffer, *Letters and Papers from Prison*, 489.
80. Bonhoeffer, *Letters and Papers from Prison*, 522.
81. Bonhoeffer, *Discipleship*, 229.
82. Bonhoeffer, *Discipleship*, 229.
83. Bonhoeffer, *Discipleship*, 229.
84. Such as the conference held in Fanö in 1934.
85. Bethge, *Dietrich Bonhoeffer: Theologian, Christian, Contemporary*, 430.
86. Bethge, *Dietrich Bonhoeffer: Theologian, Christian, Contemporary*, 430. Bethge explains that "The 'Red Card' was the declaration of personal commitment by the members in confessional congregations. In some provinces it was a green card" (Bethge, *Dietrich Bonhoeffer: Theologian, Christian, Contemporary*, 430, footnote 32).
87. Cited in Bethge, *Dietrich Bonhoeffer: Theologian, Christian, Contemporary*, 433. Statement issued on the 23rd of September 1936.
88. See Bonhoeffer, *Letters and Papers from Prison*, 364: "How do we go about being 'religionless-worldly' Christians, how can we be ἐκ-κλησία, those who are called out, without understanding ourselves as belonging wholly to the world?" The people discussed here self-identify as Christians.
89. Bonhoeffer, *Letters and Papers from Prison*, 480.
90. See Bonhoeffer, *Widerstand und Ergebung*, 535 and 558.
91. Bonhoeffer, *Ethics*, 400.
92. Bonhoeffer, *London, 1933–1935*, 388.
93. Bonhoeffer, *London, 1933–1935*, 388.
94. Bonhoeffer, *Letters and Papers from Prison*, 501.
95. Bonhoeffer, *Discipleship*, 146f.
96. Matthew 6:3: "But when you give alms, do not let your left hand know what your right hand is doing." See "Notes II," in Bonhoeffer, *Letters and Papers from Prison*, 491.
97. Bonhoeffer, *Discipleship*, 150–51. Italics mine.
98. Bonhoeffer, *Discipleship*, 152.
99. See Bonhoeffer, *Letters and Papers from Prison*, 501, quoted and discussed in chapter 3 of this book.
100. Bonhoeffer, *Discipleship*, 152.
101. Bonhoeffer, *Discipleship*, 151.
102. Bonhoeffer, *Discipleship*, 152.
103. Bonhoeffer's linking of love and the deed of simple obedience is confirmed in the German original: "Die einzige und gebotene Reflexion des Nachfolgenden geht darauf, ganz unwissend, ganz unreflektiert zu sein im Gehorsam, in der Nachfolge, in der Liebe." and "Liebe als Tat des schlichten Gehorsams [. . .]" (Dietrich Bonhoeffer, *Nachfolge*, eds. Martin Kuske and Ilse Tödt (Munich: Chr. Kaiser Verlag., 1989) 155 and 156–57).
104. "None can call themselves, says Jesus [. . .] The gap between the free offer of discipleship and real discipleship remains wide open." Bonhoeffer, *Discipleship*, 60.
105. Bonhoeffer, *Discipleship*, 62.
106. Bonhoeffer, *Discipleship*, 66.
107. Bonhoeffer, *Discipleship*, 58.
108. See Bonhoeffer, *Letters and Papers from Prison*, 480.
109. See Bonhoeffer, *Letters and Papers from Prison*, 480.
110. See Bonhoeffer, *Letters and Papers from Prison*, 486.
111. See Bonhoeffer, *Discipleship*, 62.
112. It should be noted that Bonhoeffer does not assume that everyone who identifies as Christian has encountered Christ (see his comments on the "emotional community" in Bonhoeffer, *Life Together*, 35–43). However, in the case of this specific group of people, the authenticity of their self-identification (as Christian or otherwise) is confirmed for Bonhoeffer by the fact that they give the matter consideration and do not blindly follow societal models. His use of the word "dare" is interesting in that declaring oneself to be Christian in that time

and place would have been to follow the majority of society, and not a particularly daring act. So the question Bonhoeffer raises here is: In whose eyes is it daring to call oneself a Christian? Could it be that these unconscious Christians do not dare to call themselves Christian in God's eyes? Even though, according to his definition, they do not have a real grasp of the ultimate?

113. Bonhoeffer, *Ethics*, 47–75. Bonhoeffer worked on this essay in summer/autumn 1940, and again sometime between April and the end of 1941.

114. Bonhoeffer, *Ethics*, 54.

115. Bonhoeffer, *Ethics*, 74.

116. Bonhoeffer, *Ethics*, 58.

117. Bonhoeffer, *Ethics*, 65.

118. Bonhoeffer, *Ethics*, 48.

119. Bonhoeffer, *Ethics*, 75.

120. See the introduction to this book.

121. Bonhoeffer, *Ethics*, 345–46.

122. See Bonhoeffer, *Ethics*, 347.

123. See Bonhoeffer, *Ethics*, 347.

124. See Bonhoeffer's 1936 article "On the Question of Church Communion" in Dietrich Bonhoeffer, *Theological Education at Finkenwalde: 1935–1937*, DBWE vol. 14, eds. H. Gaylon Barker and Mark S. Brocker, trans. Douglas W. Scott (Minneapolis: Fortress Press, 2013), 674. Here Bonhoeffer expresses the same general idea as previously in this article, about people separating themselves from the true Church by their actions toward the Confessing Church, but articulates it in terms of people jeopardizing their belonging to the Confessing Church by their actions toward the Reich Church: "Just as any members of the Confessing Church exclude themselves from the Church of Jesus by joining the Reich Church government, so also [. . .] do those who participate in the administrative work of the church committees" (674).

125. Matthew 12:30a and Mark 9:40.

126. Bonhoeffer, *Ethics*, 344.

127. Bonhoeffer, *Ethics*, 344.

128. It is interesting to note here that Bonhoeffer had previously addressed the question of human suffering and how it connects human beings to God in a sermon on 2 Cor. 12:9 preached in London in 1934. (See Bonhoeffer, *London, 1933–1935*, 401–4.) In this sermon, entitled "my strength is made perfect in weakness," Bonhoeffer is ambiguous about whether all human suffering entails sharing God's suffering, or whether the suffering individual has to be conscious of his connection with God in order for his suffering to entail sharing God's sufferings. Appearing to support of the former view, Bonhoeffer writes: "God has suffered on the cross. It is therefore that all human suffering and weakness is sharing God's own suffering and weakness in the world" (403). And, on the other hand, seeming to support the latter, he states: "Wherever a man in physical or social or moral or religious weakness *is aware of his existence and likeness with God*, there he is sharing God's life, there he feels God being with him, there he is open for God's strength, that is God's grace, God's love, God's comfort, which passeth all understanding and all human values" (404, italics mine). The fact that Bonhoeffer does not take care to be absolutely clear about whether the suffering individual needs to be conscious of his connection to God in order to share in God's suffering shows that at this point in his life Bonhoeffer is not paying attention to the question of the distinction between conscious and unconscious participation in God's suffering in the world. This stands in sharp contrast to the way in which he thinks about human suffering and its connection to Christ in "Church and World I."

129. "Blessed are those who are persecuted for righteousness' sake, for theirs is the kingdom of heaven" (Matthew 5:10).

130. Bonhoeffer, *Ethics*, 346.

131. Bonhoeffer, *Ethics*, 346–47.

132. Bonhoeffer, *Ethics*, 170.

133. This poem was enclosed in a letter to Bethge dated the 8th of July 1944.

134. Bonhoeffer, *Letters and Papers from Prison*, 460–61.

135. Eberhard Bethge, "The Challenge of Dietrich Bonhoeffer's Life and Theology" in *World Come of Age: A Symposium on Dietrich Bonhoeffer*, 87.

136. Bonhoeffer, *Ethics*, 170.

137. The unconscious Christians described in "Ultimate and Penultimate Things" had a previous, conscious, encounter with Christ that ultimately caused a conscious reaction of rejection of self-identification as Christian. Their subsequent, unconscious, encounter with Christ does not cause a conscious reaction like the one described in "Church and World I."

138. Bonhoeffer, *Ethics*, 349 note 44. The editors suggest "biblical marginal figures" here to complete the sentence, referring to Bonhoeffer, *Ethics*, 150, where Bonhoeffer discusses how wrong it is to persuade congregations that they should first of all try to become like biblical marginal figures. Bonhoeffer uses the term "bürgerlich Guten," translated here as "bourgeois goodness." (See Bonhoeffer, *Ethik*, 351.)

139. Ilse Tödt, Heinz Eduard Tödt, Ernst Feil, and Clifford Green, Editors' Afterword to the German Edition of Bonhoeffer, *Ethics*, 430.

140. See Bonhoeffer, *Letters and Papers from Prison*, 362.

141. Feil, *The Theology of Dietrich Bonhoeffer*, 54.

142. See Dumas, *Dietrich Bonhoeffer: Theologian of Reality*.

143. Ott, *Reality and Faith*, 66.

144. De Gruchy, *Witness to Jesus Christ*, 37.

Conclusion

The Impact of Unconscious Christianity on Bonhoeffer Studies and Contemporary Theology

INTRODUCTION

In this conclusion, I begin by presenting a summing up of my findings on unconscious Christianity in Dietrich Bonhoeffer's work and its contribution to Bonhoeffer scholarship. At the same time, I recognize that my research also opens up new questions within this field. In the second section, therefore, I suggest some possible lines of inquiry that could flow from this work, noting in particular two paths for future investigations. Firstly, I ask how unconscious Christianity might be seen as an indicator of Bonhoeffer's hopeful outlook for Christianity in the postwar years, discussing it alongside his concept of "godlessness."[1] Secondly, I return to the subsidiary but important point made in this book, that the prison fiction should be considered theological. I show that if this point is taken seriously, a study of Bonhoeffer's fiction enables a better understanding not only of the theological points he raises in the fiction texts, but also of the links between the fiction and the subsequent theological letters to Bethge.

In the closing section, I turn to the implications of unconscious Christianity for the Church in the West today, asking how theology should integrate Bonhoeffer's thoughts on unconscious Christianity into its current discourse.

FINDINGS

In constructing a definition of unconscious Christianity in this book, I have shown that rather than being a static concept, unconscious Christianity is an idea that evolves over time in Bonhoeffer's thought. I have demonstrated how unconscious Christianity differs from religionless Christianity, and how an understanding of unconscious Christianity allows a deeper understanding of Bonhoeffer's late theology. It has also become clear that unconscious Christianity represents a shift within Bonhoeffer's theology. The subsidiary point I have made is that Bonhoeffer's prison fiction should be considered theological. The following recapitulation of the different parts of the book serves as a reminder for readers of the steps by which these conclusions were reached.

Over the course of the first part of this book I built a working definition of unconscious Christianity, using the texts in which Bonhoeffer mentions it as starting points and taking into account the context in which each piece was written. The fact that Bonhoeffer addresses unconscious Christianity in different types of texts leads to different types of engagement with the idea: descriptive in "Ultimate and Penultimate Things" and *Novel*, and more theoretical and exploratory in the letter to Bethge and "Notes II." The descriptive second chapter showed that there is a discrepancy between the way in which Bonhoeffer portrays unconscious Christianity in his fiction and in "Ultimate and Penultimate Things" on one hand, and in his letter and "Notes II" on the other. In the former, Bonhoeffer does not analyze unconscious Christianity but describes the everyday lives and actions of unconscious Christians. It is true that Ulrich and Christoph refer to unconscious Christianity in a debate that contains both abstract ideas and concrete observations, but when Christoph introduces the topic of unconscious Christianity, it is simply as an observation about specific people.[2] On the other hand, in the later texts Bonhoeffer links unconscious Christianity to abstract concepts such as being-for-others, encountering Christ, and suffering alongside God in the world. Here Bonhoeffer's view of unconscious Christianity expands beyond the scope of the specific society described in the fiction, and he becomes aware that unconscious Christianity might be "a very wide-reaching problem."[3] This shows a development in Bonhoeffer's approach to unconscious Christianity, starting with a desire to communicate his idea through fiction, and then realizing that the idea that he wanted to express needed more time and thought given to it. Despite this development in Bonhoeffer's approach to unconscious Christianity, there are some aspects of unconscious Christianity that occur in several of the texts in which Bonhoeffer mentions it. For example, being-for-others and valuing the penultimate occur in more than one text, and the idea that unconscious Christians do not self-identify as Christians is a constant throughout Bonhoeffer's development of his concept.

After analyzing the different portrayals of unconscious Christianity in the late theology, at the end of the third chapter I concluded that all of the aspects of unconscious Christianity that these texts pointed to were compatible with each other, except for Bonhoeffer's identification of unconscious Christians as being likely to be members of the *Bürgertum*, a stance from which he moves away in his later writings on the subject. This is not to say that a rigidly structured definition of unconscious Christianity emerges from these texts, but rather that it is possible to form a working definition of it that allows for fluctuation over time, as Bonhoeffer investigated the idea in various forms of writing. The working definition I arrived at is as follows: Unconscious Christianity refers to the whole body of good people who have encountered Christ without being aware of it and do not self-identify as Christian. In addition, they may fulfil any of these six criteria: (1) to have faith without knowing it, (2) to be selfless and participate in Jesus's being-for-others, (3) to not seek to be other than what they are, (4) to value the penultimate, (5) to perform acts of faith without reflecting on them, and (6) to be a member of the *Bürgertum*. Bonhoeffer's linking of unconscious Christianity to Matthew 25 in "Notes II" indicates that as he progresses in his development of unconscious Christianity, Bonhoeffer suggests that unconscious Christians are recognized as righteous by God.

In chapter 4, I considered my definition of unconscious Christianity alongside other important ideas found in Bonhoeffer's prison writing, and found that it not only fits in well with them, but that it also illumines them. Thus I showed that an understanding of unconscious Christianity enables a better understanding of the prison theology in general. I compared unconscious Christianity with religionless Christianity and showed how both concepts differ from each other. I highlighted the importance of seeing Bonhoeffer's statements about unconscious Christianity as theological statements. I showed how my definition of unconscious Christianity fits with other scholars' views on the subject, and how, by taking together all the various elements contained within Bonhoeffer's thinking on unconscious Christianity, this definition forms a new step in Bonhoeffer scholarship.

Placing Bonhoeffer's work on unconscious Christianity in the context of his previous writings in chapter 5 showed that Bonhoeffer's work on unconscious Christianity was a logical next step in his theological project to answer the question "Who is Christ for us today?"[4] In this chapter I showed that he was prepared to adapt his theology to his circumstances as they changed. This was not a case of Bonhoeffer changing his theological views to fit in with his life; rather, Bonhoeffer accepted that reality must be taken seriously and be allowed to shape one's ideas and beliefs. I noted that it is impossible to conjecture in what way Bonhoeffer would have developed his thinking on unconscious Christianity had he survived the war, and that this adds to the difficulty in arriving at an inflexible definition of unconscious Christianity. I highlighted the question of self-identification in unconscious Christianity, positing that unconscious Christianity represents a shift within Bonhoeffer's thought on the nature of Christianity and how an individual can become a Christian. It is still possible to see continuity between Bonhoeffer's early writing and his work on unconscious Christianity, although I also drew attention to ways in which it is clear that unconscious Christianity is a new concept within Bonhoeffer's theology.

This book builds toward a definition of unconscious Christianity as Bonhoeffer used it in his late theology. It tests this definition against other aspects of Bonhoeffer's thought from the same time period, making sure that the analysis of the concept of unconscious Christianity proposed does not clash with other central ideas found in the late writings. It provides an overview of how unconscious Christianity fits in with the chronological development of Bonhoeffer's thought, describing it as a shift in his theology. I have sought here to present a preliminary picture of unconscious Christianity, its meaning, and its place within Bonhoeffer's theology, with each successive chapter adding a new layer to this picture.

At the end of these investigations, unconscious Christianity emerges as a concept that Bonhoeffer had not finished working on, and is therefore not fully defined and delineated. It is sufficiently well-developed in his writing that it is possible to attach a definition to it, albeit one that recognizes the tensions within itself. Several elements are held together within unconscious Christianity, and they sometimes appear to be too disparate to be comprehended within one concept. However, the tensions between them are reflected in my emphasis on the fluid nature of Bonhoeffer's thoughts on unconscious Christianity, and his development of the concept over the several years during which he worked on it. While these tensions cannot be ironed out or ignored, I find Hanfried Müller's approach to Bonhoeffer's texts helpful here: he argues for a reading of Bonhoeffer that follows the movement of his writing, and allows for tensions and contradictions within it to contain forces that push the reader forward.[5] Furthermore, taking into account the time period of several years[6] during which Bonhoeffer worked intermittently on unconscious Christianity, it is natural that he developed his ideas on the subject, and that consequently it contains different elements that do not always harmonize perfectly with each other. Despite the tensions in Bonhoeffer's work on unconscious Christianity, it is possible to state several facts about it that help to form a definition that is useful in gaining a deeper overall understanding of the late theology, and in addressing issues pertaining to that theology today.

I hope that this project will ignite interest among Bonhoeffer scholars for further research in this area. Below, I outline questions that I think are worthy of being followed up in more detail than this format allows, and that could be possible starting points for future research.

NEW LINES OF INQUIRY WITHIN BONHOEFFER SCHOLARSHIP

What Does Bonhoeffer's Work on Unconscious Christianity Teach Us about His Thoughts on the Increasingly "God-less"[7] Society That He Foresaw Gaining Ground after the Second World War?

In chapter 4, I outlined Bonhoeffer's concept of the world come of age and noted that God must still be recognized as being in the center of human existence even within this new framework. Alongside the idea of a world come of age, within which humanity no longer has need of God, Bonhoeffer writes about the rejection of the religious *a priori*[8] that results in a society that does not base itself on any religious belief or practice. In what light does Bonhoeffer view this society? His writing on the Church keeping silent for a time, while maintaining the certainty that one day it will be called upon again to speak God's renewing Word to the world suggests a patient hopefulness.[9]

So far in this book, I have not discussed how unconscious Christianity might inform our understanding of Bonhoeffer's opinion of secular society and the postwar world he so frequently referred to. This is an important question, and cannot be adequately addressed in the space remaining here. What can be done, however, is outline how unconscious Christianity might be perceived as indicating that Bonhoeffer was hopeful about the future of Christianity in postwar society. The outline I give below serves as a starting point for further investigation on this subject.

How Might Unconscious Christianity be Understood as Indicating Bonhoeffer's Positive Outlook for Christianity in the Years after World War II?

We begin with a paradox that Bonhoeffer uses to describe the world come of age. Discussing how Christians can communicate the truth about God in the emancipated world in which they now live, he writes

> [. . .] if one wants to speak of God "nonreligiously," then one must speak in such a way that the godlessness of the world is not covered up in any way, but rather precisely to uncover it and surprise the world by letting light shine on it. The world come of age is more god-less and perhaps just because of that closer to God than the world not yet come of age.[10]

Before examining the problem of how a world that is increasingly god-less can be closer to God than it was previously, the term "godlessness" that Bonhoeffer uses here should be discussed. "Godlessness"[11] in this text echoes Bonhoeffer's use of the term in his earlier essay "Heritage and Decay" in *Ethics*. In "Heritage and Decay," Bonhoeffer differentiates between "hopeless godlessness" and "promising godlessness," and provides definitions for both.[12] He observes that in Western Europe there is a "broad front of strong antichurch resentment," while at the same time "the number of those who cancel their church membership is nevertheless quite small."[13] From this situation, Bonhoeffer deduces an "ambivalence of enmity towards the church."[14] He writes:

> One cannot simply identify Western godlessness with enmity toward the church. Rather, there is also, alongside what we have called hopeless godlessness dressed up in religious-Christian finery, a promising godlessness that expresses itself in antireligious and antichurch terms. This is the protest against pious godlessness insofar as that has spoiled the churches. It thus preserves in a sure though negative way the heritage of a genuine faith in God and of a genuine church. Luther's saying belongs here, that God would rather hear the curses of the godless than the hallelujahs of the pious.[15]

For Bonhoeffer, godlessness does not necessarily entail a bad outcome. In comparing hopeless and promising godlessness he acknowledges that godlessness is negative, but shows that it can bring about a positive outcome. Martin Kuske echoes this idea in his rethinking of the parable of the Prodigal Son, in the light of Bonhoeffer's hopeless and promising godlessness. Kuske writes:

> Jesus' parable of The Prodigal Son (Luke 15) is changed: the son who leaves his father's house, proves himself, masters life, fails here and there, but is also successful. He does not lead a life that ends up in a pigsty, but puts to use his gifts and abilities in order to live with others and for others. His father hears about it and is proud that his son has proved himself among foreigners, that his upbringing has borne fruit. He visits his son and is pleased with him. His son is capable. He had made him capable of fulfilling the task of living-together-with-others. The father writes his older son a letter in which he bids him to also join his younger brother. The older son comes and lives and works together with his brother. And the joy of the father became yet greater. That is what I associate with the concept of "promising godlessness."[16]

Kuske does not disguise the negative fact that the son still wishes to leave his father's house, but the end result is no longer failure, but success, bringing about greater joy for the father, and, interestingly, a good working relationship between both brothers. Kuske illustrates how godlessness can lead to joy and companionship. Importantly, when the younger son leaves his father's house, he "puts to use his gifts and abilities in order to live with others and for others" and the father notes that "He had made him capable of fulfilling the task of living-together-with-others." There are conditions that must be met if the younger son's godlessness is to be "promising." Living with and for others is a crucial part of making godlessness promising rather than hopeless. Living with and for others is also a crucial part of both religionless

Christianity and unconscious Christianity, forms of Christian expression that Bonhoeffer thought could flourish in the world come of age. It is interesting to note that living for others, being for others, is central to both unconscious Christianity and promising godlessness, both of which are ways of being in the world come of age. It is possible to contend, therefore, that living for others must also be central to what Bonhoeffer hoped for in post-war society.

Indeed, Andreas Pangritz identifies being for others as the decisive difference between Karl Barth's and Bonhoeffer's view of what the relationship should be between the Church and a godless world. While both theologians see the Church as being orientated outward, toward the world, the way they perceive this orientation manifesting itself is markedly different. Pangritz writes:

> In Barth the "triumph of grace" appears to work itself out in missionary consciousness in the elect that is not far removed from ecclesiastical triumphalism and the eagerness to convert the "godless" world. For Bonhoeffer, the church's service for the world consists simply in "being for others." Just as Jesus "is there for others," so "the church is the church only when it exists for others."[17]

The link, highlighted here by Pangritz, that Bonhoeffer makes between the Church being at the service of the world in its simple being for others and Jesus as being "there for others" underlines just how intertwined Christology and ecclesiology are throughout the entirety of Bonhoeffer's theology, and how monumentally important this being-for-others embodied by Jesus is in Bonhoeffer's vision for the Church and society after the war.

Let us return now to Bonhoeffer's statement: "The world come of age is more god-less and perhaps just because of that closer to God than the world not yet come of age."[18] Arnaud Corbic comments on this juxtaposition of godlessness and closeness to God, positing that Bonhoeffer takes his cue from Luther's phrase *simul justus et peccator*, which presents the paradox of the condemned sinner who is at the same time justified by faith.[19] However, Corbic does not go on to explain how the state of godlessness and closeness to God could be seen as a parallel to Luther's *simul justus et peccator*. His comparison between Bonhoeffer's and Luther's paradoxes show that he considers Bonhoeffer's opinion of the world come of age as positive, but unfortunately he does not develop his argument enough to be sufficiently clear. While I agree that Bonhoeffer's assessment of the world come of age is positive, I think an important point that Corbic misses in his analysis is the work Bonhoeffer put into thinking through new ways in which Christianity could be expressed in the world come of age. In developing these new forms of Christian expression, Bonhoeffer starts portraying Christians as freed from a confined and limiting "religious"[20] idea of God. The new categories of Christianity he writes about are liberated from stifling preconceptions about the relationship between God and humanity imposed on them by hopeless godlessness, whose similarity to Bonhoeffer's negative descriptions of religion in *Letters and Papers* is clear.[21]

Could it be that Bonhoeffer was pointing toward the same idea when he wrote about promising godlessness and unconscious Christianity? Could unconscious Christians in fact be called promisingly godless? As far as their own consciousness is concerned, they intend to be godless. Bonhoeffer's definition of promising godlessness in "Heritage and Decay" includes the idea that it is fighting against the false ideas of hopeless godlessness,[22] and this could also be applied to those referred to in "Ultimate and Penultimate Things," who purposefully decline to self-identify as Christians, possibly because of a disillusionment with the Church.[23] Further exploration into how unconscious Christians exhibit a type of godlessness in their conscious approach to the world, and yet combine this with a closeness to God in their unconscious encounter with Christ, could be very fruitful.

With the help of the definition of unconscious Christianity that I have put forward here, a comparison between Bonhoeffer's concepts of unconscious Christianity and promising godlessness is now possible.

Reading the Prison Fiction as Theology

In the first part of chapter 2, I made the case for Bonhoeffer's prison fiction being considered theological. In the third chapter I also focused on what the fiction reveals about Bonhoeffer's development of his ideas on unconscious Christianity. However, the fiction contains much more that could be of import to Bonhoeffer studies. Detailed examination of the theological ideas raised in the fiction would enable greater insight into the links between the fiction and the theological letters to Bethge. Bonhoeffer first addresses in his fiction several of the ideas that he later raises in the letters. Greater attention therefore needs to be paid to the earlier texts in order to be able to trace the development of some of Bonhoeffer's most famous ideas from the prison period.

For instance, through his portrayal of Frau Karoline Brake in the opening section of *Novel*, Bonhoeffer discusses rejecting the proclamation model for communicating God's Word to the world. Frau Brake's disappointment with the Church and its preaching indicates that Bonhoeffer was writing about the need to express God's message to the world in new ways well before he formulated these ideas in terms of "non-religious interpretation of Biblical concepts."[24] In the following section I show how Bonhoeffer investigates theological ideas in his fiction before he discusses them in a more formal manner in his letters to Bethge. I do this by taking as my example Bonhoeffer's rejection of the proclamation model in *Novel*. I close the case study by listing some other ideas Bonhoeffer worked on in his fiction, which resurfaced and gained more public attention in *Letters and Papers from Prison*. I suggest that there is much to be learned from a closer study of the fiction as the theological precursor to the texts from the later prison period.

Case Study: Bonhoeffer's Rejection of the Proclamation Model in Novel

In *Novel*, Bonhoeffer sets up his discussion of the rejection of the proclamation model by introducing the reader to Frau Karoline Brake as she reflects on the Sunday morning's church service that she has just attended. Frau Brake is a wise, elderly woman, mother to Hans Brake and grandmother to the young Brakes discussed previously. She lives with her extended family in a large and comfortable suburban house, in a "mid-sized city in Northern Germany."[25] She is the mayor's widow, which indicates her important social status. Bonhoeffer's description of her, her family, and her social circle establishes her as a member of the *Burgertüm*. Bonhoeffer depicts her as kind, intelligent, diligent, with a deep sense of responsibility and a desire to seek out the truth.

Through Frau Brake's private reflections, and her conversations with other characters, Bonhoeffer introduces several themes pertaining to the Church: the misuse of power by the clergy, the preaching of cheap grace instead of costly grace, and the increasing number of people who are leaving the Church.[26] In her appraisal and rejection of the morning sermon, Frau Brake is doing more than condemning one church service amongst others. It becomes clear that she thinks the Church is not fulfilling its responsibility toward the community, because it has ceased to preach the Word of God. Bonhoeffer writes: "The congregation, the whole town, her own family was deprived of the Word of God, and that meant that their whole life must sooner or later lose its centre."[27] Frau Brake then begins to wonder whether by forsaking its responsibility the Church has also lost its authority within the community, and its expectation that the community will attend to it will no longer be met. She recollects something her grandson had said to her in a conversation on whether people should continue going to church services. The boy said: "You know, Grandma, we've outgrown this kind of preacher wisdom just like we've outgrown our Latin teachers rattling off Ostermann's exercises. I really can't understand how you can bear to listen to it Sunday after Sunday."[28] Frau Brake had tried to defend continued presence at church by arguing that it enables the hand and the heart to learn things that the head already knows.[29] However, reflecting on the conversation she imagines further exchanges, in which she says: "You mustn't confuse Christianity with its pathetic representatives." The boy replies: "Anything that has such pathetic representatives can't have much power left; I'm interested in what is alive and relevant today, not in a dead faith of the past."[30] The underlying question here is whether the Church has forfeited its claim on people by neglecting its duty. Bonhoeffer leaves this question unresolved, but is occurs continually in *Novel*'s characters' thoughts and conversations. The question of what sort of role the Church may have in the future, taking into account the mistakes it has made, is one to which Bonhoeffer returns in his sermon for his godson and in his outline for a book.[31]

Frau Brake spends a long time considering the sermon and its consequences, in contrast to the two other people she meets on her way home, her neighbor and housemaid, who don't think about or analyze it, but simply accept it.[32] Further on we read: "Now she felt her rage rising once again within her. What rubbish she had been forced to listen to again. Could one blame the children and grandchildren who, for years now, had let her go to church alone?"[33] Her anger at the falling short of the Church when it has the opportunity to preach the Word of God is clear, and through it Bonhoeffer's own anger at this situation seems to manifest itself. Frau Brake does not blame her children and grandchildren who no longer accompany her to church services. Through the younger characters, Bonhoeffer presents abandoning the institutional Church completely as one possible legitimate reaction to the state of the Reich Church. This precedes his writing on religionless Christianity by several months.[34]

Frau Brake, for her part, thinks it is still good to attend church services and try to help with the daily running of the Church, even though she knows that God's Word is no longer preached there.[35] She wants to persevere in what she sees as an essential part of Christianity. She also attempts to remedy the bad situation the Church is in by trying to get involved in its leadership.[36]

Despite the unanswered question of the Church's authority and place in society, Bonhoeffer makes it clear that "in this suburb in any event, hot air had taken the place of God's Word."[37] This is a specific case of a church in which it is impossible that people will hear God's Word proclaimed in a sermon. The Church has fallen short of the first part of its threefold mandate, as described in "Christ, Reality and Good," of "allowing the reality of Jesus Christ to become real in proclamation [Verkündigung], church order, and Christian life."[38] The central character in this section of *Novel* recognizes this to be true, and although she believes that "memory and tradition could postpone complete disintegration for a while yet,"[39] she perceives that future generations will have to find replacements for the proclamation model. In a passage that clearly speaks Bonhoeffer's own grappling with the problem, Frau Brake ponders these questions:

> But her grandchildren's generation would need to find new ways of its own, and several things these young people had said had led their grandmother to recognize the first signs of protest, even of revolt. It was not the young people's fault if things were as they were. Rather, the older people let things take

their course so unperceptively, without insight or concern. That was the worst thing about it.[40]

The idea that the older generation are at fault is taken up again by Bonhoeffer in the sermon for the baptism of his godson, when he writes:

> We have lived too much in our thoughts; we believed that by considering all the options of an action in advance we could ensure it, so that it would proceed of its own accord. We learned too late that it is not the thought but readiness to take responsibility that is the mainspring of action. Your generation will relate thought and action in a new way.[41]

Frau Brake's preoccupation with the Church, and how she should act toward it, clearly reflect Bonhoeffer's preoccupation on the same topics. How ought a Christian to act when the Church she is a member of deviates from God's Word? This question was at the forefront of Bonhoeffer's mind during the summer of 1943, and continued to be throughout his time in prison.

We don't find out in *Novel* what Frau Brake decides to do. But her acknowledgment that the proclamation model is no longer of any use to communicate God's Word to the world, and her trust in the younger generations' capacity for recognizing empty words and finding new ways in which to communicate God's Word, are the same basic ideas that Bonhoeffer develops in his letters to Bethge. People can no longer be told with words who Christ is today.[42] However, in the future there will be other ways in which to express Christ, "the language of a new righteousness and truth, a language proclaiming that God makes peace with humankind and that God's kingdom is drawing near."[43]

In showing that Bonhoeffer's rejection of the proclamation model in *Novel*, illustrated both by the characters who leave the Church and by the one who might choose to remain within it, receives a more systematic treatment in his later prison writing, I have inevitably also drawn parallels between other ideas that arise in the fiction and are dealt with again in the late prison texts. The ideas I have mentioned in passing so far are Bonhoeffer's endorsement of leaving the Church as a possible reaction to its lack of true preaching, echoed in his concept of religionless Christianity, and the new ways in which the younger generations might communicate Christ to the world, echoed in similar terms later in his work. Also of note is that, through the character of Karoline Brake and her attempts to become involved in Church leadership, Bonhoeffer confronts the problem of the clergy's misuse of power. The problem of the abuse of power more generally features strongly in all the pieces of fiction. Were someone to elaborate a thematic study of the fiction as a whole, the abuse of power and its deadly consequences would be an obvious starting point.

Joshua Kaiser lists themes occurring in the fiction, with power heading his list:

> His drama and novel fragments about the lives and relationships of a middle class family, and his short story about a lance corporal who goes to work at a military prison, contain themes such as power, community, freedom, and discernment, all of which are prominent throughout his theological and ethical writing.[44]

The misuse of power is evident in all three fiction texts. In *Novel*, the abuse of power directly brings about the death of Major von Bremer's son.[45] In *Story*, it threatens the life of another innocent young man until Lance Corporal Berg sets things right.[46] In *Drama*, there is a less obvious line drawn between the abuse of power and the death of an innocent, but the power struggle between different classes in society runs throughout the play. The working-class Heinrich storms at Christoph:

> You want to wrench us out of the community which alone makes us count for something; and you know perfectly well that once you've isolated us as individuals, you don't need to be afraid of us anymore. As individuals we're powerless in your hands, for we aren't individuals, we're the masses or nothing.[47]

Christoph perceives this outburst as a lack of trust toward the *Bürgertum*, and replies:

> Nothing is more ruinous for life together than to mistrust the spontaneity of others and suspect their motives. To psychologize and analyze people, as has become fashionable these days, is to destroy all trust, to expose everything decent to public defamation.[48]

In his outline for a book, Bonhoeffer writes about power in the context of the future Church. He states that the Church must not dominate the community, but serve it, writing: "In particular, *our* church will have to confront the vices of hubris, the worship of power, envy, and illusionism as the roots of all evil. It will have to speak of moderation, authenticity, trust, faithfulness, steadfastness, patience, discipline, humility, modesty, contentment."[49] Here, the worship of power and trust are placed in opposition to each other. Trust, portrayed in opposition to the misuse and worship of power, and the perceived misuse of power by others, are the central themes of *Drama*. In *Letters and Papers*, too, Bonhoeffer writes of the misuse of power that destroys trust. Writing to Bethge about "unchristian" Christian apologetics' efforts to convince people in the world come of age that they still need God, he states:

> Here is where the secularized offshoots of Christian theology come in, that is, the existential philosophers and the psychotherapists, to prove to secure, contented, and happy human beings that they are in reality miserable and desperate and just don't want to admit that they are in a perilous situation, unbeknown to themselves, from which only existentialism or psychotherapy can rescue them.[50]

According to Bonhoeffer, the existential philosophers and the psychotherapists abuse their positions of power to make contented people doubt themselves. They break up the trust that the secure people have in their own situations, and create misery by doing so.

There are clear parallels between Heinrich and Chritoph's argument in *Drama*, about misuse of power and lack of trust, and Bonhoeffer's warnings in *Letters and Papers* that the Church must avoid misusing power in order to dominate others and remove the trust they have in themselves. This is, of necessity, an extremely cursory sketch of some of the themes Bonhoeffer addresses in his fiction, and later develops in his letters to Bethge. However, there is still a great deal of interest to be drawn from the fiction, and much more research to be done on the continuity of theological themes between it and the later prison writing. The argument for the fiction being considered as theological writing, presented in chapter 2, lays the foundation for further research into comparing the fiction with the prison letters, and drawing out how Bonhoeffer articulates the same theological ideas in both sets of texts.

UNCONSCIOUS CHRISTIANITY, CONTEMPORARY CHRISTIAN THEOLOGY, AND THE CHURCH

In addition to raising new questions within Bonhoeffer studies, I hope the new definition of unconscious Christianity will be useful to theology more widely. Considered outside of its immediate context, it is a concept articulated by one of the twentieth century's most influential theologians according to which it is possible for people who do not define themselves as Christians to be called Christians. If unconscious Christianity can be included in the contemporary theological conversation, without falling into the obvious trap of the paternalistic discourse that could be raised by this idea,[51] it will be a useful concept in current theological debate.

It should first be noted that using unconscious Christianity as a tool to reveal to people who they really are, as though they are not competent enough to decide their identity for themselves, ignores the element of pastoral care that is evident in Bonhoeffer's development of this concept. Only in "Ultimate and Penultimate Things" does he talk about encouraging unconscious people who don't self-identify as Christians to "move toward confessing Christ."[52] As noted in chapter 4, Bonhoeffer shows pastoral concern for those who self-identify as Christians, and who come to realize that there are more forms of Christian expression than their own in the world come of age. Recognizing others as unconscious Christians will help the self-identifying Christians, because they will cease to see themselves as alone responsible for the perpetuation of Christianity in the world. Thus for Bonhoeffer, recognizing unconscious Christianity in others can be beneficial to conscious Christians.

This aspect of Bonhoeffer's presentation of unconscious Christianity leads to the final point I would like to make. The category of unconscious Christianity, and in particular the idea of being able to recognize others as unconscious Christians, is useful to confessing Christian theology in the current debates on secularization and the future of Christianity in Western Europe.[53] As confessing Christian theology tries to work out what its place is within society, discussion continues on the nature of that society and of different people within it. Questions are raised, such as: How fast is secularization taking place? How should self-identifying Christians understand people who do not profess any Christian faith but who attend church services because they find the music beautiful?[54] What should be made of "belonging without believing" and "believing without belonging"?[55] Confessing theologians whose work revolves around these questions would benefit from adding the concept of unconscious Christianity to their view of society.

The value of Bonhoeffer's theology to these discussions has already been recognized by a wide range of writers. Tom Greggs, for instance, draws on Bonhoeffer alongside Barth in his challenging and on-point treatment of contemporary soteriology, ecclesiology, and Christian engagement in the public square in *Theology against Religion: Constructive Dialogues with Bonhoeffer and Barth*.[56] Greggs makes use of several concepts from Bonhoeffer's prison letters and poetry, as well as his other works, including the differentiation Bonhoeffer makes between faith and a religious act, his work on the ultimate and the penultimate, and the commitment to worldliness that runs through his late theology. The addition of unconscious Christianity to this discussion might contribute another layer to Greggs's already rich consideration of the inter-relationships between Christians, members of other faith traditions, atheists, and others, and would add yet more theological weight to his call for the Church to have a more positive engagement with the world.

For those who are trying to construct a vision of the Church as reshaped in light of contemporary culture,[57] considering that culture to contain people who have already encountered Christ, albeit unconsciously, would be an interesting idea. For example, Pete Ward proposes a change in the way the church is conceptualized, away from the idea of "solid church" ("a gathering of people meeting in one place at one time—that is, a congregation") toward that of a "liquid church," which he describes as "a series of relationships and communications."[58] The first move to be made in order to enact the change from conceptualizing the Church as "solid" to thinking of it as "liquid," he writes, is "to take the informal fellowship, in which we experience Christ as we share with other Christians, and say this is church."[59] If Ward were to take into account unconscious Christianity in his model for a new form of church, then his suggestion that informal fellowship be called "church" would be expanded to include informal fellowship in which Christ is experienced in sharing with other Christians, whether they self-identify as Christian or not. A new section of the population would thus be included in his vision of what church is.

For theologians trying to formulate a response to the dwindling number of churchgoers[60] combined with increasing interest in, and diversification of, forms of spirituality,[61] unconscious Christianity would prove a useful category. As discussed previously,[62] by naming people as unconscious Christians, Bonhoeffer gives them a spiritual dimension, and relates them to Christ in a way that they would not attribute to themselves. Although the risk of paternalism would have to be successfully navigated and avoided, bringing the concept of unconscious Christianity into the discussion of Christianity and spirituality would be beneficial. The inclusion of unconscious Christianity in the conversation would show that confessing Christian theologians accept that there is a form of Christian expression that does not require self-identification as Christian, and that this form of Christian expression displays a wariness of identifying with the institutional Church similar to that shown in spirituality.[63]

I have shown that Bonhoeffer suggests that unconscious Christians are recognized as righteous by God.[64] Thus inclusion of the concept of unconscious Christianity would be interesting to theologians engaged in questions of soteriology. Recognizing that there is a form of Christian expression that negates the necessity of a conscious self-identification with Christianity but that is nevertheless righteous in God's sight would also be useful to thinkers in missiology, and those considering the relationship between human goodness and Christianity.

If unconscious Christianity is understood as a possible category of Christian expression within contemporary life, a new voice is added to the conversation about theology's place in the public domain. Not only are there several points of view about how theology should relate to society within confessing Christian theology, but the views articulated by unconscious Christians must be considered as Christian also. Self-identifying Christians are thus no longer solely responsible for delineating theology's place within society from a Christian perspective, but share this responsibility with unconscious Christians. Unconscious Christians' views on the matter would be sought out and presented alongside the views expressed by self-identifying Christians. On a more basic level that also echoes Bonhoeffer's pastoral concern for self-identifying Christians, if those who fear that the erosion of Christianity in Western Europe will lead finally to its disappearance come to know about unconscious Christianity, it will relieve the fear they have that only those who self-identify as Christians, and whose numbers are dwindling, are responsible for the survival of Christianity.

There are clear problems with identifying unconscious Christians in today's society that the theologians engaged in the various debates and questions mentioned above will have to decide how to tackle. The characteristic that Bonhoeffer initially associated with unconscious Christianity, and described in detail in *Novel*, of being part of a social class that inherits a cultural Christian background but no longer self-identifies as Christian, still exists, but the numbers of people who display this characteristic are vastly diminished. There are still people in Western Europe who do not self-identify as Christian but perform Christian practices on specific occasions. For instance, some people who do not call themselves Christians still choose to get married in church, following the Christian wedding ceremony. However, the number of people getting married in church in England and Wales is falling,[65] and there is no general societal expectation for people to partake in culturally Christian practices. The number of unconscious Christians whose Christianity comes to them through their unconscious cultural inheritance of it is diminishing.

However, it is obvious that engaging with Christ through actions carried out for others, participating in Christ's being-for-others and performing acts of faith on which it is impossible to reflect did not exclusively belong to people living in Bonhoeffer's era. It is still possible to be an unconscious Christian in this way in today's society. This book's definition of Bonhoeffer's developing concept of a new form of Christian expression, possible in the world come of age, is valuable in our current age, and should be included in theological assessments of Christianity in the twenty-first century.

NOTES

1. Bonhoeffer, *Ethics*, 124.
2. See Bonhoeffer, *Fiction from Tegel Prison*, 106.
3. Bonhoeffer, *Letters and Papers from Prison*, 489.
4. See Bonhoeffer, *Letters and Papers from Prison*, 362.
5. See Müller, "Concerning the Reception and Interpretation of Dietrich Bonhoeffer," 186 and chapter 5 of this book.
6. Ilse Tödt writes that "Ultimate and Penultimate Things" was written in November 1940 (see Tödt "Preparing the German Edition of Ethics" in Bonhoeffer, *Ethics*, 471). The marginal note containing a reference to unconscious Christianity could have been added at any time up until Bonhoeffer's arrest on the 5th of April 1943 while he still had access to his papers.
7. Bonhoeffer, *Letters and Papers from Prison*, 482.
8. See Bonhoeffer, *Letters and Papers from Prison*, 362.
9. See Bonhoeffer, *Letters and Papers from Prison*, 389, on the Church keeping silent for a period of time: "Our church has been fighting during these years only for its self-preservation,

as if that were an end in itself. It has become incapable of bringing the word of reconciliation and redemption to humankind and to the world. So the words we used before must lose their power, be silenced, and we can be Christians today in only two ways. Through prayer and in doing justice among human beings." See also 390, on the time when the Church will once more be able to proclaim God's message to reconciliation to the world: "It is not for us to predict the day—but they day will come—when people will once more be called to speak the word of God in such a way that the world is changed and renewed. It will be in a new language, perhaps quite nonreligious language, but liberating and redeeming like Jesus' language, so that people will be alarmed and yet overcome by its power—the language of a new righteousness and truth, a language proclaiming that God makes peace with humankind and that God's kingdom is drawing near."

10. Bonhoeffer, *Letters and Papers from Prison*, 482, letter dated the 18th of July 1944.

11. "Gottlosigkeit" is translated here as "godlessness." The German reads: "Wenn man von Gott 'nicht-religiös' sprechen will, dann muß man so von ihm sprechen, daß die Gottlosigkeit der Welt dadurch nicht irgendwie verdeckt, sondern vielmehr gerade aufgedeckt wird und gerade so ein überraschendes Licht auf die Welt fällt. Die mündige Welt ist Got-loser und darum vielleicht Got-näher als die unmündige Welt." Bonhoeffer, *Widerstand und Ergebung*, 537.

12. See Bonhoeffer, *Ethics*, 124. The German terms are "hoffnungslose Gottlosigkeit" and "verheißungsvolle Gottlosigkeit" (Bonhoeffer, *Ethik*, 115).

13. Bonhoeffer, *Ethics*, 124.

14. Bonhoeffer, *Ethics*, 124.

15. Bonhoeffer, *Ethics*, 124. The text that Bonhoeffer refers to here is: "I am saying this for the comfort of those who are perpetually troubled by the thoughts of blasphemies and are in great anxiety; since such blasphemies, because they are violently extorted from men by the devil against their will, they sometimes sound more pleasant in the ear of God than a hallelujah or some kind of hymn of praise." Martin Luther, *Lectures on Romans*, ed. Hilton C. Oswald, vol. 25 of Luther's Works (Saint Louis: Concordia Publishing House, 1972), 390.

16. Martin Kuske, "Hopeless and Promising Godlessness," in *Bonhoeffer's Ethics: Old Europe and New Frontiers*, eds. Guy Carter, René van Eyden, Hans-Dirk van Hoogstraten, Jurjen Wiersma (Kampen: Kok Pharos, 1991), 191.

17. Andreas Pangritz, *Karl Barth in the Theology of Dietrich Bonhoeffer*, trans. Barbara and Martine Rumscheidt (Grand Rapids & Cambridge: Eerdmans, 2000), 124. Pangritz cites Dietrich Bonhoeffer, *Letters and Papers from Prison*, ed. Eberhard Bethge, trans. Reginald H. Fuller, Frank Clarke, John Bowden et al. New York: Macmillan, 1972, 381f.

18. Bonhoeffer, *Letters and Papers from Prison*, 482, letter dated the 18th July 1944.

19. Corbic, *Dietrich Bonhoeffer*, 76.

20. See Bonhoeffer's comments on the "religious people" and their view of God, in Bonhoeffer, *Letters and Papers from Prison*, 366.

21. Bonhoeffer presents hopeless godlessness, which he also refers to as "pious godlessness," as spoiling the churches. He also describes it as "dressed up in religious-Christian finery" (Bonhoeffer, *Ethics*, 124).

22. Bonhoeffer, *Ethics*, 124.

23. See chapter 3 of this book.

24. See Bonhoeffer, *Fiction from Tegel Prison*, 73–80, written in August 1943, and Bonhoeffer, *Letters and Papers from Prison*, 371–74, written on the 5th of May, 1944.

25. Bonhoeffer, *Fiction from Tegel Prison*, 73.

26. See Bonhoeffer, *Fiction from Tegel Prison*, 75, 78–79, and 73–74, respectively.

27. Bonhoeffer, *Fiction from Tegel Prison*, 76.

28. Bonhoeffer, *Fiction from Tegel Prison*, 74.

29. See Bonhoeffer, *Fiction from Tegel Prison*, 74.

30. Bonhoeffer, *Fiction from Tegel Prison*, 74.

31. See Bonhoeffer, *Letters and Papers from Prison*, 389 and 500–504.

32. See Bonhoeffer, *Fiction from Tegel Prison*, 78–80. On discussing the sermon with her neighbor, Frau Brake reproaches her: "Frau Direktor, did it escape you again that the pastor said what you wanted to hear, but didn't preach the word of God?" (79).

33. Bonhoeffer, *Fiction from Tegel Prison*, 78.

34. *Novel* was written in August 1943, and Bonhoeffer introduces the term "religionless Christianity" in his letter to Bethge dated the 30th of April, 1944 (Bonhoeffer, *Letters and Papers from Prison*, 361–67).

35. See also the idea that God is withholding his Word as a punishment in Bonhoeffer, *Fiction from Tegel Prison*, 76.

36. See Bonhoeffer, *Fiction from Tegel Prison*, 75: Karoline Brake attempts to talk to the pastor about his sermons, but meets with "nothing but vain defensiveness and hollow officiousness." And "She would see that this old windbag of a preacher left this pulpit, or that a second pastor, a preacher of the word of God, would be called to the parish." Also on this page, we learn that the pastor has "thwarted her reelection to the parish council [Gemeindekirchenrat]," illustrating Bonhoeffer's concern over the misuse of power by the clergy.

37. Bonhoeffer, *Fiction from Tegel Prison*, 74.
38. Bonhoeffer, *Ethics*, 73.
39. Bonhoeffer, *Fiction from Tegel Prison*, 76.
40. Bonhoeffer, *Fiction from Tegel Prison*, 76.
41. Bonhoeffer, *Letters and Papers from Prison*, 387.
42. See Bonhoeffer, *Letters and Papers from Prison*, 362.
43. Bonhoeffer, *Letters and Papers from Prison*, 390.
44. Joshua A. Kaiser, "Bonhoeffer's Foray into Fiction," review of *Fiction from Tegel Prison* by Dietrich Bonhoeffer, *The Expository Times* vol. 123, no. 9 (2012), 461.
45. See Bonhoeffer, *Fiction from Tegel Prison*, 182.
46. See Bonhoeffer, *Fiction from Tegel Prison*, 186, 193.
47. Bonhoeffer, *Fiction from Tegel Prison*, 64.
48. Bonhoeffer, *Fiction from Tegel Prison*, 65.
49. Bonhoeffer, *Letters and Papers from Prison*, 503.
50. Bonhoeffer, *Letters and Papers from Prison*, 427.
51. See Kelly "'Unconscious Christianity' and the 'Anonymous Christian,'" 147.
52. Bonhoeffer, *Ethics*, 170.

53. I confine my comments in this section to the situation in Western Europe, conscious of the fact that the secularization question is not the same world-wide, and rejecting the idea that patterns in European religious practice are the prototype for patterns worldwide. This focus on Western Europe also echoes Bonhoeffer's own focus.

54. See Brian Mountford, *Christian Atheist: Belonging without Believing* (Winchester, UK & Washington, USA: O-Books, 2011), 20.

55. See Mountford, *Christian Atheist*, and also Grace Davie, *Religion in Britain since 1945: Believing without Belonging* (Oxford: Blackwell, 1994).

56. See Greggs, *Theology against Religion*, Part II Doctrine after Christendom: Secularism, Salvation and the Church, 97–169.

57. See for example Pete Ward, *Liquid Church* (Carlisle, Cumbria: Paternoster Press; Peabody, Mass: Hendrickson Publishers, 2002).

58. Ward, *Liquid Church*, 2.
59. Ward, *Liquid Church*, 2.

60. See Grace Davie and Linda Woodhead, "Secularization and Secularism," in *Religions in the Modern World*, 2nd edition, eds. Linda Woodhead, Hiroko Kawanami and Christopher Partridge (London & New York: Routledge, 2009), 526.

61. See Giselle Vincent and Linda Woodhead, "Spirituality," in *Religions in the Modern World*, 323.

62. See chapter 5 of this book.

63. See my comments on the unconscious Christians in "Ultimate and Penultimate Things" no longer daring to call themselves Christians in chapter 3 of this book.

64. See chapter 3 of this book.

65. For statistics on marriage trends in England and Wales, see "Trends in Religious and Civil Marriages, 1966–2011," The National Archives, archived 7 January 2016, accessed 30 June 2015, http://www.ons.gov.uk/ons/rel/vsob1/marriages-in-england-and-wales--provisional-/2011/sty-marriages.html.

Appendix

Document 1: The last page of Bonhoeffer's manuscript for the *Ethics* essay "Ultimate and Penultimate Things"
Nachlass 299 (Dietrich Bonhoeffer) A 71, 4
Staatsbibliothek zu Berlin—Preußischer Kulturbesitz

Document 2: The page of Bonhoeffer's manuscript for *Novel* on which he mentions unconscious Christianity
Nachlass 299 (Dietrich Bonhoeffer) A 70, 5
Staatsbibliothek zu Berlin—Preußischer Kulturbesitz

Document 3: Bonhoeffer's letter to Bethge in which he mentions unconscious Christianity
Nachlass 299 (Dietrich Bonhoeffer) A 81, 198
Staatsbibliothek zu Berlin—Preußischer Kulturbesitz

Document 4: "Notes II"
Nachlass 299 (Dietrich Bonhoeffer) A 86, 20
Staatsbibliothek zu Berlin—Preußischer Kulturbesitz

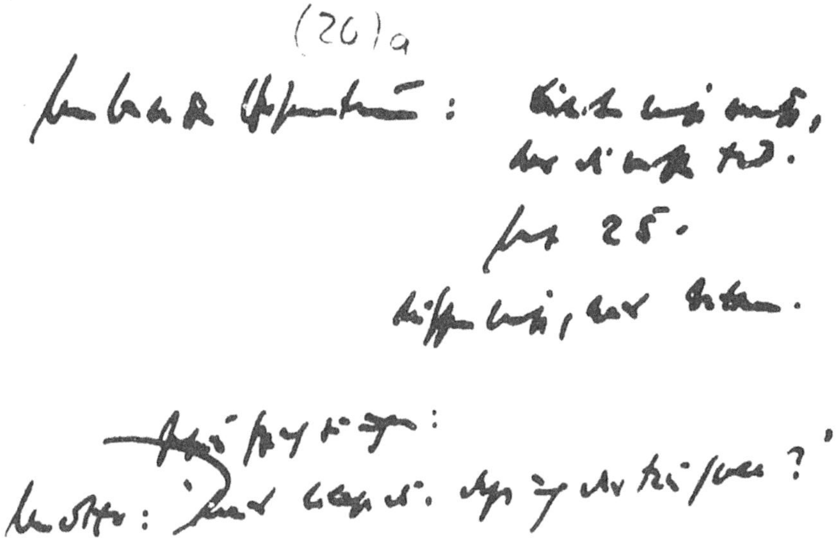
(20)a

Bibliography

Act and Being. DBWE vol. 2. Edited by Wayne Whitson Floyd Jr. Translated by H. Martin Rumscheidt. Minneapolis: Fortress Press, 1996.
Akt und Sein. DBW vol. 2. Edited by Hand-Richard Reuter. Munich: Chr. Kaiser Verlag., 1988.
Altizer, Thomas J. J. and William Hamilton, eds. *Radical Theology and the Death of God.* Indianapolis, New York, & Kansas City: Bobbs-Merrill, 1966.
Bernhardt, Reinhold. "Christentum ohne Christusglaube: Die Rede von 'unbewusstem Christentum' und 'latenter Kirche' im 19. und 20. Jahrhundert." *"Zur Kirche Gehören," Festheft für Christine Lienemann-Perrin zu ihrer Emeritierung am 18. Mai 2010.* Theologische Zeitschrift 2/66, Basel University (2010): 119–47.
Bethge, Eberhard. "The Challenge of Dietrich Bonhoeffer's Life and Theology." In *World Come of Age: A Symposium on Dietrich Bonhoeffer*, edited by Ronald Gregor Smith, 22–92. London: Collins, 1967.
———. *Dietrich Bonhoeffer, Theologe, Christ, Zeitgenossse.* Munich: Chr. Kaiser Verlag., 1967.
———. *Dietrich Bonhoeffer: Theologian, Christian, Contemporary.* Edited by Edwin Robertson. Translated by Eric Mosbacher. London: Collins, 1970.
Bethge, Eberhard, Renate Bethge, and Christian Gremmels, eds. Kabitz, Ulrich, supervisor. Geith, Ingeborg, and Willem Weijers, designers. *Dietrich Bonhoeffer: A Life in Pictures.* Translated by John Bowden. London: SCM Press, 1986.
Bethge, Renate. Editor's Afterword to the German Edition of Bonhoeffer. In *Fiction from Tegel Prison*, DBWE vol. 7, edited by Clifford J. Green. Translated by Nancy Lukens, 195–233. Minneapolis: Fortress Press, 2010.
Bethge, Renate, and Eberhard Bethge. Introduction to Bonhoeffer. In *Fiction from Prison: Gathering Up the Past*, edited by Renate and Eberhard Bethge with Clifford Green. Translated by Ursula Hoffmann, 1–12. Philadelphia: Fortress Press, 1981.
Blackbourn, David and Richard J. Evans, eds. *The German Bourgeoisie.* London & New York: Routledge, 1993.
Bosanquet, Mary. *Bonhoeffer: True Patriot.* Oxford & London: Mowbrays, 1978.
Clements, Keith. *What Freedom? The Persistent Challenge of Dietrich Bonhoeffer.* Bristol: Bristol Baptist College, 1990.
Concise Oxford English Dictionary, tenth edition, revised. Edited by Judy Pearsall. Oxford: Oxford University Press, 2002.
Conspiracy and Imprisonment. DBWE vol. 16. Edited by Mark S. Brocker. Translated by Lisa E. Dahill. Minneapolis: Fortress Press, 2006.
Corbic, Arnaud. *Dietrich Bonhoeffer: Résistant et propète d'un christianisme non religieux, 1906–1945.* Paris: Albin Michel, 2002.

Creation and Fall: A Theological Exposition of Genesis 1–3. DBWE vol. 3. Edited by John W. de Gruchy. Translated by Douglas Stephen Bax. Minneapolis: Augsburg Fortress, 1997.

Davie, Grace. *Religion in Britain since 1945: Believing without Belonging*. Oxford: Blackwell, 1994.

Davie, Grace, and Linda Woodhead. "Secularization and Secularism." In *Religions in the Modern World*, 2nd edition, edited by Linda Woodhead, Hiroko Kawanami and Christopher Partridge, 523–32. London & New York: Routledge, 2009.

Dederen, Raoul. "Karl Rahner's The Shape of the Church to Come: A Review Article." *Andrews University Seminary Studies* Vol. XIV (1976): 217–25.

De Gruchy, John. *Bonhoeffer and South Africa: Theology in Dialogue*. Grand Rapids, MI: William B. Eerdmans Publishing Company, 1984.

———, ed. *Bonhoeffer for a New Day: Theology in a Time of Transition: Papers Presented at the Seventh International Bonhoeffer Congress, Cape Town, 1996*. Grand Rapids, MI: William. B. Eerdmans Publishing Company, 1997.

———, ed. *The Cambridge Companion to Dietrich Bonhoeffer*. Cambridge: Cambridge University Press, 1999.

———. Editor's Introduction to the English edition of Bonhoeffer, *Letters and Papers from Prison*. DBWE vol. 8, edited by John W. de Gruchy. Translated by Isabel Best, Lisa E. Dahill, Reinhard Krauss and Nancy Lukens, 1–34. Minneapolis: Fortress Press, 2010.

———. *Witness to Jesus Christ*. London: Collins, 1988.

Delicata, Nadia. "Revisiting Karl Rahner's 'Anonymous Christian': Towards a Christian Theology of the Religions Grounded in the Kenotic Ethic of Imitatio Christi." Paper presented at Engaging Particularities IV: New Directions in Comparative Theology, Interreligious Dialogue, Theology of Religions and Missiology Conference, Boston College, MA, 17–19 March 2006. Chestnut Hill, MA: Theology Dept., Boston College, (2006). http://dlib.bc.edu/islandora/object/bc-ir:102756.

Discipleship. DBWE vol. 4. Edited by Geffrey B. Kelly and John D. Godsey. Translated by Barbara Green and Reinhard Krauss. Minneapolis: Fortress Press, 2001.

Dumas, André. *Dietrich Bonhoeffer: Theologian of Reality*. Translated by Robert McAfee Brown. London: SCM Press, 1971.

Ethics. DBWE vol. 6. Edited by Clifford J. Green. Translated by Reinhard Krauss, Charles C. West, and Douglas W. Stott. Minneapolis: Fortress Press, 2005.

Ethik. DBW vol. 6. Edited by Ilse Tödt, Heinz Eduard Tödt, Ernst Feil, and Clifford Green. Munich: Christian Kaiser Verlag., 1992.

Feil, Ernst. *The Theology of Dietrich Bonhoeffer*. Translated by Martin Rumsheidt. Minneapolis: Fortress Press, 2007.

Fiction from Tegel Prison. DBWE vol. 7. Edited by Clifford J. Green. Translated by Nancy Lukens. Minneapolis: Fortress Press, 2010.

Fiction from Tegel Prison: Gathering Up the Past. Edited by Renate and Eberhard Bethge with Clifford Green. Translated by Ursula Hoffmann. Philadelphia: Fortress Press, 1981.

Floyd, Wayne Whitson Jr. "Bonhoeffer's Literary Legacy." In *The Cambridge Companion to Dietrich Bonhoeffer*, edited by John W. de Gruchy, 71–92. Cambridge: Cambridge University Press, 1999.

Fragmente aus Tegel, Drama und Roman. Edited by Renate and Eberhard Bethge. Munich: Chr. Kaiser Verlag., 1978.

Godsey, John D. *The Theology of Dietrich Bonhoeffer*. Philadelphia: Westminster Press, 1960.

Green, Clifford J. *Bonhoeffer: A Theology of Sociality,* revised edition. Grand Rapids, MI & Cambridge, UK: William B. Eerdmans Publishing Company, 1999.

———. Editor's Introduction to the English edition of Bonhoeffer, *Fiction from Tegel Prison*. DBWE vol. 7, edited by Clifford J. Green. Translated by Nancy Lukens, 1–23. Minneapolis: Fortress Press, 2010.

Greggs, Tom. "Religionless Christianity in a Complexly Religious and Secular World." In *Religion, Religionlessness and Contemporary Western Culture*, edited by Stephen Plant and Ralf K. Wüstenberg, 111–25. Frankfurt Am Main: Peter Lang, 2008.

———. *Theology against Religion: Constructive Dialogues with Bonhoeffer and Barth*. London & New York: T&T Clark, 2011.

Hamilton, William. "Dietrich Bonhoeffer." In *Radical Theology and the Death of God*, edited by Thomas J. J. Altizer and William Hamilton, 113–18. Indianapolis, New York, & Kansas City: Bobbs-Merrill, 1966.

———. "Thursday's Child." In *Radical Theology and the Death of God*, edited by Thomas J. J. Altizer and William Hamilton, 87–93. Indianapolis, New York, & Kansas City: Bobbs-Merrill, 1966.

The Holy Bible, New Revised Standard Version. Oxford: Oxford University Press, 2003.

Kaiser, Joshua A. "Bonhoeffer's Foray into Fiction." Review of *Fiction from Tegel Prison*, by Dietrich Bonhoeffer. *Expository Times* 123, no. 9 (2012): 461.

Kelly, Geffrey B. "Prayer and Action for Justice: Bonhoeffer's Spirituality." In *The Cambridge Companion to Dietrich Bonhoeffer*, edited by John W. de Gruchy, 246–68. Cambridge: Cambridge University Press, 1999.

———. "'Unconscious Christianity' and the 'Anonymous Christian' in the Theology of Dietrich Bonhoeffer and Karl Rahner." *Philosophy and Theology* 9 (1995): 117–49.

Kelly, Geffrey B., and John C. Weborg, eds. *Reflections on Bonhoeffer: Essays in Honor of F. Burton Nelson*. Chicago, IL: Covenant Publications, 1999.

Kirkpatrick, Matthew D. *Attacks on Christendom in a World Come of Age: Kierkegaard, Bonhoeffer, and the Question of "Religionless Christianity."* Eugene, OR: Pickwick Publications, 2011.

———, ed. *Engaging Bonhoeffer: The Impact and Influence of Bonhoeffer's Life and Thought*. Minneapolis, MN: Fortress Press, 2016.

Kuske, Martin. "Hopeless and Promising Godlessness." In *Bonhoeffer's Ethics: Old Europe and New Frontiers*, edited by Guy Carter, René van Eyden, Hans-Dirk van Hoogstraten, and Jurjen Wiersma, 190–93. Kampen: Kok Pharos, 1991.

Leibholz-Bonhoeffer, Sabine. *The Bonhoeffers: Portrait of a Family*. Chicago: Covenant Publications, 1994.

———. "Childhood and Home." In *I Knew Dietrich Bonhoeffer*, edited by Wolf-Dieter Zimmermann and Ronald Gregor Smith. Translated by Käthe Gregor Smith, 19–33. London: Collins, 1966.

Letters and Papers from Prison. DBWE vol. 8. Edited by John W. de Gruchy. Translated by Isabel Best, Lisa E. Dahill, Reinhard Krauss, and Nancy Lukens. Minneapolis: Fortress Press, 2010.

Life Together and *Prayerbook of the Bible*. DBWE vol. 5. Edited by Geffrey B. Kelly. Translated by Daniel W. Bloesch and James H. Burtness. Minneapolis: Fortress Press, 2005.

Lindbeck, George A. "Thought of Karl Rahner, S J." *Christianity and Crisis* 25, no. 17 (October 18, 1965): 211–15.

London, 1933–1935. DBWE vol. 13. Edited by Keith Clements. Translated by Isabel Best. Minneapolis: Fortress Press, 2007.

Lukens, Nancy. "Narratives of Creative Displacement: Bonhoeffer the Reader and the Construction of 'Unconscious Christianity' in Fiction from Tegel Prison." Paper presented at the Ninth International Bonhoeffer Congress, Rome, Italy, 6–11 June, 2004.

Luther, Martin. *Lectures on Romans*, edited by Hilton C. Oswald. Vol. 25 of *Luther's Works*. Saint Louis: Concordia Publishing House, 1972.

Mann, Thomas. "Goethe as Representative of the Bourgeois Age." In *Essays of Three Decades*. Translated by H. T. Lowe-Porter. London: Specker & Warburg, 1947.

Marsh, Charles. *Reclaiming Dietrich Bonhoeffer: The Promise of His Theology*. New York & Oxford: Oxford University Press, 1994.

———. *Strange Glory: A Life of Dietrich Bonhoeffer*. London: SPCK, 2014.

Marty, Martin E. *Dietrich Bonhoeffer's Letters and Papers from Prison: A Biography*. Princeton & Oxford: Princeton University Press, 2011.

Mascall, E. H. *The Secularization of Christianity: An Analysis and a Critique*. New York: Holt, Rinehart & Winston, 1965.

Miller, Michael Craig. "Unconscious or Subconscious?" *Harvard Health Publications* (01.08.2010). Accessed 14 April 2014. www.health.harvard.edu/blog/unconscious-or-subconscious-20100801255.

Moses, John A. "Dietrich Bonhoeffer's Fiction from Tegel Prison 1943–45: His Reflections on the Dark Side of Cultural Protestantism in Nazi Germany." *The Dark Side: Proceedings of the Seventh Australian and International Religion, Literature and the Arts Conference*, Sydney, 2002. Edited by Christopher Hartney and Andrew McGarrity, 89–101. Sydney: RLA Press, 2004.

———. Review of *Fiction from Tegel Prison* by Dietrich Bonhoeffer. *The Journal of Religious History*, vol. 26, no. 3, October 2002: 341–43.

Mottu, Henry. *Dietrich Bonhoeffer.* Paris: Cerf, 2010.

Mountford, Brian. *Christian Atheist: Belonging without Believing.* Winchester, UK & Washington, USA: O-Books, 2011.

Müller, Hanfried. "Concerning the Reception and Interpretation of Dietrich Bonhoeffer." In *World Come of Age: A Symposium on Dietrich Bonhoeffer*, edited by Ronald Gregor Smith, 182–214. London: Collins, 196.

Nachfolge. DBW vol. 4. Edited by Martin Kuske and Ilse Tödt. Munich: Chr. Kaiser Verlag., 1989.

The National Archives. "Trends in Religious and Civil Marriages, 1966–2011." Archived 7 January 2016. Accessed 30 June 2015. http://www.ons.gov.uk/ons/rel/vsob1/marriages-in-england-and-wales--provisional-/2011/sty-marriages.html.

Ott, Heinrich. *Reality and Faith: The Theological Legacy of Dietrich Bonhoeffer.* London: Lutterworth Press, 1971.

Pangritz, Andreas. *Karl Barth in the Theology of Dietrich Bonhoeffer.* Translated by Barbara and Martin Rumscheidt. Grand Rapids, MI & Cambridge, UK: William B. Eerdmans Publishing Company, 2000.

Plant, Stephen, and Ralf K. Wüstenberg, eds. *Religion, Religionlessness and Contemporary Western Culture.* Frankfurt Am Main: Peter Lang, 2008.

Raina, Peter. *George Bell: The Greatest Churchman—A Portrait in Letters.* London: Churches Together in Britain and Ireland, 2006.

Rade, Martin. "Unbewusstes Christentum." *Seite zur Christlichen Welt*, 53 (1905): 1–23.

Rahner, Karl. *Theological Investigations, vol. 6, Concerning Vatican Council II.* Translated by Karl-H. Kruger and Boniface Kruger. London: Darton, Longman and Todd; New York: Seabury Press, 1969.

Reuter, Hans-Richard. Editor's Afterword to the German Edition of Dietrich Bonhoeffer. In *Act and Being*, DBWE vol. 2, edited by Wayne Whitson Floyd, Jr. Translated by H. Martin Rumscheidt, 162–83. Minneapolis: Fortress Press, 1996.

Robertson, Edwin. *Unshakeable Friend: George Bell and the German Churches.* London: Council of Churches for Britain and Ireland, 1995.

Robinson, J. A. T. *Honest to God.* London: SCM Press, 1963.

Rognon, Frédéric. "Pacifisme et tyrannicide chez Jean Lasserre et Dietrich Bonhoeffer; Seconde Partie: L'Interprétation des Incidences Théologiques." *Etudes Théologiques et religieuses* (Montpellier) 8, no. 2 (2005): 159–76.

Rothe, Richard. "Zur Orientierung über die gegenwärtige Aufgabe der deutsch-evangelischen Kirche." *Allgemeine Kirchliche Zeitschrift: Ein Organ für die evangelische Geistlichkeit and Gemeinde*, (1862): 34–68.

Sanctorum Communio. DBWE vol. 1. Edited by Clifford J. Green. Translated by Reinhard Krauss and Nancy Lukens. Minneapolis: Fortress Press, 1998.

Schlingensiepen, Ferdinand. "Die Darstellung von gelebtem Glauben und unbewusstem Christentum in Dietrich Bonhoeffers 'Fragmente aus Tegel.'" In *Dietrich Bonhoeffers Christentum*, edited by Florian Schmitz and Christiane Tietz, 251–77. Gütersloh: Gütersloher Verlag., 2011.

———. *Dietrich Bonhoeffer, 1906–1945: Martyr, Thinker, Man of Resistance.* Translated by Isabel Best. New York: T&T Clark, 2010.

Schmitz, Florian, and Christiane Tietz, eds. *Dietrich Bonhoeffers Christentum.* Gütersloh: Gütersloher Verlag., 2011.

Selby, Peter. "Christianity in a World Come of Age." In *The Cambridge Companion to Dietrich Bonhoeffer*, edited by John W. de Gruchy, 226–45. Cambridge: Cambridge University Press, 1999.

Smith, Ronald Gregor, ed. *World Come of Age: A Symposium on Dietrich Bonhoeffer*. London: Collins, 1967.
Sorum, Jonathan. "Another Look at Bonhoeffer." *Lutheran Quarterly* Volume XVIII (2004): 469–82.
Taylor, Charles. *A Secular Age*. Cambridge, MA & London: The Belknap Press of Harvard University Press: 2007.
Theological Education at Finkenwalde: 1935–1937. DBWE vol. 14. Edited by H. Gaylon Barker and Mark S. Brocker. Translated by Douglas W. Scott. Minneapolis: Fortress Press, 2013.
Tietz, Christiane. *Theologian of Resistance: The Life and Thought of Dietrich Bonhoeffer*. Translated by Victoria J. Barnett. Minneapolis: Fortress Press, 2016.
Tödt, Heinz Eduard. *Authentic Faith: Bonhoeffer's Theological Ethics in Context*, edited by Glen Harold Stassen. Translated by David Stassen and Ilse Tödt. Grand Rapids, MI & Cambridge, UK: William B. Eerdmans Publishing Company, 2007.
Tödt, Ilse. "Preparing the German Edition of *Ethics*." Appendix 2 of Dietrich Bonhoeffer, *Ethics*. DBWE vol. 6, edited by Clifford J. Green. Translated by Reinhard Krauss, Charles C. West, and Douglas W. Stott, 467–76. Minneapolis: Fortress Press, 2005.
———. "Wir leben im Vorletzten: Bonhoeffer und das unbewusste Christentum." In *Dietrich Bonhoeffers Christentum*. Edited by Florian Schmitz and Christiane Tietz, 324–37. Gütersloh: Gütersloher Verlag., 2011.
Tödt, Ilse, Heinz Eduard Tödt, Ernst Feil, and Clifford Green. Editors' Afterword to the German Edition of Dietrich Bonhoeffer, *Ethics*. DBWE vol. 6, edited by Clifford J. Green. Translated by Reinhard Krauss, Charles C. West, and Douglas W. Stott, 409–49. Minneapolis: Fortress Press, 2005.
van Buren, Paul. *The Secular Meaning of the Gospel, Based on an Analysis of Its Language*. London: SCM Press, 1963.
Vincent, Giselle, and Linda Woodhead. "Spirituality." In *Religions in the Modern World*, 2nd edition, edited by Linda Woodhead, Hiroko Kawanami and Christopher Partridge, 319–38. London & New York: Routledge, 2009.
von Klemperer, Klemens. Review of *Fiction from Tegel Prison* by Dietrich Bonhoeffer. *Union Seminary Quarterly Review* 54, nos. 1–2 (2000): 110–13.
Wannenwetsch, Bernd. "'Christians and Pagans,' towards a Trans-Religious Second Naiveté or How to be a Christological Creature." In *Who Am I? Bonhoeffer's Theology through His Poetry*, edited by Bernd Wannenwetsch, 175–96. London & New York: T&T Clark, 2009.
———, ed. *Who Am I? Bonhoeffer's Theology through His Poetry*. London & New York: T&T Clark, 2009.
———. "Who Is Dietrich Bonhoeffer for Us Today?" Introduction to *Who Am I? Bonhoeffer's Theology through His Poetry*, edited by Bernd Wannenwetsch, 2–10. London & New York: T&T Clark, 2009.
Ward, Pete. *Liquid Church*. Carlisle, Cumbria: Paternoster Press; Peabody, MA: Hendrickson Publishers, 2002.
Widerstand und Ergebung. DBW vol. 8. Edited by Christian Gremmels, Eberhard Bethge, and Renate Bethge, with Ilse Tödt. Munich: Gütersloher Varlag., 1998.
Woelfel, James W. *Bonhoeffer's Theology: Classical and Revolutionary*. Nashville: Abingdon Press, 1970.
Woodhead, Linda, Hiroko Kawanami, and Christopher Partridge, eds. *Religions in the Modern World*. 2nd edition. London & New York: Routledge, 2009.
Wüstenberg, Ralf K. *Bonhoeffer and Beyond: Promoting a Dialogue between Religion and Politics*. Frankfurt am Main: Peter Lang, 2008.
———. "'Religionless Christianity': Dietrich Bonhoeffer's Tegel Theology." In *Bonhoeffer for a New Day, Theology in a Time of Transition: Papers Presented at the Seventh International Bonhoeffer Congress, Cape Town, 1996*, edited by John W. de Gruchy, 57–71. Grand Rapids, MI & Cambridge, UK: William. B. Eerdmans Publishing Company, 1997.
———. *A Theology of Life: Dietrich Bonhoeffer's Religionless Christianity*. Translated by Doug Stott. Grand Rapids, MI & Cambridge, UK: William B. Eerdmans Publishing Company, 1998.

The Young Bonhoeffer. DBWE vol. 9. Edited by Paul Duane Matheny, Clifford J. Green, and Marshall D. Johnson. Translated by Hans Pfeiffer in cooperation with Clifford J. Green and Carl-Jürgen Kaltenborn. Minneapolis: Fortress Press, 2003.

Zachhuber, Johannes. *Theology as Science in Nineteentch-Century Germany: From F. C. Baur to Ernst Troeltsch*. Oxford: Oxford University Press, 2013.

Zerner, Ruth. "Dietrich Bonhoeffer's Prison Fiction: A Commentary." In Dietrich Bonhoeffer, *Fiction from Tegel Prison: Gathering Up the Past*, edited by Renate and Eberhard Bethge with Clifford Green. Translated by Ursula Hoffmann, 139–67. Philadelphia: Fortress Press, 1981.

Ziegler, Philip G. "'Voices in the Night': Human Solidarity and Eschatological Hope." In *Who Am I? Bonhoeffer's Theology through his Poetry*, edited by Bernd Wannenwetsch, 115–45. London & New York: T&T Clark, 2009.

Zimmermann, Wolf-Dieter, and Ronald Gregor Smith, eds. *I Knew Dietrich Bonhoeffer.* Translated by Käthe Gregor Smith. London: Collins, 1966.

Index

Abwehr, 30, 31
Act and Being, 28, 69, 86, 143
"After 10 Years," 119, 127, 128, 134n101, 134n103
anonymous Christian, 5, 6, 8, 9, 10, 12, 13, 91, 93, 115, 118, 120, 127
anonymous Christianity. *See* anonymous Christian
arcane discipline, 111, 118, 132n35

Barcelona, 28, 37
Barth, Karl, 13, 151, 169, 183, 190
being-for-others, 72, 73, 77n94, 87, 88, 89, 90, 92, 93, 94, 105, 108, 109, 113, 122, 128, 130, 135n124, 142, 154, 158, 159, 160, 161, 163, 169, 178, 183, 192
Bell, George, 32, 49n24
Berlin, 4, 23n54, 28, 37, 51n59, 122
Bernhardt, Reinhold, 17, 18, 19, 122, 123, 125
Bethge, Eberhard, 2, 4, 13, 20, 29, 35, 36, 37, 41, 58, 69, 70, 73n4, 74n6, 76n82, 106, 107, 119, 132n29, 142, 143, 148, 149, 150, 151, 152, 156, 170n11; Bonhoeffer's prison correspondence with, 4, 8, 33, 37, 46, 55, 57, 59, 62, 67, 68, 69, 71, 73, 74n21, 75n38, 76n79, 76n80, 76n82, 85, 86, 90, 91, 94, 97n66, 102, 103, 108, 110, 113, 122, 132n35, 141, 144, 148, 150, 154, 155, 157, 158, 165, 177, 178, 184, 187, 188, 189; Keith Clements's interview with, 29, 30; unconscious Christianity according to, 116, 117, 130, 133n79, 155
Bethge, Renate, née Schleicher, 20, 35, 36, 40, 41, 43, 58
Bismarck, Otto von, 37
Blackbourn, David, 32, 33, 35, 36
Bonhoeffer, Karl, 37, 40, 41, 44, 171n50
Bonhoeffer, Klaus, 31, 32, 36, 49n22, 51n57
Bonhoeffer, Paula, née von Hase, 33, 38, 51n67, 52n84
Brake, Christoph, 33, 34, 35, 39, 43, 45, 48, 56, 59, 60, 66, 67, 68, 83, 84, 85, 121, 122, 166, 178, 188
Brake, Ekkehard (Little Brother), 39, 41, 42, 68
Brake, Franz, 43, 59, 121
Brake, Hans, 28, 41, 42, 43, 45, 46, 47, 53n113, 67, 73, 91, 93, 94
Brake, Karoline, 39, 40, 47, 67, 124, 184, 185, 186, 187, 193n32, 194n36
Brake, Klara, 35, 39, 40, 42, 97n59
Breslau, 37
Bürgertum, 6, 27, 28, 32, 33, 34, 35, 36, 46, 47, 49n26, 50n36, 52n90, 57, 59, 68, 83, 84, 85, 89, 90, 95, 96n29, 130, 153, 166, 179, 185, 188; *Besitzbürgertum*, 33; *Bildungsbürgertum*, 30, 33, 47, 53n116,

207

59, 74n25; *bürgerlich*, 6, 31, 33, 34, 35, 36, 41, 46, 47, 49n26, 56, 57, 66, 79, 91, 94, 139, 151, 154

Christ. *See* Jesus Christ
"Christ, Reality and Good," 162, 163, 164, 186
Christendom, 17, 122
Christianity without religion. *See* religionless Christianity
"Christians and Heathens," 62, 68, 113, 114, 161, 165
"Church and World I," 164, 165, 166, 167, 175n137
Clements, Keith, 29, 30, 147
"The Concrete Commandment and the Divine Mandates," 158
Confessing Church, 29, 32, 140, 142, 148, 150, 152, 155, 156, 157, 174n124
Corbic, Arnaud, 183
Creation and Fall, 45, 152

death of God movement, 144, 145
Dederen, Raoul, 11
de Gruchy, John, 117, 118, 125, 126, 127, 130, 150, 169
Delicata, Nadia, 8, 11, 12
deus ex machina. *See* God
Dilthey, Wilhelm, 102, 103, 104, 106, 140, 151
Discipleship, 140, 141, 142, 147, 148, 149, 150, 151, 152, 153, 155, 159, 160, 161, 162, 168
Dostoyevsky, Fyodor, 75n33
Drama, 36, 41, 56, 57, 58, 60, 61, 66, 67, 68, 73n4, 74n14, 74n23, 75n33, 85, 88, 108, 154, 188, 189
Dumas, André, 142, 144

Ethics, 2, 4, 15, 20, 31, 58, 62, 70, 73n4, 103, 112, 118, 119, 123, 141, 142, 143, 146, 150, 157, 162, 165, 167, 168
"Ethics as Formation," 134n101
etsi deus non daretur, 102, 146

Feil, Ernst, 102, 133n73, 147, 148, 149
fiction: as a literary form, 2, 60, 62, 75n33, 121, 122; written by Bonhoeffer, 2, 3, 5, 6, 8, 27, 28, 31, 33, 35, 36, 37, 40, 41, 44, 45, 46, 47, 51n51, 55, 56, 57, 58, 59, 60, 61, 69, 72, 73, 74n5, 85, 107, 108, 110, 112, 117, 118, 121, 122, 124, 125, 129, 166, 177, 178, 184, 185, 187, 188, 189
Fiction from Tegel Prison, 32, 56
fides directa, 69, 70, 72, 86, 90, 96n47, 107, 141, 161
fides reflexa, 69, 70, 86, 107
Finkenwalde, 29, 148

God: as a *deus ex machina*, 11, 102, 111, 112, 113; as a stopgap, 72, 102, 105, 106, 113; as a working hypothesis, 11, 72, 102, 103, 104, 105; sharing in God's suffering, 72, 77n98, 109, 113, 114, 122, 132n44, 141, 142, 158, 161, 165, 174n128, 178; suffering of, 11, 72, 112, 113, 151, 158; weakness of, 112, 113, 158, 165, 174n128
godlessness, 70, 105, 108, 109, 154, 177, 181, 182, 183, 184; hopeless godlessness, 9, 77n87, 181, 182, 184; pious godlessness, 70, 77n87, 135n127, 182; promising godlessness, 7, 70, 123, 135n127, 181, 182, 183, 184; Western godlessness, 182
good, 21n17, 65, 76n68, 120, 163, 164, 165, 167; "Good," 4, 5, 119
goodness, 91, 120, 160, 167, 191
good people, 5, 20, 81, 89, 91, 94, 95, 105, 115, 118, 120, 126, 132n35, 134n89, 164, 165, 166, 167, 179; the human and the good, 20, 64, 65, 79, 80, 81, 82, 91, 95n13
Green, Clifford, 32, 35
Greggs, Tom, 105, 106, 110, 112, 114, 190

Hamilton, William, 145
Heinrich, 56, 66, 67, 68, 85, 88, 188, 189
"Heritage and Decay," 135n127, 181, 184
hidden righteousness, 159, 160, 161, 162, 168
Hildebrandt, Franz, 32
"History and Good," 58, 133n73
homo religious, 11, 113

Jesus Christ, 63, 70, 71, 81, 87, 89, 92, 112, 114, 117, 127, 141, 143, 150, 158,

163, 164, 165, 186; and the world come of age, 105; as Savior, 12; claimed for Jesus Christ, 65, 79, 81; encounter with, 72, 88, 92, 159; faith in, 18, 72, 88, 163; incarnation, crucifixion, and resurrection of, 63; incognito of, 127

Jesus's being-for-others, 72, 77n94, 87, 88, 89, 90, 91, 92, 93, 94, 95, 105, 128, 142, 154, 158, 159, 160, 161, 163, 179, 183

Jesus's parables, 71, 182; participation in the being of, 72, 88, 89, 91, 92, 93, 94, 95, 105, 128, 142, 154, 158, 159, 160, 161, 163, 179; suffering of, 143, 162, 163, 164; weakness of, 143

Kaiser, Joshua, 188
Karstensen, Ulrich, 35, 42, 48, 60, 67, 68, 73, 83, 84, 107, 136n135, 166, 178
Kelly, Geffrey B., 60, 118, 119, 120, 125, 126, 127, 128, 129, 130, 134n101, 142
Kuske, Martin, 182

Lance Corporal Berg, 57, 58, 62, 108, 109, 111, 132n35, 154, 167, 188
Lasserre, Jean, 151, 172n62
Leibholz-Bonhoeffer, Sabine, née Bonhoeffer, 29, 35, 36, 38, 40, 44, 45, 142, 153
Letters and Papers from Prison, 68, 73, 140, 142, 145, 168, 185
Life Together, 9, 70, 110, 140, 145, 173n112
London, 29, 32, 34, 37, 158, 172n53
Lukens, Nancy, 45, 58, 59, 120, 121, 122, 129
Luther, Martin, 182, 183

Mann, Thomas, 33, 34
Marty, Martin E., 143
Mascall, E. H., 13
Matthew 6, 71, 87, 89, 159
Matthew 25, 71, 73, 87, 88, 89, 90, 92, 93, 94, 95, 105, 106, 113, 119, 126, 127, 128, 179
Moses, John A, 47, 59, 74n25
Mottu, Henry, 144, 172n62
Müller, Hanfried, 146, 149, 180
music, 41, 42, 43, 44, 45, 53n101, 190

"Natural Life," 4, 62, 82, 119
New York, 37; Union Theological Seminary in, 28
nonreligious interpretation: of biblical concepts, 111; of Christian concepts, 71; of Christianity, 111, 118
"Notes II," 21n8, 68, 70, 71, 73, 79, 87, 88, 89, 90, 91, 92, 95, 97n49, 154, 178, 179, 199
Novel, 4, 6, 34, 35, 36, 38, 39, 40, 41, 47, 56, 57, 58, 59, 60, 61, 62, 66, 67, 69, 73, 74n14, 79, 82, 83, 85, 89, 90, 91, 92, 93, 94, 107, 108, 115, 118, 121, 124, 127, 153, 154, 178, 184, 185, 186, 187, 188, 192, 194n34, 197

Old Prussian Council of Brethren, 31, 62
Ott, Heinrich, 14, 168

piety, 70, 77n85, 85, 89, 147; natural piety, 69, 70, 72, 86, 94, 96n45, 122
poetry, x, 5, 6, 59, 60, 61, 62, 74n23, 190

Rade, Martin, 6, 15, 16, 18, 19, 20, 65, 82, 84, 94, 151
Rahner, Karl, 5, 6, 8, 9, 10, 11, 12, 88, 91, 93, 94, 104, 115, 118, 127
Red Card, 156, 173n86
Reich Church, 28, 29, 39, 82, 156, 157, 174n124, 186
religionless Christianity, 3, 7, 11, 13, 102, 106, 107, 110, 111, 112, 114, 115, 128, 129, 130, 144, 146, 149, 157, 165, 178, 179, 186, 187, 194n34
religiosity, 111, 113, 129, 158
religious *a priori*, 102, 104, 131n20, 181
Reuter, Hans-Richard, 141
Rieger, Julius, 32
Robinson, J. A. T., 145, 146
Rothe, Richard, 6, 15, 16, 17, 18, 19, 20, 65, 68, 82, 83, 85, 87, 94

Sanctorum Communio, 28, 34, 58, 59, 154
Schleicher, Rüdiger, 31, 32, 35, 36, 49n22
Schleicher, Ursula, née Bonhoeffer, 35
Schlingensiepen, Ferdinand, 13, 37, 38, 123, 124, 125, 140, 141, 150
secularists, 117, 126
secularity, 105, 144

secularization, 1, 2, 17, 35, 102, 107, 146, 151, 164, 190, 194n53; secular, 12, 35, 104, 106, 117, 151, 181
secularized, 17, 189
Sermon on the Mount, 87, 148
society, 1, 2, 8, 10, 11, 16, 17, 19, 20, 34, 35, 48, 56, 60, 82, 83, 85, 91, 117, 167, 178, 181, 183, 186, 188, 190, 191, 192; *bürgerlich*, 6, 94; Christian, 106; postwar, 181, 183; pre-Christian, 106; secular, 104, 181; secularization of, 1; secularized, 17; the future of, 10
Sorum, Jonathan, 27, 30, 31, 37, 48
stopgap. *See* God
Story, 6, 56, 57, 58, 60, 61, 62, 73n4, 74n6, 108, 109, 111, 118, 132n35, 132n44, 151, 154, 167, 188
suffering, 11, 12, 29, 46, 56, 57, 62, 104, 108, 109, 111, 113, 115, 121, 127, 151, 158, 164, 165, 174n128; alongside Christ, 9, 161; for the sake of Christ, 164; for the sake of others, 62. *See also* God; Jesus Christ

Tietz, Christiane, 103, 104
Tödt, Heinz Eduard, 15
Tödt, Ilse, 65, 125, 129

unbewußtes Christentum, 1, 3, 15, 65, 80, 82, 86

unconscious remnant, 65, 81

van Buren, Paul, 171n30
von Bremer, Harald, 47, 53n113, 67, 74n14, 188
von Bremer, Renate, 59, 121, 122
von Bremer, Sophie, 39, 42
von Dohnanyi, Christine, née Bonhoeffer, 31, 36, 40
von Dohnanyi, Hans, 31, 32, 36, 40, 49n22, 119
von Klemperer, Klemens, 69, 102, 107, 108

Wannenwetsch, Bernd, 61, 74n23, 96n21, 113
Ward, Pete, 190, 191
Woelfel, James W., 13
world come of age, 7, 11, 12, 31, 61, 68, 102, 103, 104, 105, 106, 107, 108, 109, 110, 111, 112, 114, 116, 117, 118, 121, 122, 129, 130, 132n29, 143, 144, 145, 146, 181, 183, 188, 190, 192; theological writing for a, 61
Wüstenberg, Ralf K., 103, 104, 111, 140

Zerner, Ruth, 47, 48, 117, 118, 121, 126, 127

About the Author

Eleanor McLaughlin is a theologian and ethicist. She is a lecturer in theology and ethics at Regent's Park College, University of Oxford, and research associate at the Oxford Centre for Religion and Culture. Her current research focuses on Dietrich Bonhoeffer's theology and disability theology.

www.ingramcontent.com/pod-product-compliance
Lightning Source LLC
Chambersburg PA
CBHW070830300426
44111CB00014B/2502